Representing Clients in Mediation

By Eric Galton

**With Overview and Appendices
By Professor Kimberlee K. Kovach**

American Lawyer Media, L.P.
Texas Lawyer Press
Edited by Diane Burch Beckham

Texas Lawyer Press

COPYRIGHT © 1994 AMERICAN LAWYER MEDIA, L.P.
[Second Printing 2000]

ISBN 1-879590-69-7
Printed in the United States of America

TEXAS LAWYER PRESS:

Editor: Julie H. Patton
Marketing Director: Rachel Parker
Customer Service Representative: Gillian Nelson

For additional information or orders contact:
Texas Lawyer Press
900 Jackson Street, Suite 500
Dallas, Texas 75202
(214)744-9300 or 1-800-456-5484 ext. 757
www.texaslawyerpress.com

This volume is intended to be a guide only. Because the law is constantly in flux, Mr. Galton and American Lawyer Media, L.P. do not warrant, either expressly or impliedly, that the law, rules, procedures and statutes discussed in this volume have not been subject to change, amendment, reversal, or revision.

OTHER BOOKS BY TEXAS LAWYER PRESS
Dallas County Bench Book – 2000 Edition
Harris County Bench Book – 2000 Edition
Tarrant County Bench Book – 1999 Edition
Travis County Bench Book – 1999 Edition
Assigned Judges Bench Book – 2000 Edition
Marketing & Maintaining a Family Law Mediation Practice
Mediation: A Texas Practice Guide
Negotiation: Strategies for Law and Business
Texas Criminal Codes and Rules, Annotated
Texas Personal Auto Policy – Annotated
Texas Legal Malpractice & Lawyer Discipline – Second Edition (1997)
Texas Legal Research

Dedication

For my wife, love and colleague, Kim Kovach, for my superstars, Justin, Seth and Noah, and in memory of my uncle, I.S. Zimler, who defined excellence in teaching.

Table of Contents

Introduction

Mediation has now become an integral part of our civil justice system. Courts, burdened with overcrowded dockets, are either suggesting or ordering parties into mediation. Institutional and individual clients, weary of the excessive costs of litigation and the delays associated with the process, are demanding that their attorneys attempt mediation or other alternative dispute resolution mechanisms. While alternative dispute resolution also includes arbitration, moderated settlement conferences, mini-trials and summary jury trials, mediation is by far the most favored ADR mechanism and will remain so. Lawyers are finding themselves in mediation rooms on a routine basis; yet, prior to this publication, no single practical reference was available to assist and guide attorneys in this brave new world of mediation.

I was a trial lawyer for fourteen years. For the first seven years of my trial practice, I was on the plaintiff's side. For the next seven years, I was on the defense side. Throughout my litigation career, I enjoyed the collegiality of the trial bar. My respect for my colleagues who labor "in the pits" and sweat out jury verdicts is immeasurable. For the past three years, I have had the extreme pleasure and privilege to preside as mediator over my trial brothers and sisters.

Alternative dispute resolution was not designed to replace or extinguish our precious jury system. Rather, ADR was intended to serve as a meaningful companion to the litigation process. ADR, particularly mediation, provides an effective method of resolving a substantial number of the lawsuits filed. Should a mediation not resolve a matter, the parties are free to test their positions in court. In this way, cases that need to be tried are tried, and cases that can be resolved in a more timely and cost-effective way through mediation are.

I decided to write this book as an expression of appreciation to my trial colleagues and as a help to them. Experienced litigators know the courthouse. But, even for the most savvy trial lawyer, the mediation process is a different, and possibly intimidating, universe. How does a trial lawyer translate his skills into the

Introduction

mediation arena? How does a litigator prepare her client for a mediation? How does an attorney maximize results in a mediation? What works? What doesn't work? When is the right time to mediate? How do you properly select a mediator? What is really going on in the mediation process? What do mediators think about? Do mediators have different styles? What special factors exist in medical malpractice mediations? Family law mediations? Consumer law mediations?

As I lecture across the country, I am routinely confronted with such questions. I wrote this book to provide practical help and answers. This book will take you from the beginning to the end of the mediation process. It was also written to be of equal benefit to the client; regardless of whether the client is an individual, a major corporation, or an insurance carrier. Further, as ADR courses increasingly find their way into the law schools, my hope is that this work will be of benefit to law students and perhaps pique their interest in the mediation process.

By the time this book is published, I will have mediated more than 1,200 cases. To date, 91% of the cases I have mediated have settled. Ten years ago, I served on the very first State Bar of Texas ADR Committee. My interest in ADR, then and now, was my strong conviction that ADR would improve and assist our civil justice system. I did not envision, when we first began our efforts to integrate ADR into Texas jurisprudence, that some day I would be a full-time mediator and make my living helping resolve disputes.

I believe that we mediators are making a favorable and substantial contribution to the administration of justice.

One of the exhilarating aspects of mediation is that no two cases are alike and the mediator must approach each case on its own merits. Mediators do not have the benefit of depositions, nor do we wear black robes. Disaster and the unknown lurk around every corner. Our only armor is our absolute neutrality, complete preservation of confidences, and our abiding and insatiable desire to facilitate a communication that results in a fair and sensible resolution.

Introduction

My primary goal in writing this book is to assist my colleagues in the bar in better understanding the mediation process and to represent clients more ably in the mediation setting. My other goal is to advance the proper use of ADR, not as a replacement for our trial system, but as a meaningful companion to it.

In the past ten years, our profession seems to have become more mechanical, as opposed to more problem solving. Computers, fax machines and other technological advances make it all too easy to spit out a set of discovery requests or a letter to opposing counsel. How often do we ask, "Does our client really need this?" or, "Is this of value to our client?"

Additionally, technological advances have de-personalized, to some extent, interactions between lawyers. It's easier to fax a letter or set a hearing than it is to pick up the telephone, call opposing counsel, and figure out a solution to a problem. I suppose I think that if lawyers took the time to meet personally with their adversaries, many disputes would be resolved without the need for a mediator.

Lawyers feel this change in their professional identities and are troubled by it. I regularly teach lawyers who aspire to be mediators. Most of these lawyers are very successful, but almost across the board they report that their practices are not satisfying or personally rewarding. Many of my lawyer students worry that they are not providing the kind of service to their clients they think they should. These lawyers are searching for more practical, cost-effective, expeditious ways of solving their clients' problems.

As disturbing as the mechanization of our practice, although perhaps a necessary response to a poor economy, is the new management trend in our profession. While business and management techniques may be necessary in maintaining an economic stability that permits qualitatively excellent work product, these techniques should not extinguish our collective sense of professionalism. Public service activities, pro bono work, and assisting our communities and schools may not neatly fit into the new management agenda, but such activities and others are essential to our concept of professionalism and must continue.

Introduction

As I see it, the ADR movement in general, and mediation in particular, are but one way our profession is attempting to humanize itself and to respond to the public's need for cost-effective and timely legal services. Client satisfaction with mediation in particular is very high. In fact, many clients who go through the mediation process wonder why mediation was not used earlier in the case. While mediation is not a panacea, it is a process that clients seem to understand naturally and feel comfortable with.

Success in mediation is no different than success in trial. Preparation is always the key. And mediation, although very different from a trial, is a process with discernible, albeit more fluid and flexible, steps. This book, in a practical way, will walk you through the process, show you how to prepare for the process, and show you how to thrive in the mediation arena.

Postscript

This book was written over the course of a year, at the beginning of which I wrote the introduction. Upon my final read, I realized that I had failed to acknowledge my appreciation and great respect for my fellow mediators.

Mediators understand that it is the process itself that makes things work. Mediators recognize that they are but caretakers of this good process. Mediators also understand that their job — walking into conflicts on a daily basis — is a difficult one. Even when resolution is reached, whether it is 6:00 p.m. or 2:00 a.m., the mediator goes home unable, because of confidentiality, to share what has occurred with anyone. Mediators must accept this and take their inner peace and satisfaction from playing some part in the resolution of conflict.

Mediators also understand that one of the inherent aspects of the mediation process is its flexibility and the fact that it permits, even demands, creativity. The more a mediator mediates, the more flexible he or she becomes. Because of this, and because a mediator's repertoire expands over time, interpreting this work as a "model form" would be a mistake. This work is a reliable guide, but the more we learn experientially, the more new chapters will need to be written.

Introduction

Mediators and mediation advocates must accept one unmistakable fact — the dispute belongs *to the parties*, not to the advocates and certainly not to the mediator. Our egos, goals and desires are, in that sense, irrelevant. We get to go home and not live the conflict. Our desire to procure "wins" at the courthouse or achieve settlements should not obscure our obligation to search for fair resolutions for the true disputants.

Further, mediation was not a creation of nor does it belong uniquely to the legal profession. Mediation advocates and skilled mediators are from all walks of life, constantly seeking appropriate forms of conflict resolution. Practically, though, many disputes rage in the context of our complex civil justice system. Knowledge of both the mediation process and our rules of law are invaluable to resolving such civil law disputes. But so may disputes arise or escalate because of a failure to communicate, and restoration of good communication is not exclusively within the province of the legal profession.

We must all keep our minds open and avoid self-serving rigidity. The future of mediation will be determined by reasoned experimentation and creativity. In all likelihood, the day will come when co-mediators from multiple disciplines will work together to find rational, satisfying and correct resolutions to all kinds of problems.

This postscript is not an apology for what I have written. We make progress one step at a time. And, as a profession, mediators must remain open to criticism, new ideas and constant re-evaluation.

For my mediation advocate readers, mediators are committed to searching for appropriate resolutions to your clients' disputes. We do the best we can, and we are fervently committed, in collaboration with you, to improving our cherished civil justice system.

Eric Galton
April 1994

Acknowledgements

I find it both a joy and privilege to acknowledge those who have provided me so much support and encouragement in the development of my mediation practice and in the writing of this book. I suppose that the mediator in me compels me to state that the order of these acknowledgements does not reflect any difference in terms of my passionate appreciation to those I will now acknowledge.

I would express my great appreciation, indebtedness and affection to the Honorable Frank Evans, former Chief Justice of the 1st Court of Appeals in Houston. Frank and I co-chaired several State Bar of Texas committees. One day, Frank asked if I knew anything about ADR. I didn't. Frank invited me to attend the very first ADR planning sessions and introduced me to and educated me about ADR. Because of Justice Evans' leadership and efforts, the Texas Alternative Dispute Resolution Procedures Act was passed. Justice Evans' vision and persistence is uniquely responsible for the ADR movement in Texas. But I am particularly grateful for Frank's friendship, advice and encouragement. Frank, you have singularly influenced my professional life and improved me as a person. I am privileged to have you as a friend and mentor.

I would like to thank Professor Kimberlee Kovach with the South Texas College of Law. Professor Kovach graciously volunteered, as one of the leading national experts on ADR, to read this work and provide me with her comments and insights — all of which were extremely helpful. Also Professor Kovach, at a very difficult time in my life, provided me with the inspiration to complete this work. Kim's passion and enthusiasm keep me going. Professor Kovach has exercised great and effective leadership in the ADR movement.

I would express my great appreciation to my law firm, Wright & Greenhill, for their supporting the development of my mediation practice, for supporting this work and for building me a mediation center devoted entirely to the mediation of

Acknowledgements

disputes. I find it encouraging that a large law firm would have the flexibility and professionalism to support a new and very different practice area.

Specifically, I would like to thank our managing shareholder, Mel Waxler, whose leadership helped me at a time when many did not understand my hopes and goals. I would like to thank my partners Chris Phillips and Pat English, who are now also fellow mediators and always provided encouragement. I would also thank my associate Mark Rogstad, who so superbly took control of my litigation practice so I could mediate. I want to express my great appreciation to my paralegal of sixteen years and my "sister," Lee Smith, whose constant friendship has always been a bright and essential part of my life. I extend my great thanks to my mediation coordinator, Debbie Kridner, who schedules and monitors my mediation practice and who has virtually defined, due to her passionate commitment, the role of mediation coordinator. And to Joyce Jarman, who not only typed this entire manuscript, but interpreted my handwriting to do it. Also, I would like to thank our Communications Director, Linda Bittner, who "got it" long before anyone else did and who endured my incessant rantings while I was convincing myself this was all possible. I appreciate your wisdom and constant kindness, Linda.

I would also like to thank several of my dearest friends. Thank you to my friend and brother Robert McEntee, who provided the wonderful music and friendship. Robert, you are the best musician I know. Thank you Rick Stein, my other brother, who is always there for me and makes sure I never take myself too seriously. Special thanks to my friends and colleagues in the Austin Mediators Society. Your constant advice and counsel has been a great help. Also, thank you Professor Randy Lowery, Professor Charles Wiggins and Professor Ed Sherman — all of whom helped me appreciate and understand the negotiation process. Thanks to the Association of Attorney Mediators and my dear friends Ross Hostetter, Mike Amis, Courtenay Bass, Ross Stoddard and Pete Chantillis. Special thanks to my local mediator colleagues, Mike Hebert, Tom Collins, Tom Forbes and Joe Milner.

I would also like to acknowledge and thank my first Mendez Junior High School Peer Mediation Class. You are the best. I would also acknowledge the school prin-

Acknowledgements

cipal, Nato Vera, and the school counselors, Marilyn Rangel, Nancy Lewis, Carolla Chapa-Burnett and Brenda Banks, for their leadership and support.

Thank you to Tracie McFadden Burns, my editor, who helped me shape this work and who was a pleasure to work with.

Thank you and love to my parents, Paul and Anne Galton, for always believing in me and to my brother, Glenn Galton, who will always be my best friend. Thank you to my uncle, I.S. Zimler, who is everything a teacher should be and who put the teacher in me and my aunt, Lillian Zimler, who never gave up on me.

Finally, all my love always to my sons, Justin Galton, Seth Galton and Noah Galton, who make my life so worth living. I love "hanging out" with you and am always aware of how special and wonderful each of you are. This book is dedicated to you because you are the magic and soul of my life.

And, oh yes, thank you to my school, Duke University, the Duke University Basketball team and Coach K. The team and its coach are a constant inspiration to me, because the program epitomizes everything good about collegiate sports.

Thank you once again to all of you. I could never have done any of this without you.

Eric Galton
Wright & Greenhill
Austin, Texas

Preface

Eric Galton's "Representing Clients in Mediation" is a significant and important contribution to the field of dispute resolution. Galton brings valuable insight to the mediation process as an advocate and neutral. His guide is both practical and informative and will assist lawyers in better understanding the mediation process and representing clients more ably in the mediation setting.

In the last 10 years, we have witnessed an increased interest in mediation that is changing the landscape of dispute resolution. Throughout the United States, we are seeing a large number of parties exercise a preference for mediation over adjudication. Nowhere is this more evident than in the Middlesex Multi-door Courthouse in Cambridge, Mass., where disputants select mediation over arbitration 47-1. Many state courts from California to Florida now require mediation in certain civil cases. In addition, the increased interest in mediation can be seen in private service providers. Judicial Arbitration and Mediation Services (JAMS), the largest for-profit provider of dispute resolution services, reports that more than 50 percent of its cases are mediated, representing an increase of almost 20 percent from 1990.

Despite this increased interest, there is still a great deal of confusion about the process and the different forms of mediation and mediation-arbitration hybrids from which to choose. "Representing Clients" excels in de-mystifying the mediation process and defining the various styles and mediation "products" that populate the field. Galton offers a detailed analysis of a mediation, walking the reader through each stage of the process and identifying potential problem areas. Practitioners should find particularly helpful the discussion of the special factors in mediating specific types of cases — from medical malpractice cases to actions involving governmental entities. These chapters, in particular, demonstrate the depth and breadth of Galton's impressive experience as a mediator.

Galton's practical advice also reflects a sensitivity to one of the distinguishing features of mediation: client participation. In mediation, the parties participate fully in the process, arguing their case and articulating negotiating position. Ultimately, the parties decide whether to settle and on what terms. This latter point emphasizes the distinguishing feature of mediation — third parties (judge, jury or arbitrator) do not settle lawsuits, parties do. Galton's "Representing Clients in Mediation" offers insight into the different style of advocacy that is required in a mediation as well as suggestions on preparing the client.

Galton also acknowledges and analyzes the impediments to settlement that, while not insurmountable, may make mediation a less effective tool. For example, the client may want a binding precedent on a specific issue so as to structure its future conduct. A client also may wish to impress other potential litigants with its unwillingness to compromise and the consequent costs of bringing an action against it. While this latter concern may be tempered once a client is aware of the significant costs (and risks) associated with trial, there still will be cases that, for a variety of reasons, clients will decide must be adjudicated in a public court.

With the understanding that mediation cannot be a panacea for the resolution of all disputes, Galton's "Representing Clients in Mediation" demonstrates that a large number of civil disputes may be mediated successfully. In so doing, he has proved his central thesis — that mediation is a valuable and important companion to our judicial system. To the many lawyers who advise clients on mediation (and that should include all of us), I predict Eric Galton's book will become an indispensable resource to our practice.

Robert D. Raven
Morrison & Foerster
Immediate Past Chair , Dispute Resolution Section, ABA

Overview

By Professor Kimberlee Kovach

A. The Role of the Lawyer in a New System of Justice

In the past, a lawyer has been viewed as an attorney and counselor at law. This title implicated that a lawyer helped individuals and entities resolve their problems. Often the resolution of the problem came in the form of legal advice or by initiating a lawsuit. Other times, the lawyer might arrange a meeting, make a phone call, or simply listen. Over the last 30 years, the lawyer's role has shifted dramatically. The lawyer became more like an adversarial mouthpiece for the client. When a client would seek assistance for a specific problem, many lawyers would focus only on the legal ramifications of the matter. Yet most problems do not involve only legal issues. Although lawyers focus on litigation, clients know there are more facets to a controversy and its resolution. Most clients want more from their lawyers.

In resolving disputes, a number of factors in addition to "the law" impact decision making. Such factors are the nonlegal consequences inherent in counseling a client and include the social, financial, psychological and moral implications of the resolution.[1] Many lawyers do not consider these factors, seeing the matter through only legal glasses. While not the only reason for public dissatisfaction with the legal profession, this narrow focus certainly adds to the negative public perception of lawyers.

In the last few years, however, a transformation in the work of the lawyer has occurred. Lawyers have focused more on client satisfaction. The change, in part, is a result of a transformation in the philosophy of the practice of law. Clients also triggered this redirection, as it can be traced to dissatisfied consumers of legal services. Regardless of the cause, an evolution of the role of the lawyer is taking place. We are beginning to witness a new definition of the role and nature of the lawyer's

---

1. David A. Binder & Susan C. Price, LEGAL INTERVIEWING AND COUNSELING 138 (1977).

work. The attorney has become more than one who advocates a certain position for her client in the courtroom. This new lawyer must be knowledgeable about all facets of a client's problem and its resolution.

Since its creation, the legal system has experienced continuous change and modification. Yet other than technological advances, the emergence and integration of alternative dispute resolution (ADR) processes into our system of justice has provided the greatest impact. ADR is changing the way courts operate, and provides a new focus for problem solving. Rather than reliance on rules of procedure, the client's problem can be addressed as a search for a satisfactory resolution. Judicially initiated ADR began primarily as a response to user dissatisfaction with the courts and the administration of justice.[2] Since these new dispute resolution processes assist in more timely and affordable settlements, clients are more satisfied. Firms have begun to require that their lawyers have a background in dispute resolution so that clients' requests for alternative solutions may be met. Integration of ADR processes within the courts have taken place. The result is the emergence of a new system for justice and the resolution of disputes. This new system of problem solving merges innovative processes and procedures with the traditional legal system.

Mediation is the primary alternative process in our new "legal" system. In order for the attorney to fit within the new justice system that includes additional dispute resolution processes, she must modify her role accordingly. The new lawyer, operating within the new legal system, must be cognizant of these changes. The lawyer must be able to ascertain when more legalistic methods are appropriate, when mediation should be utilized, and when the other ADR methods[3] are applicable. The new lawyer will represent her client in both the referral of cases to ADR and in the mediation of such matters. The lawyer will counsel her client in the preliminary decision

---

2. The milestone for the recent, court-annexed ADR movement is the Pound Conference, which took place in 1976. This was a gathering of lawyers and judges to revisit the assertions first published in 1906 by Roscoe Pound, *The Causes of the Popular Dissatisfaction with the Administration of Justice*, (1906), reprinted in 20 J. Am. Jud. Soc'y. 178 (1936).

3. In addition to mediation, the other primary ADR processes include arbitration, case evaluation, mini-trial and summary jury trial. See Ch. 20, infra.

to use an alternative forum for resolution as well as in the process itself. Just as the lawyer is aware of the rules and policies surrounding discovery or pretrial matters, so she must be knowledgeable of these ADR processes. The new lawyer must be able to be an effective advocate and negotiator in mediation and the other ADR processes, just as the more traditional lawyer is effective in a motion hearing or in trial. As the legal system transitions, so must the lawyer working within the system.

B. The Law of Mediation: A Continuous Evolution

As the mediation process and the traditional legal system become integrated, each influences the other. By participating in the creative problem-solving process of mediation, lawyers are becoming healers of conflict. They are learning innovative methods for resolving disputes; however, as mediation moves in to the legal arena, it is becoming more legalized. When participants in a mediation of a lawsuit are confronted with a problem, rather than mediate a solution, they have returned to the courts. What was designed to be an alternative to the legal process is now being shaped and guided by it. Consequently, a new area of law is in the process of development, namely the law of mediation.

The expediency of the growth of dispute resolution, and mediation specifically, is unparalleled. For instance, in 1980 there were very few state statutes with regard to mediation or dispute resolution programs. By 1990, over 300 state statutes dealing with alternative dispute resolution had been enacted.[4] In 1980, less than 10 state or local bar associations had a dispute resolution committee. Today all states but four have committees or sections on ADR, and local bar association committees are numerous and busy. Sections of dispute resolution had to be established because the number of interested lawyers became so great that committee work was impossible. Law schools have recognized the increased need for the new lawyer. For instance, in 1983 less than 25 percent of our law schools offered courses that would fall within the dispute resolution field. Nearly every law school in the nation, as well as those in many other countries, currently offer courses in dispute resolution and

---

4. American Bar Association Standing Committee on Dispute Resolution, LEGISLATION ON DISPUTE RESOLUTION (1990).

mediation. Several have clinical programs that provide the law student firsthand experience with the mediation process. With a field this new, there has been little time to decide matters with certainty.

Consequently, such rapid growth resulted in continuous change. The field of mediation has evolved from initial experimentation to implementation and is now moving to regulation. When ADR was first considered as an option to the traditional legal system, many experimented with the processes, and a number of "pilot projects" developed. This experimentation produced positive results, which caused additional programs to be implemented. More recently however, it has been realized that the broad ramifications of implementation, particularly in legal terms, had not been considered. These issues, which are now being studied, include matters of certification and regulation of mediators, ethics of all participants, and legal parameters of the process.

This introduction will provide an overview of the status of a number of current issues that surround the use of mediation. The primary focus will be on situations that lawyers are likely to encounter. However, the reader should keep in mind that with the dynamic development of the process, the status of these issues are subject to change. New cases and innovative situations are addressed on a regular basis. Legislatures and other rule-making bodies are constantly enacting new rules and procedures. Mediators themselves are examining issues in an attempt at self-determination. Moreover, the practice of mediation, by its very nature, is flexible, without rigid boundaries and regulations. Some cases and standards, even within the same jurisdiction, can produce contrary results. Therefore, the lawyer, when researching issues surrounding the process, must do so with care. She should specifically examine and research each matter within the jurisdiction or court in which she is practicing, being certain to locate the most recent information.

C. Referrals and Participation in Mediation

How disputing parties get to the mediation table is a critical part of the process. The knowledge, attitude and expectation of mediation participants, clients and lawyers can significantly impact how the matter is resolved. While consensual media-

---

tions are often preferred, mediators, lawyers and parties alike have begun a mediation convinced that it is not appropriate but, after a few hours, a satisfactory settlement results. This has been observed in cases that have not yet entered the legal system as well as in pending lawsuits.

1. Pre-litigation cases

Prior to filing a lawsuit, there are essentially three ways by which a dispute may enter the mediation process. One is the case where the parties involved in the dispute have previously agreed to mediation. There has recently been a significant increase in the use of mediation clauses. The second involves a statutory scheme that mandates mediation participation before a lawsuit can be filed. The third method of referral consists of a voluntary agreement to mediate. The parties themselves, or through their attorneys at the time of conflict, may consent to participate in the mediation process before initiating litigation.

a. Contractual

In cases where the parties contract for mediation in advance, there is usually little hesitancy about the process. The parties or their counsel are at least vaguely familiar with the process, most likely having discussed it at the time of contract. The actual mediator may even have been identified in the mediation clause. When entering into an agreement to mediate, parties should include the various details of the process in the original mediation clause, since reaching consensus is more likely before a dispute occurs.

Since the parties voluntarily agreed to mediate, presumably they will abide by the agreement. However, if one of the disputing parties refuses to participate in the process, issues of enforceability arise. Can the parties be compelled to mediate? In other words, are mediation clauses in contracts or other documents such as wills or trusts enforceable?

One case has specifically addressed this issue and held that an agreement to mediate is enforceable.[5] In this case, the mediation clause was a condition precedent to litigation and failure to conform with the agreement resulted in the dismissal of the cause of action.[6] However, this decision came several years after initiation of the lawsuit. Consequently, some mediation clauses now include liquidated damages provisions, in the event the parties try to proceed with litigation first.

Cases directly on point are sparse, although if an analogy to arbitration clauses is made, enforcement is probable. The general consensus is that most courts will enforce mediation clauses, as long as a fundamental right is not threatened.[7]

b. Pre-suit mediation programs

Pre-suit mediations may be mandated by statute or court rules. In other instances, cases of a specific nature may be required to participate in mediation as part of a program or project. For instance, some insurance companies have established programs where the first step in the claims process is mediation. As these programs become more popular, contractual provisions in policies have been added.

In some states, participation in mediation is a prerequisite to proceeding in a court, for example in some medical malpractice cases, a matter is heard by a panel prior to the initiation of a lawsuit.[8] Additionally, some employers have implemented dispute resolution systems that dictate that a complaint about the workplace must be mediated before the party can bring a formal cause of action.

c. Voluntary agreements

Individuals may agree to attempt to resolve a dispute by mediation prior to seeking legal advice. Parties familiar with the process can seek out a mediator for assistance in a matter. Additional intervention is not necessary. However, these cases are

---

5. *De Valk Lincoln Mercury, Inc. v. Ford Motor Co.*, 811 F.2d 326 (7th Cir. 1987).
6. Id. at 336.
7. Nancy H. Rogers and Craig A. McEwen, MEDIATION: LAW, POLICY, AND PRACTICE 61 (1989).
8. See for example, *Woods v. Holy Cross Hospital*, 591 F.2d 1164 (5th Cir. 1979).

---

not numerous. Although those within the ADR field are continuously educating the public about the mediation process, its use has not reached the point where most individuals involved in a dispute immediately think of this alternative. Moreover, some commentators have observed that the very nature by which individuals dispute often discourages disputants from entering mediation spontaneously or voluntarily.[9] Therefore, it is often necessary to utilize an identifiable avenue to encourage disputing individuals to access the mediation process. One such method is referral through a citizen complaint center.[10] At these centers, citizens are interviewed by a trained intake specialist and where appropriate, referred to mediation. In most situations, mediation is available at little or no cost to the disputing parties.

More attorneys are becoming familiar with the mediation process and its potential benefit to their clients. It is no longer the exception that attorneys suggest to clients that they make an effort at settlement prior to filing a lawsuit. In fact, it may now be part of the attorney's role to suggest and discuss the possibility of ADR with his client. Some have argued that the failure to do so constitutes legal malpractice.[11] Although the client may have gone to the attorney because she is ready to fight, not settle, the attorney-counselor must remember that all options of a case should be discussed with the client. While the initial consultation may not be the optimum time, allowing the client to incur sizeable legal fees before suggesting mediation is not the best option either. A specific formula for determining when to suggest alternatives does not exist. Each case and client differs and must be considered by the attorney in light of suggesting voluntary mediation.

---

9. Craig A. McEwen and Thomas W. Milburn, *Explaining a Paradox of Mediation*, 9 Negotiation J. 23, 34 (1993).

10. Citizen complaint centers are usually quasi-governmental agencies affixed to a prosecutor's or district attorney's office or courthouse. When citizens involved in a dispute call the police for assistance, they are often referred to these centers.

11. Robert F. Cochran, *Legal Representation and the Next Steps Toward Client Control: Attorney Malpractice for the Failure to Allow the Client to Control Negotiation and Pursue Alternatives to Litigation*, 47 Wash. & Lee L. Rev. 819 (1990).

2. Pending lawsuits

A pending lawsuit can find itself in mediation in a number of ways. Although currently rare, certainly the urging of mediation by the parties is an appropriate avenue to mediation. While contractual provisions either advising or mandating mediation prior to a lawsuit is technically a pre-litigation matter, in some instances the mediation will not occur until after suit is filed. During the litigation process, lawyers may suggest mediation to one another or the court may prompt mediation use. A number of courts have become active in referring pending lawsuits to a variety of ADR processes, including mediation. The court's authority to make referrals, along with the litigants' right to object and demand a trial, are issues at the core of an ongoing debate about mandatory mediation. Additional cost to the parties and the extent of participation in the process are additional matters for consideration in this context.

An initial concern is the authority of a court to mandate referral. Several states have enacted legislation that either allows or mandates courts to refer a case to ADR processes, including mediation. A sampling of those statutes, along with a brief overview of mediation activity in state courts is included as Appendix D. Some courts are required to determine whether a case is appropriate for mediation, while others have been provided complete discretion. In a few instances, the court's authority to mandate parties to participate in mediation has been challenged as has ADR in general.

When examining potential issues of mandatory referral, it is helpful to distinguish between public and private sector mediation. Public mediation covers those situations in which the mediation process is provided in a public forum[12] at very little or no cost to the parties. In these cases, the mediators are either employed by, or volunteers with, the court system in which the case is pending.[13] In private sector mediation, the mediator is in business for a profit and will provide mediation ser-

---

12. Public here meaning accessible by all, not open in terms of nonconfidential.
13. Examples include the California Mandatory Custody and the Washington, D.C. Civil Case Multi-Door Courthouse Program.

vices for a fee. There is little debate about whether an individual, with or without counsel, may voluntarily avail herself of the private sector mediator for whatever cost she determines appropriate; in essence, the principle of free market choice. However, in instances in which the court compels or mandates participation in a private mediation, substantial concerns can arise. Most of these focus on the additional cost to the parties, along with an alleged denial of the right to trial. In most cases courts can order parties to incur additional cost, but the cost is considered in light of the amount in controversy. In at least one case concerning the arbitration process, a court held that a bond as a prerequisite to trial was too heavy a burden on access to court.[14] It appears the courts will apply a balancing test to determine if the burden to the litigants is reasonable in light of the benefits of ADR procedures.

Where there is no statute or rule providing for ADR, courts have relied on their inherent power to manage their dockets to support a referral to an ADR process. When this has been challenged, there has been a split of authority. However, over the last few years, many states have enacted ADR statutes. In 1990 Congress specifically mandated all federal courts to implement cost and delay reduction plans.[15] Although not mandatory, the inclusion of ADR processes in these plans was strongly encouraged.[16]

In response to the Civil Justice Reform Act, all 94 federal courts have submitted their cost and delay reduction plans. The majority do contain ADR provisions. However, as in many situations, there are differences between design and implementation. Appendix E provides an overview of a number of plans of the federal district courts that currently contain mediation provisions. As many of these plans were recently submitted, the advocate must, however, be certain to determine whether, and the degree to which, the plan has been implemented.

In the instances where courts do mandate cases to mediation, additional questions arise, such as what constitutes participation. Participation can be described in

---

14. *Eastin v. Broomfield*, 570 P.2d 744 (Ariz. 1977).
15. 28 U.S.C.A. § 471-482 (1993).
16. 28 U.S.C.A. § 473(a)(b).

a number of ways: good faith; the exchange of position papers; meaningful partic-ipation; attendance at the mediation only; or an obligation to pay the mediator's fee.[17]

The first question of participation is whether the court can order specific parties to attend or participate. This issue has been addressed specifically by federal courts in the context of settlement conferences, first in the terms of a corporate represen-tative in *G. Heileman Brewing Co., Inc. v. Joseph Oat Corp.*,[18] and more recently with regard to a governmental official in *In re: Stone*.[19] In essence, the courts will balance the right to trial with the benefit of settlement. The next question is if parties must attend, what must they do, or essentially, what does participation mean? In *Graham v. Baker*,[20] which involved farmer-creditor mediation, the court examined a state statute that required participation in mediation. The court determined that even though the creditor refused to cooperate with the mediator, the mere presence of the creditor satisfied the participation requirement of the statute.[21]

In *Decker v. Lindsay*,[22] the court was directly confronted with a challenge to a requirement of good faith mediation. In this case, the court's power to mandate par-ticipation in a mediation was limited to attendance under the Texas enabling statute. The decision made clear that the court cannot compel a good faith participation.

However, other jurisdictions do compel the good faith participation of the par-ties. For example, in Maine the court has the duty to determine whether the parties made a good faith effort at mediation. If good faith is found to be lacking, the court may order a re-mediation, dismissal, or other sanction.[23] As courts continue to

---

17. Edward F. Sherman, *Court-Mandated Alternative Dispute Resolution: What Form of Participation Should Be Required*, 46 SMU L. Rev. 2079 (1993).
18. 871 F.2d 648 (7th Cir. 1989).
19. 986 F.2d 898 (5th Cir. 1993).
20. 447 N.W.2d 397 (Iowa 1989).
21. Id. at 401.
22. 824 S.W.2d 247 (Tex.App.--Houston [1st Dist.] 1992).
23. 1993 Me. Rev. Code § 636.

implement ADR, and in particular mediation procedures, questions such as these will continue to arise. Currently no recognizable trend has been established.

3. Effect of Mediation Referral on Pending Litigation

A recent trend involving court-referred mediation is the tolling of action while the matter is in mediation. For example, in Colorado, if the court is informed that the parties are engaged in good faith mediation, any pending hearing can be continued.[24] Indiana provides that when a civil case is referred to a dispute resolution center, the court, subject to a few exceptions, shall suspend action on the case.[25] Moreover, in some instances a request or an agreement to mediate can temporarily stop the running of a statute of limitations.[26] A Montana statute also tolls an applicable statute of limitations when either the parties agree to mediate or a court orders mediation in family cases.[27] Trial and discovery time deadlines are stayed in Oregon courts.[28] Of course, even in those jurisdictions that do not provide tolling, advocates may consider entering into an agreement to stay all litigation until after mediation is completed.

D. Confidentiality and Mediation

When people discuss the beneficial aspects of ADR, confidentiality is generally included. The private nature of the process is even more explicit in mediation than other ADR procedures. Mediation has always been considered confidential, and at times, the words are used almost synonymously. Most people operate under the assumption that the mediation process is confidential, even if it is not.[29] However, a close examination of what specifically is meant by confidentiality may be very confusing.

---

24. Colo. Rev. Stat. § 13-22-311(3) (1991).

25. Ind. Code § 34-4-42-3 (1993).

26. Ind. Code § 34-4-2.5-20(b)(2) (1993); Wash. Rev. Code § 7.75.080 (1992); Wash. Rev. Code § 7.70.110 (1994).

27. 1993 Mont. Laws Ch. 199 § 2(4).

28. Or. Rev. Stat. § 36.190(3) (1993).

29. Lawrence Freedman and Michael Prigoff, *Confidentiality in Mediation: The Need for Protection*, 2 Ohio St. J. Dis. Res. 37, 42 (1986).

Overview

Most mediation programs within the courts as well as in the community setting began with an assumption of confidentiality. As time passed and in-depth analysis occurred, confidentiality in mediation has become questioned. In fact, it is possible that mediators have specific duties to disclose. While a detailed analysis of confidentiality in the mediation process is beyond this introduction and is treated at length elsewhere,[30] some consideration will be provided to acquaint the reader of the recent trends and underlying policies.

The case law reveals that where there exists a statute providing for confidentiality in mediation, the courts will generally uphold it.[31] What is more problematic, is the determination of the type, or the extent, of confidentiality. Whether confidentiality is viewed in legal or lay-person terms can add to the confusion. From the non-attorney's standpoint, being informed that the mediation is confidential could mean a variety of things. Many people see "confidential" as something secret; information that should not be disclosed to anyone — ever. Disputing parties may believe that absolutely no one but those present in the mediation will know what occurred. At the other end is a view of confidentiality that means the discussions occurring in mediation are not revealed to the court, but can be disclosed to the rest of the world. Another perspective is that only those present, plus individuals directly related to and affected by the dispute, can know about the mediation.

1. Exclusion or Privilege

The legal environment has two distinctions with regard to confidentiality: exclusion and privilege. Often, in discussing the confidential nature of the mediation session, the two are not distinguished. Confidentiality is discussed and even guaranteed; yet it is not made clear whether the confidentiality is in terms of establishing an evidentiary exclusion, which could prohibit anything stated at the mediation from being admitted at trial, or, whether it is in the context of a mediation privilege, with ramifications that could prevent disclosure for almost any purpose.

---

30. Supra, Note 7 at Chap. 8.
31. Id. at 119.

The advocate should be certain whether either or both is in effect before advising his client.

a. An evidentiary exclusion

Exclusions are dictated generally by rules of evidence. One method by which information disclosed during a mediation may be excluded from evidence at the trial of a case is by the application of a rule of evidence. Rules of evidence have historically provided protection for discussions which attempt to settle a matter. Specifically Federal Rule of Evidence 408, which has state counterparts, provides that:

Evidence of (1) furnishing or offering or promising to furnish or (2) accepting or offering or promising to accept. a valuable consideration in compromising or attempting to compromise a claim which was disputed as to either validity or amount, is not admissible to prove liability for or invalidity of the claim or its amount. Evidence of conduct or statements made in compromise negotiations is likewise not admissible. This rule does not require the exclusion of any evidence otherwise discoverable merely because it is presented in the course of compromise negotiations. This rule also does not require exclusion when the evidence is offered for another purpose, such as proving bias or prejudice of a witness, negating a contention of undue delay, or proving an effort to obstruct a criminal investigation or prosecution.[32]

Mediation is, in essence, a structured negotiation that relies on compromises. Therefore expansion of Rule 408 specifically to the mediation appears consistent with the general purpose and policy of the rule.

---

32. Federal Rule of Evidence 408.

However Rule 408 has limitations, and reliance on only Rule 408 to protect the entire mediation can be detrimental. For instance, one court has held that Rule 408 does not apply to the entire negotiation; all statements made are not covered by the rule.[33] Therefore, if Rule 408 alone is to be relied upon for confidentiality, care must be taken that all statements are related to the compromise. Much stated at the mediation, particularly the offers and exchanges, if not contingent upon one another, would not normally be protected by Rule 408. Although there are broader mediation evidentiary exclusions,[34] these are rare.

Under Rule 408 and similar state statutes, statements are only excluded if used to prove validity of the claim or amount. Statements can be admitted if they are offered for another purpose, such as impeachment.[35]

Moreover, an evidentiary exclusion only limits admissibility of information at a trial. Disclosures and testimony in other situations are possible. Exclusions, however, would prohibit all participants from testifying. It is the information that is excluded, regardless of whose testimony is sought. A privilege, on the other hand, may cover a number of situations, but is limited to prohibiting a specific individual from disclosure.

b. Privilege

A privilege is a legal concept that provides a broader scope of confidentiality by protecting against a number of disclosures. Privileges are created by law in recognition of certain relationships that are built on trust and a need for protection of privacy. While initially created by common law, many privileges are now created by statute. States have begun to enact statutes providing for confidentiality in mediation and some of these have been recognized as a mediation privilege. In some

---

33. *Thomas v. Resort Health Related Facility*, 539 F.Supp. 630 (E.D.N.Y. 1982), held that the evidence of an offer for reinstatement during a settlement meeting was deemed outside 408 because it was not contingent upon compromise.

34. See Maine R. Evid. 408(b), which excludes evidence of mediation discussions for any purpose.

35. Federal Rule of Evidence 408.

instances, a mediation privilege may even include the files and records of a mediation program.[36]

Another relevant factor in considering protection by a mediation privilege is the determination of who holds the privilege. In other relationships that enjoy privileged communications there are only two parties, such as the doctor and patient or lawyer and client. The implication and rule is that the holder of the privilege is the patient or the client; it is that individual who may waive the privilege. In the situation of mediation, there are always more than two parties. Can the privilege be held by the mediator, without regard to the parties? Are the parties able to waive it? Must all parties agree for the waiver to be effective? One case that tangentially approached this issue was *Fenton v. Howard*[37] where, in a conciliation court, the neutral was not compelled to testify although the parties waived the confidentiality.[38] Some of these questions have been at least preliminarily answered by recently enacted state statutes. For example in Colorado, all parties and the mediator must consent in writing before disclosure can be compelled.[39] On the other hand, Wyoming has made it clear that the privilege is held only on behalf of a party.[40]

In nearly all reported cases, the courts have upheld the confidentiality of the mediation. They have done so primarily by enforcing a statute or agency rule.[41] Even in the instance where a mediator was ordered to provide deposition testimony, the court left open the possibility that the result would differ if there had been a state statute providing for confidentiality.[42] However, some experts contend that the cases to date do not indicate a trend toward a generic common law mediation priv-

---

36. Rogers & McEwen, supra, note 7 at 115.
37. 575 P.2d 318 (Ariz. 1978).
38. However, the dissenting opinion was clear in its position that the privilege belonged only to the parties.
39. Colo. Rev. Stat. § 13-22-307 (1991).
40. Wyo. Stat. § 1-43-103 (1993).
41. See *NLRB v. Joseph Macaluso, Inc.* 618 F.2d 51 (9th Cir. 1980); *United States v. Gullo*, 672 F.Supp. (W.D.N.Y. 1987).
42. *State v. Castellano*, 460 So.2d 480 (1984).

ilege or that courts will create such a protection. Rather these cases generally have involved labor negotiations, and evidence a confirmation of an explicit legislative intent to encourage settlements through mediation.[43]

2. Confidentiality Agreements and Court Orders

Another means to acquire confidentiality in mediation is through a confidentiality agreement. While most agreements to maintain the secretive or confidential nature of matters going before the court have not been upheld, some argue that mediation should be an exception. Because of the current confusion and difficulty surrounding issues of confidentiality in mediation, if the parties wish to assure themselves and the mediator of protection, an agreement is recommended. In fact, the ABA Standards of Practice for Lawyer-Mediators in Family Disputes indicate that a mediator should ask the parties for such an agreement. However, these standards also contain a provision that places a duty upon the lawyer-mediator to inform the parties of the limited effectiveness of the agreement as to third parties.[44] There are several issues for consideration when contemplating a confidentiality agreement as an avenue for protection.

If the parties have voluntarily entered into a confidentiality agreement, and the subject matter to be protected is not a matter about which testimony should be compelled, it is likely that a court will uphold and enforce it.[45] It is likely that courts will enforce confidentiality agreements against those who sign the agreement.[46] However, it may not have any effect on non-parties to the agreement.

Enforcement of the agreement may be simple in the trial process. However, if the disclosure is made or threatened outside of litigation, it is more difficult for the courts to restrain disclosure. More probable will be an alternative new cause of

---

43. Rogers & McEwen, supra, note 7 at 119.
44. *ABA Standards of Practice for Lawyers - Mediators in Family Disputes* (1984).
45. *Simrin v. Simrin*, 233 Cal. App. 2d. 90, 43 Cal. Rptr. 376, (5th Dist. 1965) upheld such an agreement in the context of counseling. A previously existing agreement not to subpoena a rabbi who acted as marriage counselor was enforced.
46. Rogers & McEwen, supra, note 7 at 136.

action for a breach.[47] The problem is that often the harm is already done. In response to this concern some confidentiality agreements provide for liquidated damages.

In instances where enforcement by a court is not likely, there nevertheless may be benefit to executing a nondisclosure agreement. For example, the written agreement may serve as a deterrent. In this case, a party may maintain confidentiality because they have agreed to, not because they are legally bound to. Confidentiality agreements may also deter third parties from seeking information.

Somewhat related to party-executed confidentiality agreements are orders of the court. Specifically, courts can order the parties to maintain confidentiality in the nature of a protective order. Some courts routinely include in their order of referral to mediation a provision that the process is confidential. Of course this type of protection is limited primarily to the litigation process. As in other cases of challenge, the courts will apply a balancing test. The burden to show compelling need for the information is far greater on those who stipulated to the protective order than outside parties.[48]

3. Discovery

In the majority of pending litigation cases, confidentiality issues arise during the discovery process. Many statutes that provide for confidentiality in either an evidentiary exclusion or privilege include a discovery exception. Specifically, if a matter is otherwise discoverable, then the fact that it is discussed in a compromise or mediation does not protect it from discovery. The basis of the exception is to keep parties from discussing information during the mediation process, solely to invoke the rule of confidentiality later. However, the problem here is that the exception for "matters otherwise discoverable" is often so great that in essence it leaves little protected material.

---

47. Id. at 137.
48. Id. at 133.

4. Duties to Disclose

Assuming that confidentiality is established as either an exclusion or privilege, there may be instances where the law, nevertheless, establishes a duty on the part of the mediator to make disclosures.

Under the evidentiary exclusion, there should be very few instances, other than a statutorily imposed one, where the mediator must disclose, that is, testify in a court. The California Trial Custody Program is one such exception. In this program (which some may claim is not true mediation), if an agreement is not reached between the parties, the mediator may make a specific recommendation to the court.[49] Likewise, where a criminal defendant needs the testimony of a mediator as a defense, the court may require the information from the mediator.[50]

In some cases, statutes mandate the disclosure of certain information. The most common is a duty to report child abuse. Some of the statutes that establish confidentiality in mediation include specific provisions that exclude from confidentiality those matters that are otherwise required to be disclosed.[51] What is more difficult are situations where there is no legal duty to disclose, but the mediator may feel an ethical or moral duty to make certain disclosures. If an advocate determines that the subject matter of a mediation may fall within this area, he should clarify with the mediator the parameters of confidentiality and its exceptions.

5. Policy Considerations

The law surrounding confidentiality in mediation is uncertain and in the process of change. When the courts are confronted with confidentiality questions, policy issues are likely to be considered. The underlying purpose of the mediation process is settlement. Some contend that only if the process is confidential and the items dis-

---

49. Cal. Civ. Code § 3183 (1994).
50. *State v. Castellano*, 460 So.2d 480 (Fla.App. 2nd Dist, 1984).
51. See Tex. Civ. Prac. & Rem. Code Ann. § 154.073(b) (Vernon Supp. 1993) and Utah Code Ann. § 78-31b-7(3) (1992).

cussed therein are protected as secret, will the parties be willing to make disclosures and openly discuss their underlying interests, needs, wants and desires.

In part, a need for confidentiality in mediation is similar to the policy considerations underlying Federal Rule of Evidence 408. With the assurance of confidentiality, parties and lawyers are more willing to discuss matters openly and propose settlements. The longstanding exclusionary rules surrounding compromise discussions is one of the stronger policy considerations for establishing confidentiality in mediation. Protection of the relationship between the mediator and the parties is another reason why many propose that the mediation process should be a confidential one. However, problems of fraud and the right of the public to be informed of certain matters provide arguments for a more public mediation process.

6. Current Statutes and Cases

If courts and legislatures establish a mediation privilege, there is a question about the specific nature of that privilege. Although courts have displayed a trend to create qualified privileges, about half of the mediation privilege statutes appear to be absolute, failing to indicate an awareness of any need for a more balanced approach.[52]

Many states have enacted legislation that distinctly applies to the mediation hearing. Those states which have passed statutes, most include a specific provision which excludes statements from evidence. These include Texas, Oklahoma, Washington, Wyoming, California and Florida. Local mediation programs have specific rules as well. There are currently no reported cases where the court has compelled the mediator to testify in court where such a statute exists.

When deciding to mediate, if confidentiality is an important factor, the lawyer should first research the current statutes and case law. In the rare situation where the mediation takes place outside of the jurisdiction where the case is pending, then both jurisdictions should be checked. If it is unclear as to the specific information

---

52. Rogers & McEwen, supra, note 7 at 124.

that would be protected, the attorney should consider a protective order or confidentiality agreement.

There exist five primary ways to assure "confidentiality" in mediation. These are:

- Statute

- Local Court Rule

- Court Order

- Case Law

- Agreement

The lawyer should consider if any of these are in effect, and the specific extent of protection afforded to the mediation participants.

E.   The Mediated Agreement: Its Form and Enforceability

The agreement that results from a mediation can take a number of forms. The specific nature of the agreement should be considered by the lawyer and his client. In pre-litigation cases, there is little choice; a mediated resolution will be either a written or verbal agreement. In pending cases, however, more options are available. The case can be dismissed, and an independent agreement or contract executed; the mediated agreement can constitute an agreed judgment of the case; the final judgment can incorporate the mediation agreement by reference; the judgment may merely refer to the agreement; or the judgment may include only a portion of the agreement. Counsel for the parties should take care to determine with precision the form of the mediated agreement and particularly its relationship to, and effect upon, the pending lawsuit.

Periodically concerns about the enforceability of the agreement have been raised, and recent cases have addressed this issue. For the most part, any agreement reached during a mediation will likely be governed by general contract law. Some state legislatures have confirmed this identical nature of a mediated agreement and contract by including such a provision in a statute.[53]

Alternatively, other states have come to the conclusion that an agreement reached through mediation should be treated differently than contracts or agreements reached without a mediator's assistance. For example, Minnesota provides that a mediated agreement is NOT enforceable unless it states that it is, and includes specific language that the parties were advised of their legal rights, that a mediator has no duty to protect their rights or provide information, and that the mediator urged the parties to consult with an attorney.[54] Moreover, in debtor/creditor mediation, Minnesota adds a requirement that allows the parties 72 hours to withdraw from the agreement.[55] Utah requires that if an ADR agreement is to be enforceable as a contract, it must include such an acknowledgment and be in writing.[56] When preparing for mediation, the advocate should refer to local statutes. However, even in cases where there may exist some question about enforceability, because the parties have participated in the process, they own, and are therefore psychologically committed to the agreement. In most cases, parties are satisfied with the process and comply voluntarily with the agreement.

Courts have confronted these issues as well. When the mediation concerns a pending lawsuit, the rules of procedure for settlement agreements generally are applicable. In *Rizk v. Millard*,[57] the settlement agreement reached at mediation was not signed by the parties. The court held that since Tex. R. Civ. Pro. 11 requires any settlement agreement to be signed, the agreement was unenforceable by the trial court in the pending case. However, the court left available to the parties the option of enforcement of the new contract. Likewise, in *Barnett v. Sea Land Service, Inc.*[58]

---

53. See Tex. Civ. Prac. & Rem. Code § 154.071(d) (Vernon Supp. 1993) and Utah Code Ann. § 30-3-28(4) (1993).
54. Minn. Civ. Code § 572.35 Subd. 1 (1988).
55. Minn. Civ. Code § 572.35 Subd. 2 (1988).
56. Utah Code Ann. §78-316-5 (1991).
57. 810 S.W.2d 318 (Tex.App.--Houston [14th Dist.] 1991).
58. 875 F.2d 741 (9th Cir. 1989).

the court's holding, based primarily on Local Rule 39.1(d)(3), was that unless a settlement reached in mediation was reduced to writing, it is not binding upon the parties.

In a later Texas case, *In the Matter of the Marriage of Ames*,[59] the appellate court held a signed mediated settlement enforceable and further ruled that the trial court must enter a decree that embodies the agreement. One party attempted to withdraw consent after the agreement was executed. The court emphasized that settlement agreements reached in mediation are enforceable and binding. When confronted with the question of whether the trial court may review and modify the agreement of the parties, the court emphasized that the court should render a judgment consistent with the parties' agreement. The issue of court review in terms of mediation has rarely has been presented to the courts. However, at least one legislature has instructed its courts to conform judgments to mediated agreements.[60]

F. Ethical Considerations in Mediation

At first glance, a consideration of ethics involved in mediation will focus on the mediator. The ethical aspects of the mediator's work has been the subject of a number of articles.[61] Several organizations such as the Academy of Family Mediators, SPIDR (Society of Professionals in Dispute Resolution), state and local bar associations, and other organized groups of mediators have enacted or are in the process of drafting and enacting codes of ethics for mediators. An attempt is being made to enact a code applicable to mediation in all civil cases. This is a combined effort of three primary organizations: AAA (American Arbitration Association), SPIDR and the ABA Section of Dispute Resolution.

---

59. 860 S.W.2d 590 (Tex.App.--Amarillo 1993).

60. N.C. Gen. St. § 50-13-1 (1992).

61. See Robert A. Baruch Bush, The Dilemmas of Mediation Practice: A Study of Ethical Dilemmas and Policy Implications, A report on a study for the National Institute of Dispute Resolution (1992); Robert A. Baruch Bush, *Efficiency and Protection, or Empowerment and Recognition?: The Mediator's Role and Ethical Standards in Mediation*, 41 Fla. L. Rev. 253 (1989).

Yet the ethical considerations present in a mediation go beyond the mediator. It is possible that ethical guidelines and rules may be appropriate for organizational providers of mediation services, referring entities such as courts and employers, and for participants in the process.

With regard to the ethical standards for mediators, since a number of organizations have promulgated codes of ethics or standards of conduct, one mediator may be governed by a number or codes. While the majority are consistent, there are occasions of contradiction. The advocate may want to ascertain prior to the mediation what code, if any, the mediator follows.

Primary ethical issues facing mediators include conflicts of interest; providing professional information or advice; parameters of referrals; confidentiality; and fees. While agreement exists that mediators should avoid conflicts of interest, there is little consensus on exactly what constitutes a violation. Prohibitions may include mediating any dispute involving a previous client, even if an unrelated matter, and acquaintance with the attorney advocates. Most codes in existence ban the mediator from providing the disputants professional advice, while some remain silent on the issue. Advertising should be truthful and fees reasonable. In most cases, contingency fees are prohibited. Most of the previous issues are also appropriate matters for consideration by private organizational providers of mediation services.

Because courts have become active in the referral of cases to mediation, many believe that they, too, should be governed by standards which assure ethical behavior. Special standards for the courts have been promulgated,[62] and while only aspirational, it is anticipated that courts will more carefully examine issues surrounding the implementation of mediation within the court system. These standards suggest that a court determine that a case is properly referred to mediation; that the mediator to whom a case is referred is competent, and that the court does not receive confi-

---

62. See National Standards for Court-Connected Mediation Programs, Center for Dispute Settlement and Institute of Judicial Administration (1992).

dential information.[63] These standards might also be applicable where other public entities such as governmental agencies refer parties to mediation.

In those instances where private individuals or organizations make referrals to providers of mediation services, there may be ethical issues raised concerning quality assurance or referral fees.

Ethical concerns for the lawyer advocate may also arise in the mediation setting. Most likely, these are identical to those in the traditional representation and settlement of cases. Certainly any guidelines regarding ethics in negotiation would likewise be applicable in mediation. For the attorney advocate, some of these matters are related to issues of liability.

G. Issues of Liability

As with most other providers of professional services, mediators have become concerned with issues regarding liability. It seems that the most common claim would be that of negligence. However, determining if the mediator's actions may be negligent can be difficult since there has yet to be established definitive standards of conduct. Other possible causes of action include breach of contract, libel, slander, fraud, false imprisonment, breach of fiduciary duty and tortious interference with a business relationship.

Although most of these have not yet been tested, some states have established immunity — mostly for volunteer mediators.[64] At least one state supreme court has protected court-annexed mediators.[65] In addition, two courts have provided guidance on this issue. When a mediator handles a case pursuant to a court referral, judicial immunity is extended to the mediator.[66]

---

63. Id.

64. For example see West's Colo. Rev. Stat. Ann. § 13-22-305(6) (1993); Iowa Code Ann. § 679.13 (1993); and West's Rev. Code Wash. Ann. § 7.75.100 (1992).

65. Rule 6.2, Alternative Dispute Resolution Rules, Supreme Court of Georgia, March 9, 1993.

66. See *Howard v. Drapkin*, 222 Cal. App. 3d 843 (2d. Dist. 1990) and *Wagshal v Foster*, 1993 WL 86499 (D.D.C.)(not reported in F. Supp.).

Liability concerns can also arise for the lawyer advocate. For instance, the traditional areas of potential liability in the representation of clients are also present in the mediation environment. For instance, an issue which has not yet been resolved surrounds the decision-making authority of the lawyer versus the client. Clearly a lawyer has a duty to advise the client about specific settlement offers on the table.[67] But what is less clear are decisions to pursue settlement options.[68] In terms of the client, if, as many now advocate, he is to make the decisions as "owner of the case," he must have information. The client must be able to evaluate all options available to him for the resolution of a matter. Participating in the mediation process can directly provide the client with that information. One of the benefits of mediation may be that it can protect a lawyer from later claims of malpractice, since the client participates in the process, and in most instances and under most models, will be the decision maker.

As added protection for the advocate, the client's unambiguous consent to the settlement will be present. In nearly all instances, the mediator will have both the client and lawyer sign the memorandum of agreement. As the use of mediation increases and the attorney advocate sees the benefits of using mediation, cases resolved by the process continue to increase. As participants in the process, no doubts attorneys representing clients in mediation will be actively shaping the new "law of mediation."

Kimberlee K. Kovach
South Texas College of Law

---

67. See *Rizzo v. Haines*, 520 Pa. 484, 555 A.2d 58 (1989).
68. Supra, note 11.

Overview

Chapter 1

Mediation Styles

Let us begin by stating what mediation is not or should not be. Mediation should not be coercive. Mediation is not "snake-charming" or voodoo. Mediation, as a dear and wise colleague jokingly referred to it, is not a séance. Mediation is not a spiritual awakening, although resolution favorably impacts the spirit. Mediation is not "wimpy," "touchy-feely," or for the weak of heart. We do not sing songs at a mediation — although if it would result in resolution, I would play my guitar and sing.

Mediation is a process just as litigation is a process. But mediation may be practiced in a number of different, acceptable methods, just as there are myriad different, equally effective litigation styles. Simply stated, mediation may well mean different things to different mediators.

Your initial inquiry, in terms of your own evaluation of a mediation alternative or as a question to a prospective mediator, is *what kind of mediation approach do I want for my particular case*? In terms of a global definition of mediation, mediation is a process in which a neutral third party attempts to facilitate a discussion between the parties and their counsel that will result in resolution of the dispute.

All mediators, regardless of style, must remain impartial and neutral. But the variable word in the global definition is "facilitate." Mediators adopt different approaches, methods, and styles to "facilitate" a resolution.

Regrettably, in these early days of the mediation revolution, we are already developing buzz words to describe different mediation styles. Equally sad, some mediators are already given to declaring their style to be superior or their style to be "real mediation." Over time, such declarations no longer will be made for one simple reason. Mediation, by its very nature, requires a multiplicity of different styles and approaches to accommodate and deal with a multiplicity of different kinds of

Chapter 1
Mediation Styles

cases. One mediation style may be absolutely perfect for one particular case and absolutely wrong for another kind of case. Truly excellent mediators will receive training in all mediation styles in order to be able to tailor the right method to a particular case. Further, a case may require a mediator to use a number of different styles and approaches in the same mediation.

Nonetheless, until such better times come, you need to know and understand the various mediation "styles" in order to evaluate what is correct for your case and to identify a mediator who is skilled in such an approach.

§1.1 "Case Evaluation" or "Evaluative Mediation"

One acceptable mediation style is referred to as "case evaluation" or "evaluative mediation." Note that variations in these buzzwords are already entering our vernacular. For ease of reference, I will refer to this style as "case evaluation" mediation, the goal of which is to assist each party in fully evaluating its case. Even for those who practice this method, the definition may vary slightly, but generally, case evaluation mediation includes:

1. Use of the separate caucus. The separate caucus is a process in which the mediator places the parties in separate rooms, moves from room to room, and meets privately with each side. Everything said in a private caucus is confidential, save and except for what the party in the caucus room authorizes the mediator to communicate to a party in another caucus room. See Chapter, §4.4, page 33 for an explanation of the separate caucus room.

2. Case evaluation within the separate caucus. In a separate caucus (and outside the presence of the other parties and their attorneys), the mediator will ask the party to identify the strengths and weaknesses of its positions. The mediator, through the use of questions, may challenge the party's assessment of strengths and weaknesses or point out additional problems that the party may not have considered.

3. Offering opinions. Even in case evaluation mediation, the mediator should not offer an opinion as to an outcome or suggest who will win or lose. Certain case evaluation mediators believe that they may offer outcome opinions if both sides consent. In my view, such practice adversely affects neutrality and prevents the parties from reaching their own conclusions — the opposite of what the process intends. Also, a mediator's prediction as to outcome is often no better than an educated guess that counsel for the parties might make. While the mediator may have the benefit of a perspective an advocate might not have, the advocate has the benefit of a much greater knowledge of the case itself.

4. "Aggressive mediation." Case evaluation mediation is often described as "aggressive mediation"; i.e., the mediator challenges and questions the positions of the parties more actively than in other types of mediation. A less kind description of case evaluation mediation is that the mediator "hammers" both sides in the caucus rooms. An over-aggressive case evaluation mediation style runs the risk of being perceived as coercive and heavy handed. Remember: Mediation should not be coercive. Effective case evaluation mediators develop questioning techniques that get points across without appearing to be coercive.

5. Involving lawyers. Case evaluation mediations anticipate that the lawyers on all sides will be active participants.

6. Collaborative session. Case evaluation mediation typically includes an initial collaborative session in which all parties begin in the same room. Often, the parties are segregated immediately after such initial session and do not directly interact. The mediator may elect to reconvene the parties together at a later stage in the process.

§1.2 "Pure Form Mediation"

The other major mediation method is typically described as "empowerment mediation," "pure form mediation," or "community model mediation." For ease of reference, I will refer to this method as "pure form mediation." The elements of pure form mediation typically are:

1. The mediator attempts to "empower" the parties to identify constructive options and solutions.

Chapter 1
Mediation Styles

2. The majority of the process occurs in a group, community session.

3. While pure form mediators may use the separate caucus, they do not consistently rely upon the separate caucus.

4. The parties' lawyers may become involved in the process, but the lawyers' roles are de-emphasized. Some pure form mediators attempt to exclude the lawyers from the process entirely.

5. Pure form mediators will rarely, even if the parties consent, offer opinions.

6. Pure form mediators attempt to make the parties themselves fully responsible for generating options and solutions.

My hope is that you already intuitively appreciate why I believe that drawing rigid lines based on stylistic differences is not helpful in terms of the efficacy of the process. You may have a case in your office in which a case evaluation approach may be perfect. You may have another file in which a pure form approach may be more suitable. But the best of all worlds is to identify a mediator who is versed in all styles and who has the capacity to be flexible. I have begun several mediations on a case evaluation track and during the process discovered, based on the personalities of the participants, that a community, more directly party-interactive, approach would be more effective. From the mediator's perspective, any variation of the process that is more likely to attain resolution should be the "right" process for that dispute.

Chapter 2

Determining Whether and
When to Mediate

About two years ago, I published a paper setting out some objective guidelines for determining whether a case was appropriate for mediation. Today, some 1,200 mediations later, I find that the criteria I set out in that article were too rigid. I have mediated and resolved enough cases that would not have met my own guidelines to know that specific criteria are not particularly helpful. In my opinion, and at the risk of being self-serving, almost every case is suitable for mediation, especially if the mediation occurs at the appropriate time and the necessary players attend the session.

§2.1   Inappropriate Cases for Mediation

The cases that may not be appropriate for mediation are:

1. A case in which the real decision-maker, for whatever reason, either can't or won't attend the session itself.

2. A case involving a governmental entity in which a political issue absolutely prevents serious discussions or in which a budgetary reality may obstruct settlement.

3. A case in which an ostensible settlement had been reached previously, but one side has already breached that agreement.

Even within these limited categories, I believe certain cases could be successfully mediated. The real trick is setting the mediation at the right time and to have the necessary players at the session.

Chapter 2
Determining Whether and When to Mediate

§2.2 When to Mediate

In terms of when to mediate, my experience has been the sooner the better. For example, I have mediated complex hospital liability cases even before an answer to the lawsuit has been filed, and more than 90% of those cases have resolved. In those cases, the hospitals had already made internal investigations, consulted with counsel, and made a preliminary evaluation of the case. Of course, I have also mediated hospital liability cases in which some, but not all, of the discovery had been done. In those cases, the limited depositions taken also permitted a preliminary evaluation of the case.

Additionally, the mediation session itself always provides additional information that results in a re-evaluation. "Sooner," of course, is a relative concept, and when to mediate "sooner" must be made on a case-by-case basis. The guiding principle should be: "At what point does the decision-maker possess enough information to make a reasonable, preliminary evaluation?"

Both subjective and objective factors also point to the validity of mediating as soon as is practical.

§2.3 Subjective Reasons for Early Mediation

1. Parties are more flexible and oriented towards resolution earlier in the dispute. Ideas and opinions about a party's position harden over time and re-evaluation becomes more difficult as time progresses.

2. Parties become more committed to "the case" itself as time progresses. The attitude becomes "I've gone this far, why not go all the way to trial?"

3. Parties are more likely to settle their dispute and obtain closure the farther away trial and final resolution appears to be. People have a natural and innate desire to resolve their problems. As the trial moves closer, many litigants see the trial itself as providing closure.

Chapter 2
Determining Whether and When to Mediate

4. In many instances, the litigation process itself breeds distrust and creates close-mindedness. On occasion, a party may grow to dislike opposing counsel, and this may create a new layer of rigidity.

§2.4 Objective Reasons for Early Mediation

1. Cost containment is the most compelling factor. In some instances, the litigation costs incurred can become an impediment to settlement. Monetary savings through early resolution is an incentive towards settlement.

2. Attorneys' fees are less of a factor at the front end of the litigation process. The claimed attorneys' fees themselves may become an additional obstruction to resolution. Lawyers may be more willing to discount or re-adjust their fees earlier in the litigation.

3. Court dockets don't always move as quickly as we may hope. A party may have a specific, objective need for an early resolution.

The appropriate time to mediate, considering all these factors, is the *earliest practical time* at which the parties are in a position to evaluate their case.

§2.5 Benefits of Early Mediation if No Settlement

1. Early mediation narrows the dispute, thereby reducing litigation costs.

2. Mediation lays the predicate for post-mediation negotiations.

3. Mediation creates more positive lawyer-lawyer dynamics, which makes scheduling discovery more painless.

4. As the parties continue with discovery and negotiations, they may elect to mediate again later in the case.

Chapter 3

Selecting a Mediator

Presently, no certification standards exist for mediators. The Alternative Dispute Resolution Procedures Act, Texas Civil Practice & Remedies Code §154, *et seq.,* sets out the qualifications of a mediator in §154.052. See Appendix D, page 235.

I would expect, especially in states that have a comprehensive ADR statute and in which mediation is used heavily, that certification standards or guidelines will be created over the next several years. This chapter, however, is not designed to suggest standards or guidelines. Rather, it is intended to help you, the lawyer, ask the right questions in order to assess whether a particular mediator is qualified and well suited for your case.

Because I acknowledge that there may well be good faith differences of opinion regarding the criteria I will set out, I have attempted at least to identify such issues and have also provided you with the basis for some of my opinions.

§3.1 Appropriate Mediation Training

Unequivocally, specific mediation training is essential for anyone who holds himself out to be a mediator. Some lawyers, feeling they have been negotiating all their practice lives and seeing potential revenue in a mediation practice, simply declare themselves to be "mediators" without receiving any specific mediation training. Mediation, as you will come to understand better in later chapters, is a process. As with any other process, appropriate training and study is necessary. Fortunately, many excellent mediation training programs are offered across the United States. Law schools, the American Arbitration Association, local dispute resolution centers, and private organizations offer superior mediation training.

Most mediation training courses involve a 40-hour program. In Texas, §154.052(a) of the Alternative Dispute Resolution Procedures Act requires 40 hours of training.

Chapter 3
Selecting a Mediator

Most 40-hour programs include lectures, along with a substantial number of interactive practice skill exercises. Students are asked to role play using hypothetical problems in order to understand the mediation process and mediation techniques better.

Many training programs also require, and I think it to be essential, that attendees observe at least three mediations conducted by an experienced mediator after the training in order to receive certification from the training group. Mediation, as you might suspect, is experiential, and such observations greatly enhance the benefits of the training received.

§3.2   Actual Mediation Experience

Obviously, newly and appropriately trained mediators may well do a superior job mediating their first dispute. Learning to mediate, however, is very much like learning to try lawsuits. All of us who have litigated appreciate the difference between how we approached our first jury trial and how we approached our 50th jury trial. Mediators, like trial lawyers, become more confident with experience and develop new methods, approaches, and ideas with each mediation.

As a result, actual mediation experience is indeed a factor, especially if the dispute is complex and involves multiple parties. I feel somewhat reluctant to overemphasize experience. Three years ago, some kind parties were willing to permit me to operate on them for the first time. Fortunately, the parties and I both survived and the dispute in fact settled.

Mediators, myself included, are prone to keeping statistics about the number of disputes they have mediated and the percentage of those cases they have resolved. In my standard introduction at a mediation, I will mention that I have mediated more than 1,200 cases and that 91% of those cases have settled. I began to "keep score" initially because I was curious, as a longtime proponent of ADR, to see how many cases indeed did resolve. Also, I wanted to keep track, for my own sake, of how I was doing. As time has progressed, I tend to use my "record" to instill confi-

Chapter 3
Selecting a Mediator

dence initially in a group of new mediation parties by indicating I do have substantial experience and success in mediating disputes.

I am hesitant, however, to suggest a "magic number" of mediations before a mediator "comes of age." I recall often hearing as a fledgling litigator that you were not really a trial lawyer until after you had handled your 25th jury trial. I cannot seriously argue with such wisdom, but I cannot suggest that a mediator does not "come of age" until after his 50th mediation.

I will, in this regard, share this thought with you. I felt capable and competent after my 25th mediation. After my 50th mediation, I revisited my methods and received additional training to develop new techniques. After my 100th mediation, I felt I could see certain patterns in certain kinds of cases. After my 300th mediation, I realized (although I think I knew it all along) that you will never know it all, and perhaps the most exhilarating aspect of mediation practice — like trial practice — is that you learn something new every time you mediate a dispute.

Success records in mediation also are like a trial lawyer's track record. I have always believed that you are not really a trial lawyer if you haven't lost your share of cases. Mediation will not resolve every case. I loathe statistics and inherently distrust them. And, in this new area, save and except for statistics involving Settlement Week (an organized program by a local or state bar that provides pro bono mediations by volunteer lawyers), reliable statistics (at least to the extent I would vouch for them in this book) regarding the success of private mediation are not available. In talking with my experienced colleagues across Texas, however, I think it is safe to suggest that qualified mediators resolve in excess of 70% of the cases they handle.

In summary, I would think a question is raised if a mediator has failed to resolve more than 50% of his cases. Further, I think the training, background, qualifications, and breadth of experience are far more important and reliable criteria than a proffered success ratio.

Chapter 3
Selecting a Mediator

§3.3 Practice Background

Two important questions are raised when asking about a mediator. Should or must the mediator be an attorney? And should the mediator, if he is an attorney, have a litigation background as opposed to, for example, a transactional law background?

1. The attorney mediator. Under §154.052 of the Alternative Dispute Resolution Procedures Act, a mediator need not be an attorney. The "must" part of my first question, therefore, is quite easy to answer. The more difficult question is whether a mediator *should* be an attorney.

This book is written for the practicing lawyer who presumably is representing a client in a dispute that is either already in litigation or that is likely to go into litigation if a resolution is not reached. The cases I have mediated have included medical malpractice/hospital liability, products liability, vehicular collision, consumer law, borrower-lender, commercial/contract, and family law disputes. Many, if not most, of these cases involved issues of both law and fact. My 16 years of law practice were invaluable to me in order not only to understand the issues in the case but, more important, to evaluate the attendant strengths and weaknesses of certain positions and to play an effective devil's advocate role in the separate caucus. See Chapter 4, pages 33-45.

Further, while many cases are not "just about money," most cases, at least the kinds of cases I mediate, are resolved on some monetary basis. My background as a litigator who tried more than 300 cases (for seven years as a plaintiff's lawyer and seven years as a defense lawyer) enables me to evaluate better what a jury might think about the evidence and what a potential award range might be. Simply stated, my litigation background is a great aid, in conjunction with my mediation skills, in getting cases resolved.

So, again, should a mediator be a lawyer? One of the best mediators I know is a psychologist who is not a lawyer. He mediates family law matters, employer-employee disputes, and sets up conflict resolution mechanisms for institutional clients. He is brilliant, talented, and capable, but I suspect that if confronted with a dispute that involved complex issues of law and the need to appreciate probable trial outcomes, my friend would refer the matter to a skilled mediator who was also a practicing attorney. In summary, I believe most complex civil cases should be handled by a mediator who also is (or was) a practicing attorney.

2. The litigator as mediator. Now, should the mediator have a litigation background? Many of the most successful mediators in Texas have substantial litigation backgrounds. But many successful mediators also were highly skilled transactional and administrative lawyers with no real litigation experience. Most of these mediators with no actual litigation experience were exposed to litigation during their practices and are therefore familiar with trial procedures and jury outcomes. As a result, I think the selection criteria should not be based on whether a highly qualified and skilled mediator was or was not a litigator.

You should evaluate a candidate's skill and experience as a mediator and satisfy yourself that the candidate has an adequate working knowledge of the subject matter of your dispute. Further, if the prospective mediator requires confidential pre-mediation submissions as I do, a highly competent transactional lawyer/mediator will be able to get up to speed on the specifics of your dispute.

Ultimately, as mediation grows and evolves, we will see the development of a broad continuum of mediation services. Some mediators will develop special expertise in mediating medical malpractice cases. Other mediators may develop special skills in mediating family law cases. I am not advocating a new layer of bureaucracy; i.e., sub-specialiazation within the area of mediation. Skill in the mediation process and the process itself will always be and should always be the guiding principle. Over time, you may well be able to match the "right mediator" to the type of case you are handling.

§3.4   Style as a Selection Criteria

I have already stated my hope that the mediation practice will accommodate a variety of styles and my strong belief that mediators should become versed and skilled in all mediation methods.

1. Using separate caucuses. But I also strongly believe that a mediator must be skilled in and willing to use the separate caucus when mediating civil litigation matters. Most civil litigation matters cannot be resolved without the use of the separate caucus at some point in the mediation. I see no problem with a mediator who uses other acceptable methods in conjunction with the separate caucus, but in my opinion, a mediator must at some time privately caucus with each party, undertake a strength-weakness analysis of each party's case, and identify and understand those issues that the parties may never be willing to discuss in the presence of the other side.

Why must a mediator use the separate caucus? Simply because mediation does not settle every case. And a party, despite its good faith participation in the mediation process, may not be willing to disclose certain matters to the other side because the case may not settle and such matters may prejudice the party's position at trial. In such instances, a party will share such information with the mediator only under the protection of an absolutely confidential separate caucus. This confidentiality helps give the mediator an understanding of the entire case, without which he cannot resolve the dispute.

Further, because of human nature, certain sensitive issues will be discussed only in private quarters. For example, one party may identify a sensitive and/or emotional issue and authorize the mediator, because of the nature of the mediator's role, to discuss that matter privately with the other side rather than fatally damaging the mediation by raising the issue directly and antagonizing the other party.

Finally, I also strongly believe that money should be discussed only in the separate caucus and communicated through the mediator. Nothing cuts to the bone more than a monetary offer, and, as we will discuss in a later chapter, lawyers, based on traditional negotiating styles, almost always open the monetary bidding with "high ball" or "low ball" proposals. While lawyers are accustomed to this "negotiation dance," parties may react poorly or emotionally to such opening gambits.

Chapter 3
Selecting a Mediator

The ancient Greeks understood this phenomenon well. When the Greeks had bad news to deliver, they sent a messenger. Often, the messenger who delivered the bad news was killed. Fortunately, mediators who deliver opening monetary gambits to a party in a separate caucus room are not killed — at least not so far. But the separate caucus permits the mediator to take the sting out of such an initial proposal and to encourage the parties to understand that the process, and the negotiation, is only in its early stages.

2. Lawyer participation. I strongly believe you should select a mediator who encourages lawyer participation during the mediation process. Some mediators are trained, and zealously believe, that lawyers should play a passive role, or even be excluded, in the mediation process. In civil litigation matters, I don't think you should select a mediator who adopts such a practice.

As I see it, lawyer participation in the mediation process is critical for many reasons, including:

(1) Parties feel more secure and confident with their lawyers present and actively participating.

(2) Mediators should *never* dispense legal advice to parties. Mediators do not even have to consider doing so if a party's counsel is an active participant. Inevitably, questions of law, trial strategy, or possible trial outcomes arise during a mediation. A party absolutely needs the benefit of counsel during such moments.

(3) Because it generates new information, the mediation process permits the lawyers to re-evaluate the strengths and weaknesses of their case.

(4) Lawyers are often co-decision makers, along with their clients, regarding settlement. Parties want, and need, to know whether a proposal is fair in light of the totality of the case.

(5) Without the lawyers present and actively participating, a party may feel there is an imbalance of power, and this feeling alone may obstruct resolution.

Chapter 3
Selecting a Mediator

---

(6)   Lawyers who are litigators are learning to appreciate how to translate their trial skills into the mediation arena. Positive "mediation advocacy" by counsel increases the chances of resolution. Chapter 10, "The Mediation Advocate's Role in Negotiations," is devoted to this newly developing practice area of mediation advocacy. See pages 81-83.

My ardent belief that lawyers participate does not mean that the parties should not participate. The parties themselves must participate fully. The dispute belongs to the parties, not the lawyers.

Mediation, unlike any aspect of litigation, affords the parties an opportunity to look, see, touch, and feel the other side's case directly — perhaps for the first time. The parties themselves go through a re-evaluation process during mediation. They are the ultimate decision-makers and may have interests not known to their counsel. But for the parties to benefit fully from the mediation process, they must feel comfortable, protected, and secure. Lawyers provide the requisite comfort and security. And, contrary to popular belief, lawyers are genuinely and passionately dedicated to finding good resolutions for their clients. After more than 1,200 mediations, I have encountered only one obstructionist lawyer. Overwhelmingly, lawyers excel and constructively participate in the mediation process.

3. Lawyers available, but separate. I have only one exception to the lawyer participation rule. In certain cases, the lawyers suggest that the mediator work with the parties without the lawyers present, but with the lawyers available in a caucus room. I do not oppose such a practice and have successfully mediated many cases in this manner. Some of the reasons that lawyers have suggested such an approach in their particular case are:

(1)   A lawyer may candidly admit that he evokes such a strong negative reaction in the other party that the chance of resolution may be fatally contaminated.

(2)   The parties may have a long-term relationship, be equally sophisticated, and have no imbalance of power issues between them. The lawyers may

believe that the parties may be more likely to "open up" without their lawyers present.

(3)   The essence of the dispute does not involve an issue of law or even a seriously contested factual dispute. Rather, the dispute is fueled by a personal/ emotional factor that the lawyers believe will more likely be resolved with the mediator meeting alone with the parties.

§3.5   Mediation Fees

A mediator must be fully willing to discuss and explain his fee structure. While this section is not intended to suggest a standard for mediator fees, regrettably, mediator fee abuses already have begun to occur. One of the guiding principles of ADR is that it should provide a *cost-effective* alternative to litigation. Experienced, talented mediators save parties tremendous litigation expense and should be fairly paid for their efforts. Nonetheless, certain mediator fee practices are, in my view, not only inconsistent with the cost-effective principle, but wholly inappropriate.

First permit me to outline what I consider to be appropriate mediation fee practices.

1.   Hourly billing. Many mediators, myself included, bill on an hourly rate (plus any expenses). Hourly rates generally range between $150 and $350 per hour, depending upon the experience and philosophy of the mediator. For a year and a half I charged $180 per hour, and then raised my hourly rate to $220 per hour. My rate, and this is true for many mediators, is divided evenly by the parties; i.e., in a two-party case, each side pays $110 an hour, and so on. I do not escalate my hourly rate based on the number of parties, but some mediators do.

I do not believe adjusting an hourly rate based on the number of parties to be an unethical practice, but I personally do not approve of it. Admittedly, a six-party case may be more complicated than a two-party case and, to be sure, sometimes co-defendants are antagonistic and the mediator is conducting several mediations during the same session. Often, however, several of the parties are aligned and the mere fact that six parties are involved makes no difference. In fact, the presence of mul-

Chapter 3
Selecting a Mediator

tiple defendants, each of whom may contribute in varying degrees to a settlement pot, may make resolution less complicated.

2. Flat fees. Another acceptable fee approach used by many mediators is a "per day" or "per half day" flat fee approach. Again, flat fee ranges generally vary between $1,000 and $2,500 for a full mediation day. As with the hourly rate, you must determine whether the flat fee rate is a total charge to be divided by the parties or whether it is a per party flat rate. You also need to know what constitutes a "half day" and what constitutes a "full day." Finally, you need to know whether the flat rate is adjusted based on the number of parties.

3. Amount in controversy. Some mediators increase their hourly rates or flat fees based on the amount in controversy. I find this to be wholly inappropriate, although I will explain what I understand to be the rationale behind such a fee approach.

The mere fact that a party makes a pre-mediation demand of $100,000, $1 million or $10 million means only one thing — that is the party's opening bid. A case in which there is a $10 million pre-mediation demand may settle for $10 million, zero, or some place in between. The mediator, prior to the mediation itself, does not know where the case will land monetarily. Often the parties do not know. But in my opinion, to adjust an hourly rate or flat fee upward solely on the basis of the amount of the demand is inappropriate. The mediator's job and the process of mediation is not altered by the amount in controversy. In fact, most mediators will tell you that "high stakes" cases are actually easier, in some instances, to mediate. Why? The parties may have far more at risk and greater incentives to resolve the dispute. Additionally, high stakes litigation often, but not always, involves more experienced counsel who know how to evaluate a case fully.

So what is the rationale offered for an increased fee based on the amount in controversy? The most frequently espoused reason is that high dollar cases take longer to prepare, more discovery is involved, the trial itself will take weeks or months, and each side will incur massive litigation costs; ergo, a substantially increased mediation fee is a drop in the bucket compared to such costs.

My reply to this rationale is: What difference does it make that the parties are going to incur massive litigation costs? Isn't sparing the parties such costs the whole point of mediation? Creating an outrageous mediation fee is wholly inconsistent with a guiding principal of ADR.

In one instance in Texas, I was able to verify that a mediator in a five-party case charged each party $1,000 per hour based on the fact that a $50 million claim was asserted. I will admit to being just a little jealous, but I do not approve, and such practice, while possibly aiding a college fund for the kids, I find unacceptable.

4. Amount of the ultimate settlement. But a more outrageous fee practice actually exists in which the mediator's fee is based on the amount of the ultimate settlement. This practice is *clearly* unethical. A mediator's ultimate duty is to remain fully impartial. How may a mediator operate on what is in essence a contingency fee and remain neutral or, even if that is possible, be perceived as neutral? In my opinion, such a fee practice should be statutorily prohibited.

5. Post-mediation fee agreements. Finally, I have learned of one other fee approach that is not on its face unacceptable, but that I find troublesome. In another "high stakes/complex case" in Texas, a mediator set no fee in advance of the mediation. The mediator agreed to mediate the case and *after* the mediation let the parties set what they thought to be a fair fee. The mediator agreed in writing to be bound by the parties' decision. After a two-day mediation that resulted in a resolution, the parties agreed that the mediator was entitled to a $40,000 fee. Wow. Double wow!

Again, I do not know whether my concerns are motivated by jealousy or ethics. In the case I just described, the mediator made no suggestion of what he thought his fee should be. And, as I understand it, the parties were glad to pay the fee and thought it was richly deserved. My reservations with such an approach are that I believe the parties should know in advance the extent of the cost, a mediator's fee should be cost effective, and consumers of mediation services do not, at least yet, have a good sense of what a fair mediator's fee might or should be. I ponder what might have happened, in the case just described, if the parties had set the fee at

$1,000. Perhaps I simply need to test this approach and report to you in a later supplement of this book if I found myself feeling unethical or impure. With my luck, however, I would probably receive the $1,000 fee.

§3.6 Ability to Provide Adequate Time

Another factor in the mediator selection process is to identify a mediator who will commit the necessary time, without interruption, to the process. As you might expect, it is extremely difficult to predict just how long a mediation will last in a given case. Some disputes may be resolved in four hours or less. Most disputes in my experience, however, require four to eight hours of mediation. Some disputes may even require 12 or more hours, or sometimes several days.

Regardless, you want and need a mediator who is able to commit whatever time is necessary to mediate your dispute. Currently, some lawyers have received mediation training in order to add a new component to their practice. For example, a lawyer may have decided to mediate when he is not trying cases or closing transactions. Mediation is not a process that may be done "between depositions."

In your initial call to a prospective mediator, you should determine whether the mediator is willing to reserve a specific date and to agree to take whatever time is necessary for your mediation. From your perspective and the perspective of the parties, scheduling a mediation may require substantial effort. Often, mediation participants will be coming from different parts of your state or from out of state. You do not want a last minute call from a mediator that his "trial ran over."

§3.7 Ability to Provide Adequate Facilities

The mediator also should be able to provide you with the facility/neutral site for the mediation. In my opinion, a neutral site is imperative, and conducting the mediation at one of the party's counsel's office should be avoided if at all possible. The other parties will feel uncomfortable with having the mediation on another side's "home turf."

Typically, assuming the mediator uses the separate caucus, two or three conference rooms are necessary to conduct the mediation. In complex, multi-party cases,

Chapter 3
Selecting a Mediator

20 or more people may participate in the mediation. The mediator must have access to an area that will accommodate such large groups comfortably. Further, the conference rooms should either be non-contiguous or sound-proofed to prevent a party in one room from hearing what occurs in the other party's separate caucus.

Environmental factors, while not controlling the ultimate outcome of a mediation, are important to the process. For many parties and counsel, the mediation may be their first experience with the process. In any event, parties, at least initially, may feel as apprehensive about the mediation as they would feel going to trial. As a result, a comfortable, positive mediation environment is important. The parties should feel that the mediator is prepared, thought has been given to the process, and proper arrangements have been made for the participants.

Also, the mediator should be willing to instruct his support staff that he will not be interrupted, in person or by telephone, during the mediation process itself. Momentum and focus are critical in mediation practice. I do not permit any interruptions when I am mediating a case.

Finally, the mediator should provide, at the expense of the parties, sustenance during the mediation. Mediation is hard work for everybody and can be emotionally and physically draining to the parties.

Initially, the mediator should provide for coffee, soft drinks, and water in each room and arrange to have staff replenish such items. Because of the momentum factor, I do not like to break for lunch and instead have food delivered to each room. If the mediation is going to continue late into the day, the mediator should provide some light snacks for the participants. Participants in a mediation get tired and it seems, not surprisingly, that food helps.

The mediator also should be sensitive to the fact that we now live in a rigid world of smokers and non-smokers. A non-smoker will be offended if a smoker lights a cigarette in his room. Conversely, a smoker will go absolutely nuts if he does not have a place to smoke during the mediation. The mediator should arrange for one or two designated smoking areas.

§3.8   Required Pre-Mediation Submissions

Your selection process should include retaining a mediator who will require the parties to provide a pre-mediation submission. Chapter 5, pages 54-60, is devoted entirely to the art of preparing a proper pre-mediation submission.

I require each attorney to provide me a confidential pre-mediation submission at least three days prior to the session. Although I will describe the pre-mediation submission in detail in Chapter 5, the submission includes a statement of the issues and the party's positions on such issues, copies of current pleadings, any essential appellate decisions or statutes, and any critical documentary evidence. The mediator does not share the submission with any other party and destroys the submission after the session.

I require a pre-mediation submission for two specific reasons. First, although I have an extensive litigation background, I want to be specifically educated about a particular case in advance of the session. In this way, the attorneys do not have to waste valuable time educating me at the session and the parties are comforted by the knowledge that I have a full and complete understanding of the issues in the case. The submissions permit the mediator to get a "flavor" for the case, which is helpful in pre-planning what approaches or methods might be most appropriate.

Second, the pre-mediation submission compels counsel to focus on the case in advance of the session. Many attorneys, because they do not know much about the mediation process or have not participated in a mediation, believe all they have to do is show up and the process, by some magic or voodoo, will make things happen. Preparation is the key to success in almost everything — and this is especially true in mediation. By requiring a pre-mediation submission, I know that every counsel has gone through an analysis of the case before the session. I absolutely believe that such pre-mediation evaluation is critical to a successful mediation outcome.

§3.9   Conflicts

A final, and perhaps obvious, selection criterion is that the mediator should not have any interest or conflict with the particular case. As stated before, the mediator's greatest asset is neutrality, and any hint of interest or conflict will undermine the process.

What is or is not a conflict, or a conflict sufficient to exclude a particular mediator, is to some extent ambiguous. A mediator who previously practiced law may have had either a direct or tangential relationship with a particular individual or institutional client. Or, if a mediator practices in a law firm, the firm may have had a direct or tangential relationship with a particular client. Mediators who work in law firms should run conflicts checks as they would do in their law practice.

While what constitutes a conflict may be subject to debate in a particular case, full disclosure by the mediator is subject to no debate. The mediator should apprise all parties of any matter that might even suggest a conflict and permit the parties to assess whether, as a result of such disclosure, a mediator should be excluded. In my view, if any party perceives any trace of a conflict, the mediator should refuse to serve. The goal of any mediation is to maximize the opportunity for resolution and any factor, including a conflict, that will in any way obstruct such a goal should be avoided at all costs.

§3.10 Making the Selection

Having now considered these selection factors, you may be pondering the most efficient method for selecting a mediator. I would propose the following steps:

1.   Other lawyers. Many lawyers in your community probably have significant mediation experience and have had a chance to work with several mediators. Ask these lawyers to provide you with their candid assessments of the mediators who have presided over their cases. I believe you should call several lawyers and receive several opinions.

2.   Judges. While for ethical reasons I would discourage contacting a judge who is presiding over your case, other judges may be aware of those reputable mediators practicing in your community. In certain counties, the courts may have a list of trained mediators along with a description of each mediator's experience.

---

3. Mediator list. Create a list of several mediators. Simultaneously, consult with opposing counsel and advise them of the process you are undertaking. Opposing counsel may have substantial mediation experience. The mere fact that opposing counsel suggests positive experiences with certain mediators should not be a basis for exclusion. In truth, the fact that opposing counsel feels comfortable with a certain mediator may enhance the opportunity for resolution.

4. Interview. Contact the mediators on your list by telephone and interview them. Paragraph II of the Mediation Checklist in Appendix A, page 183, provides you with a succinct set of questions to ask based on this chapter.

5. List. Arrive at a list of at least three mediators acceptable to you to present to opposing counsel.

The ultimate goal, of course, if to select a mediator that all counsel are comfortable with and respect. The fact that all counsel consensually agree upon a certain mediator increases the chances for resolution.

§3.11 Judge Selects the Mediator

In certain jurisdictions throughout the United States, courts are not only compelling the parties to mediate on the court's own motion, but certain courts are dictating who shall mediate the dispute. Beyond the possible judicial impropriety associated with such a practice, I find it unacceptable, if not outrageous, for the following reasons:

1. Citizens have the absolute right to select their lawyers. Similarly, citizens should have the absolute right to participate in the selection of their mediator.

2. Mediation, unless it is pro bono, costs money. As you are now aware, mediators' fees vary. Basic consumerism demands that citizens be able to shop for an appropriate mediator. Further, a mediator thrust upon the parties has no reason to discuss or consider modifying the fee.

3. Certain mediators may be more "right" for a particular case than others.

---

4. Finally, parties and their counsel are more likely to respect and respond to a mediator whom they have had a hand in selecting. Parties may rebel against a mediator who they perceive is forced upon them. As a result, the process, which is far more important than the mediator, is unnecessarily thwarted.

Chapter 4

The Mediation Process

Mediation, as stated several times already, is a process. While a skilled and fully trained mediator is essential, the process itself is what makes things work. Like trial practice, which is in many ways experiential, the mediation process must be experienced in order to be fully understood. Regardless, in order for this work to be valuable to you, I must generally describe the process from beginning to end, acknowledging again that different mediators may stylistically vary or alter the model I will now set forth based on the case itself.

The following illustration is a linear model of the mediation process. My purpose is not to create or imply a rigid model or form, but rather to provide you with a series of reference points so that you, the advocate for a party in mediation, may understand every facet of this process.

THE MEDIATION PROCESS

Mediator Introduction

Lawyers' Opening Statements

Collective Session

Separate Caucuses

Possible Additional Collective Sessions

Possible Lawyers' Caucus

Drafting the Agreement

In this chapter, I will take you on a detailed tour of each of these phases of the mediation process.

Chapter 4
The Mediation Process

---

§4.1 Mediator Introduction

Typically, all parties and their counsel will initially assemble in the same room and the proceedings will commence with the mediator making an introduction. If the mediator is following good form, her introduction usually takes no more than 15 minutes.

1. Explaining the process. Specifically, the mediator in her introduction is attempting to accomplish the following:

(1) Provide some information on her background, expertise, and credentials. The purpose of this part of the mediator's introduction is to humanize the mediator and to help her establish control of the process.

(2) Explain the role of the mediator. The mediator will emphasize her neutrality, will explain that she is not the judge or jury, will assure the parties that she will not offer absolute opinions, and will describe her role as a facilitator.

(3) Explain fully the confidentiality aspects of the mediation process.

(4) Generally outline the sequence of events that will occur during the day. The mediator will explain the various phases of the mediation process, just as a trial lawyer will tell a jury during voir dire how the trial will unfold. The mediator will also explain the special aspects of the separate caucus during this part of the introduction.

(5) Obtain several commitments from the parties. The mediator will ask the parties if they are willing to allocate whatever time is necessary to permit the process to work, whether they possess the requisite authority to resolve the dispute, and whether they are willing to make a good faith effort to resolve the dispute.

More globally, the mediator's introduction is designed to make the parties and their counsel as familiar and comfortable with the mediation process as is possible. Many lawyers, and most clients, have not been through a mediation. As a result, the mediator must assist the participants in fully understanding what is about to take place and to appreciate that the mediation process is a protected, confidential, and safe environment. The mediator will not be able to have the parties open up and participate if the parties have any doubts or fears about the process itself, confidentiality, or the mediator's neutrality.

2. Pre-mediation issues. Good mediation practice requires that the mediator and all counsel attempt to resolve several important issues prior to the mediation itself. These issues may be handled by a pre-mediation conference call or an exchange of correspondence. The issues that should be resolved prior to the mediation are as follows:

(1)   The authority to settle issue *must* be resolved before the mediation. The issue of who has the authority to settle a case for the party is a thorny one; so thorny that I have devoted an entire chapter to the topic (see Chapter 6, pages 61-68). But to summarize the issue for purposes of this chapter: All parties should confer, agree on who will attend the session, and be comfortable that the persons who will attend the session have authority to resolve the dispute. If the proper parties or representatives are not present, the mediation process likely will not work. The mediation may have to be postponed or rescheduled. Parties or representatives may have had to travel great distances to attend a session. A mediation that breaks down because the necessary parties or representatives are not present may further heighten tensions and animosity. Therefore, the authority issue and who should attend the mediation should be *fully discussed* before the session itself.

(2)   All mediation participants should make realistic travel plans before the session. A mediator never knows how long the mediation process itself will take. Some disputes may be resolved in four hours or less. Most disputes seem to require five to eight hours for the process to run its course. Some complex disputes may even require several days of mediation. Counsel and the mediator should discuss in advance of the session the time parameters that may be involved, and travel and lodging plans should be made accordingly.

**Chapter 4
The Mediation Process**

---

§4.2 Opening Statements by Counsel

The opening statement by counsel is one of the most important facets of the mediation process; yet, in my experience, talented and highly skilled counsel routinely ignore the great opportunity associated with their opening remarks. For more information on this issue, see Chapter 9, pages 75-80.

To be sure, counsel's opening remarks are in part designed either to educate the mediator about the dispute or to educate the mediator further in the event a confidential pre-mediation submission has already been provided. *But* the second and most important aspect of the opening statement is that it permits each party a direct opportunity to set out for the other party (*not* the other party's lawyer) how counsel sees the case and the basis for such view. Rarely in the litigation process does counsel ever have an opportunity for such direct contact.

We are now crossing into the territory I call "mediation advocacy"; i.e., effective representation of a client in the mediation process. Certainly, mediation is not the courtroom. But how does the experienced attorney (be she a litigator, transactional lawyer, or other) translate her skills into the mediation forum? This is a list of my "do's" and "do not's."

   1. Do not address your opening statement to the mediator. The mediator is not the judge or the jury. And, if you have provided the mediator with a confidential pre-mediation submission, the mediator already knows how you see the case.

   2. Do not address your remarks to opposing counsel. Opposing counsel has already read your pleadings, read your written discovery, heard your questions at depositions, and probably has spoken to you at length about the case. Further, the opposing counsel may or may not be the "decision-maker."

   3. Do not discuss legal issues in "law talk" — if you discuss issues of law specifically as issues of law at all. You do not discuss issues of law in "law talk" to a jury. Do not do so at a mediation.

Chapter 4
The Mediation Process

---

4. Do address your remarks to the opposing party. In a mediation, who is your jury? Not the mediator. Not the lawyer. Of course, the jury is the other party — be she the claimant, the insurance adjuster, the corporate executive, etc.

5. Do *not* engage in personal attacks on the other party. Be prepared. Be organized. Be confident. Be constructive. Emphasize risk and your belief in your position. Attacks preempt and obstruct listening by the other side. You are making a good faith appeal. No one who is insulted will listen, re-evaluate, consider your position, or be inclined to negotiate.

6. Do use charts, blow-ups, and well-presented handouts. Impress with preparation and organization — not harsh words.

7. Do acknowledge you understand how the other side feels. Understanding does not equal agreement.

8. Do acknowledge that you are present to listen and are willing to do so. People have two fundamental interests in a mediation — to be listened to and to be understood. Most people feel "no one listens" or "understands" in the litigation process.

9. Do emphasize your good faith participation in the mediation process and your hope for resolution. This is *not* an expression of weakness; rather, you are expressing open-mindedness and a desire for a sensible solution.

10. Do not address sensitive issues. Prior to the mediation, consider what sensitive issues or "nerves" exist on the other side. Do *not* address such issues; rather, permit the mediator to do so in a separate caucus. The mediator's neutrality provides her with greater latitude. And, consider human nature. No one will admit she is a thief, a con artist, a malingerer, engaged in negligence that killed another human being, etc. Psychologists call this denial. Accusations make people close up. Your words, much to the surprise of most lawyers, are not magical. And if the party you are so confronting detests you, you will be doing a disservice to your client. *Again*, and I know I am repeating, impress by organization, preparation, listening, understanding, and exhibiting (although you were schooled to do the opposite) a

---

touch of your humanity. You will be amazed how much better your message will be received if you adopt this approach.

11. Do express or extend sympathy or concern to those who have either been hurt or experienced a loss. Such an expression is not an admission of liability.

12. Do introduce yourself. Provide some background on who you are. Humanize yourself.

13. Do acknowledge your belief in and support of the mediation process.

14. Do emphasize why you believe resolution will be in everyone's best interest.

15. Do explain your role as an advocate on behalf of your client.

16. Do explain that in anticipation of the mediation, you have thoroughly and objectively re-reviewed the case and that you have had your client do so as well.

17. Do not ever discuss money in your opening statement. Money cuts to the heart. Money is cold. And your reference to money will be the only thing remembered.

18. Do not ever use absolute words. Words like "never" and "won't" only get in the way.

We are all aware of the legendary trial lawyers and their accomplishments before juries. Often stories are told, if not transcripts made, of great summations. But mediation outcomes may be profoundly affected by great opening statements. In mediation, you are not selling the other side on the correctness of your position. The other side, regardless of your legal abilities or oral skills, will always rule against you. Instead, you are communicating your integrity as a human being, your preparedness, your willingness to listen and understand, your good faith participation in the mediation process and your interest in a sensible resolution.

Chapter 4
The Mediation Process

§4.3   Initial Collective Session

I will hasten to admit that I rarely hold a collective session immediately after the lawyers' opening statements. For some mediators, the concept of having the parties "vent" and express their thoughts and feelings is a critical element of the mediation process. The thinking, of course, is that with such feelings vented and therefore "out of the way," the parties will be predisposed towards more rational thought regarding resolution of the dispute.

Being honest, though, I would suggest that I am (perhaps as a function of my legal training) too nervous to permit such an exchange. I would much prefer to allow such venting to occur in separate caucus outside the presence of the other side. I suppose I believe that venting is all right and necessary — but, isn't that accomplished if I hear it and no damage is done by the other side hearing it? If the feelings need to be expressed to the other side, the mediator is able to deliver the message in a, no politics intended, "kinder and gentler" way. Also, putting on my negotiator's hat, I do not believe that invectives put people in the mood to negotiate constructively. In more blunt terms, call me a "malingerer," a "quack," a "liar," or a "crook," and I will be inclined to use any resource available to prove you wrong — regardless of the risk.

As an experienced trial lawyer, I do not see mediation as ESP, voodoo, or a group therapy session. Anything told to me as a mediator in the privacy of the separate caucus is fine because only I hear it and it won't hurt my feelings. Further, despite the confidentiality of mediation, lawyers may be leery that their clients' candid statements in mediation may be used against them if the case does not resolve. For these reasons, I omit the collective session and move into the separate caucus except in the following situations:

1. When little or no discovery has been done. Mediation should never be transformed into a deposition or an adversarial hearing. *However*, the collective session may be useful in exchanging otherwise discoverable evidence for purposes of evaluation.

2. When the parties have a long-standing business relationship or friend-ship. Certainly, business disputes may be very acrimonious and even divorce-like. But the parties in such situations have a great need to communicate directly with each other before going into the separate caucus. Sometimes the parties may not be prepared to negotiate until such direct words are exchanged. If such direct commu-nication occurs during the initial caucus, the mediator must control the discussion and keep it focused. Alternatively, if the mediator is concerned that such direct ex-change might be very destructive, she may elect to move the parties into separate caucus, get a sense of what will be communicated directly, help each party focus her thoughts, and then reunite the parties for a direct exchange after the initial separate caucus.

3. It may be appropriate to discuss the procedural posture of the case, what discovery is remaining to get the case ready for trial, the length of the trial, the like-lihood of appeal, and the remaining costs. The parties may benefit from a candid discussion of both the time and costs associated with the continuation of the dispute. Simply stated, the parties may need an initial collective caucus to appreciate the real opportunity afforded to them by resolving the dispute through mediation in terms of both time and cost savings.

4. When an acknowledgment of the negotiation posture may be appropri-ate. In some instances, the issue of who made the last offer, the amount of the offer, and the like needs to be clarified. A party virtually never will bid against herself. The parties should agree whose court the ball is in.

5. When the party has a real interest in "public shaming" as a pre-condition to resolution. Chapter 12, pages 98-101, is devoted to a full discussion of the par-ties' non-monetary interests. Of course, mediation is a private, confidential pro-ceeding. But a party with such an interest may view the mediator as a member of the public. The party may have an absolute need "to tell on" the other side; i.e., Dr. Jones is a quack, Bob Smith is an unethical car dealer, etc.

Such situations, as previously discussed, are explosive. And, fortunately, most claimants may fulfill this need by expressing such feelings to the mediator in separate caucus. But in a small group of cases (and the mediator must be able to identify such a case intuitively), the party will not be able to begin to resolve the dispute until this public shaming interest is met. The mediator, recognizing such a situation, may engage in some damage control. The mediator, anticipating harsh words may be said, should advise all parties that candid expressions, no matter how harsh, are appropriate and better stated under the aura of the confidentiality of a mediation. The mediator may also encourage the parties that such candid expressions should, if at all possible, be stated constructively. The mediator, in essence, is attempting to lessen the degree of rancor expressed or to prepare the other party for what is about to occur.

6. When a party needs to express grief. Some litigants feel that "no one cares" or that the other party does not fully understand the extent of their hurt or loss. A party who feels this way may not be able to consider resolution without having the opportunity to express such feelings directly to the other party.

§4.4   The Separate Caucus

I have already made you aware of my bias, but let me say again that the separate caucus is the essence of mediation. The parties and their counsel are placed in separate quarters and the mediator goes from room to room meeting privately with each side. Everything said in each separate caucus is confidential, save and except for what a party authorizes the mediator to communicate to a party in another room. The mediator must communicate *only* authorized communications and must take whatever precaution necessary to avoid any unauthorized disclosures. The mediator will separately caucus with each party several times. In complex cases, I may have nine or ten separate caucuses with each party.

While every mediation is different and the mediator may vary protocol in a particular case, the separate caucus usually has three general phases: the initial strength/ weakness, objective evaluation caucus; the preliminary negotiation caucus; and the closing/resolution caucus.

Chapter 4
The Mediation Process

§4.5 Initial Strength/Weakness Caucus

The initial separate caucus with each party is typically the most lengthy phase of the mediation process. The mediator usually will visit with each party for at least 30 minutes, and sometimes as long as an hour. Because of the mediator's goals in the initial caucus, the mediator may, especially in a difficult case, have to hold two (and sometimes more) strength/weakness caucuses with each party. I find I almost always can accomplish my mission in one such caucus. The mediator has several goals in the initial caucus and it is indeed a highly critical phase of the process.

1. Bonding with the parties. A mediator will initially make an effort to obtain the trust and confidence of the party. The party already may have confidence in the mediator, but the party may need to get to know the mediator better (and vice versa) before she is willing to "open up." The party needs to be reminded of the confidentiality of the caucus and the mediator's impartiality. The mediator is also looking for insights into the personality of the party and to identify some of her interests unrelated to the dispute; i.e., children, golf, basketball, travel, music, etc. The purpose of this, of course, is for the mediator to "bond" a bit more with the party. Bonding results in a party feeling more relaxed with the process and more comfortable with the mediator.

Someone once said every time he mediated he made new friends. The statement, which does not negate neutrality, is very true. Bonding is not artificial or a "psych job." Bonding in mediation is like making new friends. In mediation, each party has had to deal with a difficult dispute that, in many instances, is the most significant problem in her life. The mediator, because of her neutrality, training, and skill, becomes a friend who is there to help everyone.

The mediator bonds with the party not through any tactical plan, but by demonstrating that she has listened, is willing to listen, and is willing to understand (not agree). The mediator bonds with the party by demonstrating preparedness, professionalism, neutrality, and compassion. Many parties have reported to me, upon completion of a successful mediation, that I was "the first person who really listened." While such a statement may not be completely true, the party perceived and believed that was the case. Most parties want out of the litigation process and find it confusing and uncaring. The mediator is perceived as the person who may well get the parties out of the box.

2. Venting. Many parties really do need to vent their feelings to the mediator. And most people want to do so right away. Parties feel — correctly — that the dispute belongs to them, and they are often tired of all the "lawyer talk."

Good mediators understand that a party wants such an immediate opportunity to speak. A good mediator may walk into the caucus, look at the party, and simply ask, "Mr. Williams, how do you feel about this dispute?" Typically, the question triggers a flood of information, often emotionally charged, and the party begins to feel more a part of the process itself. The party comes to understand quickly that the mediator is listening and not sitting in judgment.

In the separate caucus, venting occurs with no destructive consequences. But venting, beyond the relief it affords the party, also usually identifies many of the party's interests and needs. Often, a venting party repeats important words or thoughts, which is not accidental. Good mediators write down key words or phrases and recognize that while the dispute may "be about money," such words are often the emotional matter that fuels the dispute. Simply, venting permits identification of interests. And while such interests may appear "silly" or "subjective" to the lawyers involved, they are very real and very important to the parties.

Parties in mediation sometimes tell me that no one, including their own lawyers, ever asked them what the case was really about. Lawyers, and I am not being critical, are more trained (and more comfortable) in clinically and objectively evaluating a case. For the lawyer, regardless of how caring she may be, the client's problem becomes a "case" or a "file." For the client, the problem may be her entire life. Lawyers speak in terms of issues and positions. Beneath the line of issues and positions is the realm of interests. More often than not, the client's motivations are in the realm of interests and often the keys to resolution are found in this territory as well.

Chapter 4
The Mediation Process

---

3. Identification of the decision-maker. At this critical stage, the mediator is also attempting to identify who the decision-maker or decision-makers are in each room. In civil litigation, the decision-maker or decision-makers may be any of the following:

(1) The party only.

(2) The lawyer only.

(3) The party and the party's lawyer.

(4) Someone not in the room (God forbid).

In most instances, the party and the party's lawyer will make the decision. Ideally and ethically, the party should make the final decision. In some disputes, the party may be the only decision-maker and in other disputes the party's lawyer may be the only real decision-maker. In certain disputes, the party and the party's lawyer may have very different views of the dispute and its resolution.

Identification of the decision-maker (or decision-makers) is critical because it is the decision-maker's negotiating style and interests that need to be identified and met if resolution is to occur. Most of the time, identification of the decision-maker is an easy task, but sometimes the determination is not so obvious. If uncertain, the mediator should ask who is going to make the decision.

Permit me now to explore with you two difficult situations — a dispute in which the lawyer is the sole decision-maker and a dispute in which the lawyer and her client are at odds.

4. The lawyer as decision-maker. Undoubtedly, the dispute belongs to the party and not the lawyer. But clients, as they should, often rely heavily upon their lawyers to guide and advise them. In certain instances, a client may possess little formal education. In most instances, the client possesses virtually no formal legal education. As a result, it is not surprising that in certain cases the party's lawyer is going to make the decision — "I'll do whatever my lawyer says."

Chapter 4
The Mediation Process

In the great majority of cases, the lawyer functioning as the decision-maker is no problem. The fact that a lawyer has control over her client is usually a great help in a mediation. But, what happens when a lawyer puts her interests ahead of the client's interest and obstructs the mediation process?

A mediator must *never* come between a lawyer and her client. A mediator must *never* embarrass or humiliate an attorney in the presence of her client. A mediator *must* respect the attorney-client relationship and *actively support* that relationship in a mediation. In instances in which the mediator perceives an attorney is placing her interests ahead of the client's interests, however, the mediator may wish to hold a private meeting with the client's counsel to discuss such issues openly and diplomatically.

5. When the lawyer and client are at odds. A more common, and less troublesome, situation is when the mediator perceives that an attorney and client are at odds with each other. In fact, many lawyers suggest mediation because they have lost control over their clients. In such instances, the client is the decision-maker, but she may not be listening to her counsel and often has unrealistic expectations and goals. Typically, a lawyer will cue in the mediator at the first caucus that such a situation exists, or the dynamics in the room will make the problem strikingly obvious.

The mediator's role in such situations is *not* to dispense legal advice or to play the "second lawyer." Rather, by posing specific and appropriate questions, the mediator should attempt to focus the party on the objective realities of the case so that the party will see both the weaknesses and strengths of her position.

6. Identification of negotiating style. This book is not intended to discuss the negotiation process fully. Other excellent works are devoted uniquely to that topic. But one way of looking at mediation is as a supervised negotiation, with the mediator governing the negotiations.

Everyone has a different negotiating style. Some negotiators are very aggressive. Other negotiators are very conciliatory. Some negotiators wish to exploit; others fear being exploited. Many negotiators have done little formal study on the negoti-

---

ation process. Often, a person's negotiation style is reflective of her personality. As such, a mediator rarely can change the negotiating style of a party to a mediation and probably should never even try.

But from the mediation perspective, the negotiating style is not the rub; rather, the negotiating "pace" of the decision-makers is the critical issue. Pace is best illustrated by thinking of mediation like a dance. If you enter a dance hall and the band begins to play, you will usually observe four general classes of dancers:

(1)   Those who will get on the floor and really dance as soon as the band starts to play.

(2)   Those who may dance a little bit, sit down and talk, and then begin really to dance on their own.

(3)   Those who have to be dragged out on the floor, but once they are, they really dance.

(4)   Those who never dance.

Negotiating pace is just like the dancers I have described. Some parties to a mediation want to get down to business quickly; others may want to settle in a bit before getting into serious negotiations. Certain parties need to be dragged into the negotiations. Fortunately, very, very few people are unwilling to negotiate at all.

The mediator may, in a certain sense, be thought of as a band leader. The mediator must know the negotiating pace of the parties to play the right music; i.e., Springsteen, country and western, a very slow waltz, etc. A good mediator must be chameleon-like, versatile, and flexible. A mediator with the ability to play only a slow waltz may well frustrate parties who want to rock 'n' roll, and resolution may not occur for that reason alone. Good mediators, if they do not intuitively know each party's pace, ask the parties what kind of tempo they want.

Many times, the parties' pace is the same — all parties want to get right down to serious discussions or all parties want a slow, deliberate negotiation. But the more challenging situation, which often occurs, is when each party has a different (some-

Chapter 4
The Mediation Process

times radically different) negotiating pace — one party wants to "cut to the chase" and the other party wants to go slow and be deliberate. This stylistic pace clash may damage any chance of resolution unless it is identified and addressed at the outset — the "fast dancer" will be frustrated by the "slow dancer's" unwillingness to get down to business, and the "slow dancer" will feel as if the other party is rushing or pressuring her into a bad decision.

In separate caucus, the mediator (with authorization from each party to disclose) should openly discuss with each party these stylistic differences and encourage each party to respect the style of the other and not to become frustrated. If the mediator sews together such an agreement in the first caucus, the parties' stylistic differences will not, in themselves, create a fatal impasse.

7. The "winner's curse." Many mediations, especially personal injury matters, involve one party agreeing to pay the other side money. The issue is how much. A claimant never wants to leave something on the table. An insurance adjuster never wants to pay too much. An interesting phenomenon based on this premise explains many of the initial rounds of negotiation in mediation. Consider the following story, which I first heard from Professor B. Randolph Lowery of the Pepperdine University School of Law:

Suppose we find ourselves magically transported to the Neiman Marcus department store in Houston — a rather pricey place to shop. You walk into the leather goods section and see a briefcase that you really like. You can just imagine walking into the courtroom proudly holding the briefcase. But your daydream abruptly ends when you look at the price tag and see $500. Even if you have the money, you know you are very hard on your briefcases and are unwilling to pay $500 for an item you will shortly beat into a pulp. So you don't buy the briefcase.

The next week you find yourself in Mexico. You are walking through the shopping area and enter a leather goods store. You see a briefcase in the very back that looks very much like the one you saw at Neiman Marcus. You closely inspect and touch the briefcase. If the briefcase is not identical to the one you saw at Neiman's,

---

it is very, very similar. This briefcase, however, has one unique characteristic. It has no price tag.

You begin to get very excited. You think about the $500 price tag at Neiman's. You think about negotiation. You think about Mexico and the negotiating culture you find yourself in, and you come to a command decision. You take the briefcase from the display counter, you walk over to the sales clerk, you hand her the briefcase, and with utter conviction in your voice you say, "I'll give you $200 for this briefcase."

The sales clerk says only one word: "Sold."

How do you feel? Five steps away you think you could have bought the briefcase for $170. Ten steps away you think $130. You are at the door and think $100. By the time you are outside the shop, you are upset with yourself and have totally forgotten the $300 you saved by not buying the briefcase at Neiman Marcus.

This phenomenon is often referred to as "the winner's curse." And "the winner's curse" often explains the initial bids exchanged during the mediation process; that is, until the defendant says "no" to $1 million or the plaintiff says "no" to $50,000, the "real" negotiation cannot commence.

Of course, the interesting problem is that after the winner's curse bids are exchanged, who will be the one to make the first "credible" proposal?

Winner's curse bids create a tit for tat negotiation, which is illustrated by the following hypothetical negotiation:

1. The plaintiff demands $1 million.

2. The defendant counters with $50,000.

3. The plaintiff counters with $975,000.

4. The defendant counters with $75,000.

5. The plaintiff counters with $950,000.

6. The defendant counters with $100,000.

7. And so on.

You have been in such negotiations. Each counter takes more time to get, both parties become frustrated, and the only outcome is that a very large gap will remain and both parties will feel the negotiation is going nowhere. Mediators usually hear one or both parties say "we are wasting our time." And of course, no one wants to make the *first* "credible" move.

In a negotiation, what is a "credible" number? A credible number is not a number a party may be willing to pay or accept, but is instead one that encourages a party to perceive that the negotiation is moving into the realm of reason. Interestingly, most cases resolve at the mid-point between the first two credible proposals. I am not suggesting a baby split. If one party starts at $1 million and the other party counters with $200,000, the mediator does not set a goal of $600,000. Mediators do not set dollar goals to begin with. But, hypothetically, if one party believes a $500,000 proposal to be credible and the other party believes a $300,000 counter to be credible, the very likely resolution is $400,000.

Back to the issue of who makes the first credible proposal. Interestingly, I have observed the opposite of what you may have thought or still think. My observation is that the party who makes the *first* credible proposal *controls* the negotiation. Why? Neither side perceives the opening tit for tat winner's curse bids to be good faith proposals. Thus, the party who makes the *first* credible proposal, instead of demonstrating weakness, scores a lot of points with the other side and subsequent, more de minimus proposals are excused or tolerated.

Another way of saying this is that the one who makes the first credible proposal controls the velocity of the negotiation. Consider the following illustration:

1. The plaintiff opens with $1 million.

2. The defendant counters with $50,000.

3. The plaintiff counters with $975,000.

4. The defendant counters with $75,000.

5. The plaintiff counters with $950,000.

6. The defendant, with a hopeful settlement goal of $250,000-$300,000 makes the first "credible" move to $150,000, still leaving $100,000-$150,000 of elbow room.

7. The plaintiff, encouraged by the move, counters with $850,000.

8. The defendant, now permitted to control the velocity of the negotiation, counters with $175,000.

9. The plaintiff counters with $750,000.

10. The defendant, to demonstrate that he is close to an end, counters with $190,000.

The plaintiff in this illustration, will believe that $200,000-$250,000 is the defendant's likely goal. The plaintiff, if he or she is seriously interested in resolution within that range, must make a substantial drop to keep the negotiations alive. If the mediator is doing her job, she will discuss a dramatic drop to $400,000-$450,000 with the plaintiff. Of course, I have used an illustration in which the defendant controls the velocity. The plaintiff can just as easily control the velocity by making the first credible proposal.

The "Harvard theory" of negotiations states that 91% of all cases settle around the midpoint between the first two credible proposals. I know that such an approach is in opposition to many of your views; but, based on observing more than 1,200 mediations, I know the strategy works.

§4.6 Strength/Weakness Analysis

Another essential aspect of the initial caucus is a strength/ weakness analysis. In this regard, the mediator does not render ultimate opinions; i.e., who will win or lose the lawsuit, whether an absolute limitations defense bars recovery, or whether a witness' credibility is subject to an absolute challenge, etc.

Chapter 4
The Mediation Process

Remember, the mediator's job is not to determine the legal issues but to assist the parties in identifying potential weaknesses as well as obvious strengths. As we all know, most litigants have little difficulty identifying their strong points. The mediator simply plays the role of devil's advocate by asking "what if," "what about," "do you think," or "why do you believe" questions.

Generally, the mediator is asking open-ended questions designed to permit the party to identify weaknesses on her own. Weaknesses may involve specific issues in the case, such as whether a jury will accept or believe an expert witness' testimony, whether a defendant will be able to attribute negligence fully to a third party, whether a certain piece of evidence will be admissible, etc. Weaknesses may also involve a more global assessment of the case, such as whether the claim has more limited value in the county in which the case will be tried, whether proof problems may be ignored because of the nature of the injuries or sympathy, whether a party may not desire a public trial for personal reasons, etc.

Because of the mediator's neutrality, most parties are willing participants in the strength/weakness analysis. Most lawyers are eager players in this phase as well because they are interested in a neutral perspective of their case. Advocates, as we all know, may become too close to a case and lose their objectivity. And, as stated before, a lawyer may have some weaknesses in a case that he identified to the client, but may need the mediator's help in getting the client to understand them. Also, the opening statements and information exchange prior to the initial caucus may produce new information or evidence that may require a re-evaluation of the case. More often than not, however, the opening statements do not produce significant new evidence; rather the opening statements produce a more clear, coherent, and full understanding of the other party's position. Also, the opening remarks are usually the first time the client has heard a complete characterization of the other side's position. Finally, in many instances, the mediation is the first time an insurance adjuster has physically seen the claimant. As we know, the impression a claimant will make may affect the valuation of a case.

The strength/weakness analysis is therefore critical to the negotiations themselves. Parties come to a mediation with an opening offer that is usually inflated or deflated for negotiating purposes, but that also reflects to some extent their sense of the value of the case.

Consider that a party's assessment of a case is like an imaginary box. The box contains the evidence, the witnesses, the law, subjective factors, and the like. The party's advocate has attached a value to the box. For the value of the box to change at all, the contents of the box need to be changed. The value of the box may represent a "problem free" box. Putting problems in the box changes the value — the box may contain inadmissible evidence, for instance. As those problem items are removed from the box, the box becomes a different box and, as a result, the value attached to it must necessarily change.

A party does not re-assess or change value for no reason. Of course, reasons outside of the contents of the box may result in value changing; i.e., unwillingness to accept any risk, a desire to avoid delay, avoidance of litigation expenses, a desire for confidentiality, etc. But beyond such factors that a mediator may identify in her introductory remarks, re-evaluating the case with the mediator's help is how the essential change occurs.

Based on my experience, parties often do not fully appreciate risk, the other side's position, or the defects in their case without the direct interaction the process affords. The neutral's strength/weakness questions are accepted and welcomed *because* she is a neutral and is not contaminated; that is, the neutral is not the other side.

I would make one final, strong statement regarding the strength/weakness phase of the first caucus. The mediator should *never, never, never* attempt to impose her view of a facet of the case or the whole case on a party. In fact, a mediator should rarely even suggest her view. A mediator who is skilled in good questioning techniques does not even need to suggest her view of an issue. In countless mediations, I have heard a party respond to my question by saying, "You know, I haven't really thought of this before." Such responses encourage me to believe the box is already

Chapter 4
The Mediation Process

beginning to change, values will change, and with persistence and effort, the case will likely settle.

§4.7 Money, Expectations, Hopes, Dreams and Motivations

As you probably realize by now, the initial caucus is a critical aspect of the mediation process. Consider mediation to be like building a house. The initial caucus is like building a good foundation.

Ultimately, most resolutions involve the payment of money. In the initial caucus, the mediator will explore monetary issues and attempt to obtain each party's first monetary proposal. Good mediators will go through the strength/weakness analysis before monetary discussions. And good mediators will attempt to identify the non-monetary interests that are motivating the party and that are affecting the party's monetary values.

We all have expectations in life — some of which are realistic and some of which regrettably are not. To be sure, parties to a mediation have preconceived monetary expectations. In the first caucus, a mediator may take the following approach regarding monetary expectations:

1. Whether we are here mediating for two hours or 12 hours, what are your monetary expectations?

2. Why do you have such monetary expectations?

3. Are these expectations realistic?

4. What are your monetary needs?

5. What do you realistically expect, whether we are mediating for two hours or 12, the other side to offer?

Monetary values are in part objective and in part subjective. Value may be claimed in non-monetary ways, but money is often more convenient and is something everyone understands. Ultimately, in any negotiation, the situation boils down to what someone is willing to pay and what someone is willing to accept.

The mediator's goal is to have credible (as you now understand that term) monetary negotiations occur as soon as is practical. The five questions listed above, obviously framed a bit differently by each mediator, will be asked in either the initial caucus or the second caucus. And if the mediator is worth her salt, a credible monetary dance will have begun.

§4.8 Subsequent Caucuses

The strength/weakness analysis, which is part of the initial caucus, occurs continuously, albeit in a more focused form, throughout all caucuses. Typically, one or two issues, out of an initial potpourri of many issues, become the primary focus of subsequent evaluation. A facet of liability, including the issue of causation, may become the essence of subsequent evaluation. More often than not, though, damages become the major focus of the subsequent caucus. And, logically, this is as it should be.

Damages, whether liability is virtually conceded or not, relate most particularly to the ongoing monetary proposals or counter-proposals. The mediator in second, third, and fourth caucus rounds is making a determined effort to get the monetary negotiations going, to move the parties off their "winner's curse" opening, and to encourage one of the parties to make the first, credible significant move. Needless to say, depending upon the negotiating styles of the parties, this not an easy process. Ostensible impasse usually occurs during these subsequent caucus rounds, which the mediator must be able to break. Chapter 14, pages 104-112, is devoted entirely to breaking impasses, and you may wish to read that chapter at this point.

You probably would guess that impasse is the bane of most mediators. Although mediators are trained how to avoid impasse, some live their lives dreading it. In my opinion, mediators should learn to live *for* impasse. After all, ostensible impasse will occur in every mediation, often several times, and if the parties could resolve their dispute by themselves a mediator would not be needed.

As you realize, all declared impasses are not real impasses at all. Mediators become used to parties declaring "I will never" or "I will not." Mediators, not dis-

Chapter 4
The Mediation Process

respectfully, learn to ignore or discount such declarations. The mediator must keep pushing through such barriers — after all, if the mediator does not try to, who will? If they use good form, mediators will push on without being coercive by constantly re-visiting issues and maximizing communication. When everyone else feels they are "wasting their time," mediators maintain optimism and encourage the parties to continue on. I cannot tell you how many times I have heard "we are wasting our time" in the seventh hour and had the case resolve in the ninth hour. Style, pace, tempo, and re-evaluation explain this.

Admittedly, certain aspects of this process are inexplicable. For instance, sometimes the most complex cases, which the mediator may think will require 12 hours or more to resolve, are concluded in four hours. Conversely, seemingly simple cases sometimes require twice as long as a mediator might expect. Another example: Sometimes people who have no ability to communicate or who are overtly hostile can develop a real ability to talk and understand each other during the process. Despite having mediated over 1,200 cases, I still cannot fully explain this except to say that it is created by the process itself.

As you might think, the mediator must be especially careful in all caucuses to preserve confidentiality and make only authorized disclosures. Losing confidentiality is like losing virginity — it happens only once. If a mediator walks into a second or third caucus with you and states "I know I shouldn't tell you this, but," you should consider terminating the session. If the mediator is divulging the other side's confidences, the mediator is probably divulging your confidences.

Good mediators are obsessively meticulous about maintaining confidential information, but mediators are, like everyone else, human beings and on rare occasion capable of mistakenly divulging a piece of confidential information. Should a mediator make such a mistake, she should visit immediately with the party whose confidential information she has inadvertently disseminated and admit the mistake. Most of the time, a party will appreciate such candor, admire the mediator's integrity, and wish to continue with the process. On the other hand, if a party's belief in the process or the mediator is fatally contaminated by the admission, the mediator should consider closing the session. Perhaps another mediator will have a better chance to succeed.

The mediation advocate should feel free to make suggestions like the ones below to the mediator in subsequent caucus rounds. The mediator is the captain of the ship and will make the final call, but she should always be interested in hearing any idea that will increase the chances for a successful resolution.

1. The advocate might suggest, for whatever reason, that the mediator might get together with the parties without the lawyers present.

2. The advocate might suggest a lawyer caucus (described in §4.10) to review a point of law with opposing counsel or to discuss a particularly sensitive issue.

3. The advocate might wish to have the mediator present a document or an appellate decision to opposing counsel.

4. The advocate might suggest that a more direct, expedited negotiation would be more helpful.

§4.9   Mediation Advocates' Opinions — What to Tell

Confident mediators, sure of their own skills, may even ask the mediation advocates what they think will work or admit to being a little lost and in need of direction. Such confessions are signs of strength, not weakness. The mediator may be sensing that an unidentified issue or interest is blocking progress, but the only way she will find out is by asking for help. Many mediators have strong intuitive skills. Some mediators have uncanny intuitive skills. But mediators are not psychics and cannot read minds. As stated before, one of the greatest tools in the mediator's toolbox is the same as the litigator's most important tool — the ability to ask the right question.

From the mediation advocate's point of view, especially in the later caucuses, a constant tension revolves around the issue of how much information to give away. In modern discovery times, very few secrets exist. But the other side may not have

Chapter 4
The Mediation Process

done its homework. Or the other side may have failed to identify a witness. Or the other side may have a real limitations problem of which it is unaware. Does the mediation advocate save such matters for trial? Or does the mediation advocate give such information out to increase the probabilities of resolution?

Because it is the mediator's job to move matters towards resolution, she will always want authority to disclose such information, and you should not blame a mediator for being persistent. But such a decision is clearly the mediation advocate's call and the mediator should not be coercive.

So how does the mediation advocate make this call? I would suggest the following analysis:

1. Is the information likely to be discovered?

2. If a pleading or discovery deadline has been missed, how likely, if such information is disclosed, is your opponent to cure the problem?

3. Just how devastating is your opponent's error? Does the mistake blow your opponent out of the water? Seriously hurt your opponent? Or does the mistake create just a slight degree of discomfort?

4. How are the negotiations going? Has progress been made? If so, will such disclosure push things to conclusion? Has no progress been made? If not, will such disclosure get things going?

5. Consider the timing of the disclosure. Do you make all the progress you can make and use the disclosure as your final blast? Do you set your depth charge early and use it as a basis of an aggressive negotiating posture?

6. Ask the mediator her impression of the information itself and the potential impact of such disclosure, not whether you should disclose the information. Sometimes an advocate thinks something is an H-bomb when it really is a firecracker. Sometimes an H-bomb is an H-bomb. Most often, the reality lies somewhere in between. But beyond giving away a secret, the mediator may advise you that disclosure of the information may be a negative in terms of the negotiation instead of a positive, because of the opponent's emotional response for example.

Returning to the monetary aspects of the subsequent caucus, the mediation advocate must accept one fundamental principle — each party bears responsibility for the proposals it makes and should not be surprised or angered by an in-kind counterproposal. In other words, minimal increases in an offer usually result in minimal decreases in a demand. Ultimately, if the parties continue to negotiate in such a fashion, a considerable gap will remain and an impasse may well occur. The mediator, as her role requires, is continuously attempting to get both sides to negotiate on a credible basis.

§4.10 Lawyer Caucuses

Some mediators may call a lawyer caucus at some time during the caucus phase of the proceedings.

Lawyer caucuses sometimes are called because a resolution is stalled by a legal issue. Of course, the mediator is not the judge and will not rule on a point of law. But the mediator may believe that counsel are not fully understanding each other's legal positions and that additional discussion would be beneficial. Typically "law talk" sails over clients' heads and sometimes mediation advocates feel they cannot fully discuss points of law in the initial group setting. A lawyer caucus provides a forum for a more expanded discussion of legal issues. Admittedly, a mediation that gets bogged down in extended legal debates may be doomed to failure, but in certain instances, focusing or clarifying the legal issues may be helpful.

A lawyer caucus may be useful in breaking a negotiation impasse. Most often, the mediator is provided a monetary proposal and is authorized to deliver the offer to the other party. Of course, the benefit of such an approach is that the mediator, to some extent, deflects a negative reaction to an offer and encourages a party to continue on with the negotiation.

The liability with such a messenger approach, however, is that a party does not get to see "up close and personal" the other party communicate the message. Suppose, hypothetically, negotiations have proceeded using the mediator as the messenger. Further assume that at some late point in the negotiations a party is going to make a "take it or leave it" proposal. From the other party's vantage point, the question is whether the opposition really means take it or leave it. A mediator in such a situation may call a lawyer caucus and have the lawyer delivering the message communicate it directly to the opposition. Further, such a situation provides the parties yet another opportunity to interact, to discuss the proposal, and perhaps to re-evaluate their positions once again.

In other circumstances, a mediation advocate may wish to suggest a lawyer caucus in order to have a private meeting with the mediator. Typically, a mediation advocate may make such a request when she wishes to let the mediator know she is having a problem with her client. Mediators, as already stated, must never come between an attorney and her client. But as previously discussed, an attorney may believe her client has an exaggerated or incorrect view of the case and would like the mediator's assistance in helping the client better understand things. Often, mediators are intuitively aware of such situations, but sometimes a mediator may be uncertain and will hold back so as not to interfere with the attorney-client relationship. A private meeting with the mediator permits the mediation advocate to explain fully those areas in which her client may need some additional reality checking.

I need to make one caveat about lawyer caucuses: Lawyer caucuses should be used sparingly and selectively, and should be brief. The dispute, of course, belongs to the parties. Parties may become apprehensive and concerned if too many lawyer caucuses occur or if such caucuses take too long. The parties will wonder what is going on behind their backs and may begin to feel disenfranchised from the process.

§4.11 Additional Collective Sessions

One of the inherent advantages of mediation is its flexibility. As the mediation evolves, a mediator must always be thinking of ways to maximize communication and thereby increase the chances of a successful resolution. The mediation process in fact improves communication and assists parties who had no desire or ability to understand each other's positions in engaging in a meaningful dialogue. Further, the mediation process unearths interests, feelings, and motivations that may not have been known or expressed prior to the mediation.

As participants settle into and become comfortable with the mediation process, they may become more willing and able to have a helpful and constructive discussion later in the day. Additionally, a party may indicate to the mediator in caucus a real need to communicate something to the other side. The mediator may assist the party in considering the most constructive way of getting such a message across.

Consider the following examples in which such subsequent collective meetings might be useful:

1. A mediator in private caucus learns that the plaintiff's primary motivation in filing a medical malpractice complaint was his feeling that the physician didn't care and never expressed regret. The mediator obtains authorization to tell that to the physician and her counsel. In caucus with the physician, the mediator learns that the physician, while denying liability, wanted to express regret, but did not do so out of fear that such expression would be misconstrued as an admission of liability. The mediator then may wish to reconvene the parties so that the physician, under the safety of mediation, may communicate regret and concern for the family.

2. In a partnership dispute, the mediator in caucus learns that a matter unrelated to the business issues was the real genesis of the current dispute. The mediator also learns that this matter has never been communicated to the other partner and the other partner has no idea that his former associate was angry about the matter. The mediator may decide to bring the parties back together so that such issue may be directly communicated and discussed.

3. The mediator may feel that both sides are not negotiating in a manner likely to obtain resolution, and therefore may elect to re-assemble all the participants in order to suggest that if negotiating progress is not made that an impasse will result and no resolution will be reached. In many instances, the participants will elect to continue the negotiations as opposed to declaring an impasse.

Chapter 4
The Mediation Process

§4.12 Memorandum of Agreement

Assuming the mediation results in a resolution of the dispute, a memorandum of agreement should be prepared and signed by all parties and their counsel. Most mediators have standard memorandum of agreement forms. I have included in Appendix C, pages 211-212, a copy of the memorandum of agreement form I use.

Of course, the memorandum of agreement is not the final release, and dismissal documents will be prepared by counsel after the mediation. The memorandum of agreement, however, should be clear and specific enough to avoid any post-mediation controversy as to what was agreed to at the mediation session.

In most cases, the memorandum of agreement will simply set out that the claimant will release any and all claims and dismiss the suit with prejudice in exchange for a specified sum of money. In complex business disputes, the memorandum of agreement will likely include numerous other specific items.

While the memorandum of agreement should be clear and specific, the parties should not attempt to create the final release documents at the session. In one mediation I conducted, an agreement almost fell apart because counsel attempted to draft the final agreement at the session.

I also think it is better practice for the mediator to draft the memorandum of agreement, as opposed to counsel for the parties. A memorandum of agreement drafted by an attorney for one of the parties may be subject to question. If counsel insist upon drafting the memorandum of agreement, all counsel should collaborate on its preparation. After all parties and counsel have executed the agreement, the mediator should provide copies to all participants.

Chapter 5

Pre-Mediation Submissions

This chapter begins four chapters devoted to the concept of mediation advocacy; that is, how a lawyer effectively represents his client in the mediation setting. As I see it, by the year 2000, lawyers will specialize in mediation advocacy as much as they now specialize in civil litigation. Mediation advocacy is *not* trying your lawsuit; however, many of your trial skills, with some modification, translate well into the mediation environment.

Many mediators require counsel to submit confidential (for the mediator's eyes only) pre-mediation submissions. I insist upon such submissions for two reasons. First, regardless of my litigation background, I want to be specifically educated about the dispute so as to not waste time at the session. Second, and probably more important, I want the lawyers to focus on and objectively evaluate their case prior to the session. Some lawyers incorrectly perceive their role in mediation is just to show up. Lawyers who labor under such misimpression will be ill prepared, reduce the chances for a successful resolution, and unable to participate in the process. In contemporary mediation practice, lawyer involvement is intensive and essential. Preparation and effective mediation advocacy improves the chances for resolution. In my view, this is as it should and must be.

Pre-mediation submissions are not designed to influence or persuade the mediator as to the correctness of your cause. The mediator must remain neutral and never will rule on a point of law or a disputed fact. In this sense, the pre-mediation submission is not a trial brief. On the other hand, providing controlling appellate decisions and a memorandum of law may be very useful in assisting the mediator in understanding the strengths and weaknesses of your position.

I require counsel for each party to include the following in their pre-mediation submission:

Chapter 5
Pre-Mediation Submissions

---

1. A brief and concise statement of the client's assessment of the issues involved in the case and his position on such issues. What is "brief" depends upon the nature and complexity of the case. "Brief" in a more simple case may mean four pages or less. "Brief" in a mutli-million dollar dispute may mean 25-30 pages.

2. Copies of the current "live" pleadings. "Live pleadings" do *not* include every pleading ever filed. Rather, "live pleadings" are the most current affirmative and defensive pleadings on file.

3. Copies of helpful appellate decisions, if certain issues turn on matters of law. As with a trial brief, the mediation advocate should *not* provide *every* appellate case ever decided on a certain point; rather, the mediation advocate should selectively choose the most useful opinions. Such appellate decisions assist the mediator in better understanding the relative strengths and weaknesses of your positions. In this regard, appellate decisions that are not favorable to the mediation advocate's position should also be provided.

4. *Critical* documentary evidence. "Critical" could mean the controlling contract or correspondence, *excerpts* from significant depositions, a chronology of events, an important scientific/medical article or report, and the like.

5. A history of the negotiations to date. What have the proposals and counter-proposals been? And who, in the mediation advocate's thinking, bid last? I have an absolute rule in mediation that no party should ever be compelled to bid against himself.

6. An objective assessment of the party's strengths and weaknesses. What are the party's strongest points? And what are the perceived weaknesses?

7. Subjective factors and interests that may appear in the mediation: What are the party's non-monetary interests? Are there any sensitive spots (I call them "nerves")? Do any of the parties have an extreme dislike for each other? For any of the lawyers? Why?

Chapter 5
Pre-Mediation Submissions

As you will realize from this list, the pre-mediation submission not only helps the mediator understand the case, but also helps the mediator in developing a strategic plan (and alternative plans) for your specific case. A pre-mediation submission may result in a mediator deciding to keep the parties together longer in the collaborative session, or the mediator may decide to move more quickly into caucus. The mediator may decide direct interaction between the parties might be useful, or he may decide "venting" in the group session may be disastrous or extremely helpful.

Further, a pre-mediation submission is much more effective if it is placed in a three-ring binder, contains a table of contents, and is tabbed and segregated accordingly. As a mediation advocate, keep in mind that your pre-mediation submission is your first opportunity to assist, not influence, the mediator. You should make every effort, especially if your submission is a lengthy one, to have your pre-mediation submission in the mediator's hands at least three days prior to the session itself. You want the mediator to have adequate time to read and evaluate your written materials.

Please keep in mind that the mediator *never* shares the submission with the other side, nor does the mediator imply its contents in caucus. The submission is usually destroyed after the session. And if the mediation does not produce resolution, the submission is always valuable to the attorney, either in whole or in part, as a trial notebook.

Having described the pre-mediation submission generally, I will now provide you with a checklist for each section.

Checklist

I. Brief Statement of Issues and Positions

A. Include a factual summary.

B. If the sequence of events is essential (almost always in medical negligence cases), include a chronology of events. Even if the case does not resolve, such chronology will be helpful at trial.

C. What are the legal issues in dispute?

D. What is your position on such legal issues?

E. What are the factual issues in dispute?

F. What is your position on these factual issues?

II. Copies of Current, Live Pleadings

A. Include only the most recent amended affirmative and defensive pleadings.

B. Include, subject to confidentiality, pleadings that may be filed if the matter is not resolved; i.e, a motion for summary judgment.

C. If a motion for summary judgment, a brief in support of such motion, and/or an opposing motion and brief are already on file, include such pleadings in this section.

III. Pertinent Appellate Decisions

A. Those decisions most supportive of your position.

B. Those decisions that oppose your position, to whatever degree.

C. In cases in which a legal point has not been finally resolved or there are conflicting opinions, include the following:

1. Helpful law review articles.

2. Recent seminar articles.

3. Opinions from other jurisdictions.

IV. Critical Documentary Evidence (this will vary from case to case)

A. The contract or correspondence that creates an agreement.

B. Medical bills (essential in a personal injury (PI) mediation).

C. Physicians' reports or medical records (PI).

D. Reports regarding future medical expenses and treatment (PI).

E. Lost wage statements (PI).

F. Reports on future lost earnings and possible employment opportunities or lack thereof (PI).

G. A life expectancy table (PI).

H. Reports from treating psychiatrists, psychologists, counselors, etc.

I. Economist reports.

J. *Excerpts* from critical expert/witness reports or depositions.

K. A chronology.

L. Critical photographs.

M. Any models, charts, diagrams, etc.

N. "Day in the Life" videos.

O. Curriculum vitae for important experts.

P. Invoices that support alleged damages.

Q. Time sheets, report summaries, and the like that support attorneys' fees.

R. Excerpts from responses to interrogatories, requests for production, or requests for admissions.

V. Negotiation History

A. Outline the series of demands and offers.

B. Indicate clearly which party made the last bid.

C. Include any history of any informal negotiations that have not resulted in a specific proposal.

D. Include your best educated guess as to what the other side might be willing to pay or take and why you think so.

VI. Objective Strength/Weakness Analysis

A. From a *factual* perspective, outline your strengths and weaknesses. For example, do your witnesses make good, credible presentations? Or do your witnesses testify poorly? Are they then subject to rigorous cross-examination? Do you have a strong expert? What about the other side's witnesses?

B. From a legal perspective, what are your strengths *and* weaknesses? What potential legal problems do you have; i.e., limitations, causation, immunity, etc.?

C. Does the venue play any part in your assessment of strengths and weaknesses? Are juries liberal? Conservative? What is the orientation of the judge?

D. How quickly will your case come to trial?

E. Is an appeal possible, likely, or certain?

F. Has the other side committed a procedural blunder?

G. Insurance coverage problems.

VII. Subjective Factors

A. Do the parties dislike each other intensely? Why?

B. Did the parties, prior to the dispute, enjoy a positive relationship? Why and on what basis?

C. Have any of the parties developed a personality problem with any of the counsel? Why?

D. Is there a personality problem between counsel? Why?

E. What is the negotiating style of your client? The other side?

F. What are your client's non-monetary interests and needs?

G. What are the sensitive, sore spot issues? Why?

H. Does your client have unrealistic expectations? The other side? Why?

I. Are there political, personal, or emotional issues fueling this dispute?

J. Why do you think settlement at mediation is in your client's interests? The other side's interests?

You will find from your review of the specific aspects of the pre-mediation submission that preparation for mediation is as essential as preparation for trial. The lawyer's role (that is, the mediation advocate's role) is essential. Because of the absolute need for preparation, you "feel like a lawyer" as much in the mediation setting as at the courthouse.

If you are nodding your head at this moment, you are already understanding the most important thing: Mediation is an identifiable process, *lawyers play a valuable role in the process*, and you can effectively represent, and thus help, your client in the mediation setting. You will *need* to. By the end of this decade, I predict at least half of all filed cases will receive mediation treatment. No longer is there a debate as to whether mediation "works." A lawyer, if he is to survive, must know the process and prepare for it.

Chapter 6

Who Should Attend The Mediation —
The Authority to Settle Issue

One of the most controversial and nettlesome problems in mediation practice is the issue of who has authority to settle the case.

As previously stated, mediation is predicated upon a party's decision-maker having the opportunity to look, see, touch, and feel the other side's case for purposes of possibly re-evaluating her position. For the decision-maker, many observations in mediation are subjective; i.e., how the other party looks, how the other party communicates, how well prepared the other lawyer seems to be. These more subjective observations cannot really be reported second hand. After all, seeing is believing.

Additionally, negotiation is itself a process that people sense and feel beyond the mere monetary proposals themselves. Negotiation participants feel frustration, progress, momentum, and have a direct sense of how close an agreement might be and what would or might make a difference. A non-participant cannot, regardless of the thoroughness of a report, feel such things. The non-participant has not been through the process, nor has the non-participant invested in or committed to the process. More simply stated, a non-participant, from a distance, can nix a deal she has not worked to build. Even more simply, it's easy to say "no" over the telephone.

The tension, of course, is created by economics. A true decision-maker may have to travel great distances at substantial costs to attend a mediation. And there may be several decision-makers, which serves to multiply both cost and inconvenience. Further, the mediation process, while resolving the vast majority of cases, does not guarantee resolution in every case. Cost, inconvenience, and skepticism create the attitude that a representative with conditional or "subject to" authority who is geographically closer is more sensible and practical.

Chapter 6
Who Should Attend The Mediation — The Authority to Settle Issue

In previous articles I have written and speeches I have given discussing the authority issue, I have attempted (in true mediation fashion) to reconcile these opposing views and effectuate a compromise. For example, I have suggested that a more local representative with limited authority attend the session with the final decision-maker available by telephone throughout the session. And I have suggested that an individual who is part of a decision-making team and whose opinion will be respected attend the session.

Actual mediation experiences, however, have finally brought me to an inescapable conclusion — the final decision-maker physically needs to attend the session. I have observed local representatives without full authority become immeasurably frustrated when the true decision-maker on the other end of the telephone "doesn't get it." I have heard local representatives suggest to the true decision-maker "if you could only have seen the way our client looked." Of course, the true decision-maker has seen nothing. How can the non-participating true decision-maker believe a "bottom line" is in fact a bottom line without having participated in the negotiations and staring down the other side? The true decision-maker may believe the local representative wasn't tough enough, has an engagement that night, or is being misled. How may such thoughts by a non-participant be dispelled?

I have had local representatives have me talk, by telephone, to the non-participating true decision-maker. The true decision-maker hasn't met me, doesn't know me, and hasn't observed my use of the process. As a result, the true decision-maker has no basis for real trust in my words. The true decision-maker may believe the mediator is just trying to get the case settled or that the mediator is not being hard enough with the other side.

Again, I appreciate the fact that if a claimant makes a million dollar demand that is perceived as being ludicrous, why send a representative from New Jersey to Texas with million dollar settlement authority when a local representative with up to $200,000 authority may attend. Until the mediation process is attempted, however, no one knows what the fair value might be. The mediation process itself produces new information. Some new information is objective and easily communicated by telephone; some is subjective and difficult to communicated over the telephone. But the feel of the negotiation process and trust in the mediator can never be communicated telephonically.

I am no longer of the view that the economic argument makes sense. A million dollar demand case may not be a million dollar case, but it will be defended as if it were in terms of litigation costs. A trip from Ohio to Texas costs less than one or two depositions and conceivably may avoid $50,000 to $200,000 or more in defense costs. Convenience may be dealt with by proper scheduling. Skepticism may be assuaged by attending the mediation and resolving the million dollar demand case for $125,000. In any event, substantial costs are saved if the case settled via mediation.

The situation is complicated in instances in which multiple decision-makers are involved; i.e., a board of directors, a city council, a state agency, a group of beneficiaries, a class of claimants, etc. Obviously, I am not advocating sending 20 board members from California to Texas to attend a mediation. A rule of reason must apply to multiple decision-maker situations, and should also be applied even in the single out-of-state decision-maker context.

As a result, I will craft, as best as I am able, suggested approaches to both situations. My goal, of course, is to maximize the potential success of the mediation process.

§6.1 Single Out-of-State Decision-Maker Cases

1. Every effort should be made to have the true decision-maker attend the session.

2. If the true decision-maker will not be able to attend, the following should occur:

(1) All counsel should discuss such matters and agree upon an acceptable representative prior to the mediation session.

Chapter 6
Who Should Attend The Mediation — The
Authority to Settle Issue

---

(2)   The acceptable representative should be a person who has the trust and confidence of the true decision-maker.

(3)   The true decision-maker, although not attending, should be fully briefed on the case prior to the mediation session.

(4)   The true decision-maker should be "available" by telephone throughout the mediation. "Available" means telephone accessible *at any time* during the mediation; this means available at lunch, after normal business hours, and even if in a meeting — no meetings that cannot be interrupted should be scheduled.

(5)   After each separate caucus, counsel should telephone the true decision-maker with status reports. Do not make the only call to the true decision-maker at the end of the negotiations.

(6)   The true decision-maker should be encouraged to communicate directly with the mediator.

(7)   The true decision-maker should hear by speaker phone the opening statements of all counsel.

§6.2   Multiple Decision-Maker Cases

1.   All counsel should discuss, well in advance of the mediation session, whose final approval is necessary to endorse a "subject to" agreement.

2.   Counsel representing the party with multiple decision-makers should identify that person (or persons) who has the full confidence of the decision-making group.

3.   Having identified such person or persons, counsel should communicate to opposing counsel, in advance of the session, who will attend the mediation and obtain an agreement on that issue.

4.   The entire decision-making body should be fully briefed on the case prior to the mediation session.

Chapter 6
Who Should Attend The Mediation — The Authority to Settle Issue

---

5.   If at all possible (depending upon the size of the decision-making group), the non-attending decision-makers should be available by telephone throughout the mediation session.

6.   If the group is too large (e.g., a board of directors or a state agency or committee), counsel for the group should make arrangements in advance for rapid approval or disapproval of an agreement after the mediation session.

I do not intend for these guidelines to be taken as rigid rules. Every case and situation is different. The guiding principle is to have the true decision-makers present if at all possible. Failing that, the mechanism is to discuss the situation fully with opposing counsel in advance of the session, identify the appropriate representative, fully advise the non-participating decision-maker or decision-makers about the case prior to the session, have such non-participants accessible by telephone during the session, keep the non-participants posted during the session, and have a built-in rapid approval or disapproval system prior to the session.

These matters cannot be resolved at the mediation session itself. Planning is essential.

The "who should attend" issue involves matters other than the authority to settle issue. Permit me to address each of these issues in capsule form.

§6.3   Should the Claimant/Plaintiff Attend?

The answer to this is obvious — absolutely "yes." The claimant must have an opportunity to listen to the other side's position, to participate, to express her interests, to vent, to participate in the negotiations, to work with the mediation, and to make the final decision. Further, if a claimant's spouse or an important family member upon whom the claimant relies are really part of the decision-making process, they should attend the session as well.

§6.4   Should the Insured Attend?

Many times I find the insurance representative attends the mediation session, but the insured does not. My suggestions in this regard are as follows:

Chapter 6
Who Should Attend The Mediation — The Authority to Settle Issue

1. If the insured's consent is a prerequisite to settlement, the insured must attend the session.

2. If the insured's consent is not a prerequisite, the insured should always be afforded the choice of whether to attend, and should be strongly encouraged to attend in almost every case. The reasons are obvious: The insured may provide helpful information to counsel at the session; the insured (through an expression of regret, for example) may meet certain non-monetary interests at the session; and the insured is entitled to participate in the negotiations and the process itself. The insured owns the dispute and is at risk.

3. In certain instances, the insured may not be able to attend because of illness, cost, or business conflict. As long as the insured is in no way the true decision-maker, the insured's non-participation may not adversely affect chances for resolution.

§6.5 Should Experts Attend?

Obviously, mediations should not be transformed into trial proceedings, *but* a critical expert's participation at the session may be very helpful and improve chances for resolution. Let me offer some examples.

1. In a construction case in which certain building defects are alleged, the experts on both sides may be able to offer helpful insights and creative solutions at the session itself.

2. In a case in which emotional injuries make up the substantial portion of the damages claim, a psychologist's or psychiatrist's participation may be helpful.

3. In cases in which lost wages or diminution of earning capacity are in dispute, an economist's attendance may be useful.

The decision to bring such experts should be made *carefully* and *selectively*. The real question is whether such experts' participation will be critical and useful at the session. Should counsel elect to bring an expert to the session, counsel should communicate that intention to opposing counsel *prior to the session*.

Chapter 6
Who Should Attend The Mediation — The Authority to Settle Issue

§6.6 Should Structured Settlement Professionals Attend?

If the settlement will involve, either in whole or in part, a structure, structured settlement professionals on both sides should attend or be available by telephone. In many instances, both sides may wish to bring their own structure professionals.

As most of you know, the initial question is always what the value or cost of the structure is in today's dollars. Additionally, structures may be adjusted in numerous ways to meet certain needs and interests. I have always found the participation of structured settlement professionals to be very helpful.

§6.7 Should the Profoundly Injured Child/Claimant Attend?

This issue is a sensitive one for obvious reasons. No one wants to put a profoundly injured child through a possibly traumatic event, but claimant's counsel may want the decision-maker to see and observe the child. My suggested guidelines in this regard are as follows:

1. If the attendance will be traumatic or physically taxing on the child, do not bring the child. Counsel may instead elect to play a videotape of the child at the session.

2. If the child will not be unduly taxed by attending, bring her. However, I would suggest the following:

(1) Notify opposing counsel in advance of the session of your intention.

(2) Introduce the child at the *beginning* of the session.

(3) Make arrangements for someone to remove the child or care for her outside the room after such brief introduction and any questions.

(4) Do not permit the child to remain during any other part of the session.

(5) If, because of the illness or injury, the child will distract her parents during the session, arrange for a caretaker.

Chapter 6
Who Should Attend The Mediation — The
Authority to Settle Issue

§6.8   Should the Defendant/Doctor Attend?

Physicians need to practice medicine and have special demands on their time that may make it difficult for them to attend mediation sessions. Many insurance policies, however, require the physician's consent to settle. In many instances, the physician's presence demonstrates she in fact cares. The physician may very much want to attend. My suggestions in this regard are:

1.   In my opinion, the physician should always attend, especially if she wants to. The chances for a successful resolution are dramatically increased if the physician attends.

2.   The physician *must* attend if she has not provided consent to settle.

3.   If the physician *has* provided consent to settle, she may choose not to attend if medical emergencies or patient care demands otherwise.

4.   If the consenting physician will not attend, counsel for the physician should communicate this to the claimant's counsel prior to the session.

5.   The claimant should be advised that the physician's non-attendance is not because she is indifferent, but because she needs to care for patients. Again, every effort should be made to have the physician attend the session.

As will be specifically discussed in Chapter 16, pages 117-130, I have found the initial attendance of the physician to be very helpful because it demonstrates her interest, compassion, and concern.

Chapter 7

Preparing the Client for Mediation:
A Checklist

As a trial lawyer, you would never permit your client to sit for a deposition without adequate preparation. Yet I routinely preside over mediations in which clients have been prepared badly or not at all. If the goal of the mediation is a final resolution of the dispute, the mediation is one of the three most important aspects of the litigation process, along with the deposition and trial. As such, a client must be fully and completely prepared.

As you may have begun to realize, I am a firm believer in checklists. As a former litigator myself who understands the demands upon your time, I have determined that a checklist approach is the most effective way of assisting you with mediation advocacy. In this regard, I would envision that you would meet with your client the day before (or a few days before) the mediation, have an extended conference to prepare for the mediation, and cover the following topics:

    1. Who the mediator is, the mediator's background, and the mediator's practice experience.

    2. The personality of the mediator, if you know him.

    3. Where and when the mediation will be held.

    4. Your best guess as to how long the mediation will last. Explain to the client that your time projection is only an estimate and that while many mediations may take a day or less, to make contingency plans to work past 5:00 p.m.

    5. Who will be attending the mediation and for what purpose.

    6. The mediator's role. Include the following:

Chapter 7
Preparing the Client for Mediation: A Checklist

(a) The mediator is impartial/neutral and will remain so throughout.

(b) The mediator is not the judge or jury and will not render a decision or judgment.

(c) The mediator is attempting to facilitate a discussion geared towards a final resolution.

(d) Mediation is binding only if the parties reach a final agreement. If not, the parties proceed with the litigation without jeopardy.

(e) The mediation, by statute or written agreement, is a confidential proceeding.

(f) The mediator, because of confidentiality, may never be a witness.

(g) The mediator will play devil's advocate in separate caucus and will have the parties identify their strengths and weaknesses.

7. **The mediation process.** In this regard, explain and outline the following:

(a) The mediator's introduction.

(b) The lawyers' opening statement.

(c) The initial separate caucus.

(d) Subsequent caucuses.

(e) Lawyer caucuses.

(f) Subsequent collaborative sessions.

(g) The memorandum of agreement.

8. **The lawyer's role at mediation.** Include the following:

(a) Your role is different than your role will be at trial.

(b) You will not be objecting to evidence.

Chapter 7
Preparing the Client for Mediation: A Checklist

(c) You will not be putting on your full case or even a large part of your case.

(d) You will present an opening statement, which will be aimed at getting a favorable resolution for your client.

(e) You will assist your client and the mediator with the negotiations.

(f) You will participate in caucus in an objective strength/weakness analysis.

(g) You will listen to what is said at mediation for purposes of any re-evaluation.

(h) You will talk openly and candidly with the mediator in caucus.

(i) You will make all decisions as to what is disclosed at mediation.

(j) You understand the dispute belongs to the client.

(k) You will permit the client to make the final decision, subject to your advice and counsel.

(l) Your role, by its very nature, will be much more conciliatory than it would be at trial.

(m) You may express understanding or empathy with the other side in order to effectuate a positive resolution. Such understanding does not mean agreement and you are not selling out your client.

(n) If a resolution is reached, you will assist with the preparation of the memorandum of agreement.

(o) You may choose to avoid sensitive issues that may adversely affect the chances of resolution.

(p) Your approach may well be different at trial if a resolution is not reached.

(q) You will be respectful towards the mediator and the process.

9.   **The client's role at mediation.** Include the following:

(a) The client is there to listen.

(b) The client is there to evaluate and re-evaluate his case.

(c) The client is there to participate directly in the negotiations and discussions.

(d) At the request of the mediator, the client may be asked to make a statement in the collective session. If so, the client should prepare his remarks and express his feelings, but attempt to do so in the most constructive fashion.

(e) In separate caucus and because of the confidentiality of the process, the client should speak freely and openly to the mediator.

(f) The client should expect and want the mediator to play devil's advocate in separate caucus. The client should desire an objective review and analysis and not consider it to be a breach of neutrality.

(g) If an agreement is reached, a memorandum of agreement that will be reviewed by the client will be prepared and executed.

(h) The client should enter the mediation process with an open mind and give the process a chance to work.

Client preparation for mediation that covers these topics ensures several things. First, the client will be more comfortable with the mediation process. Second, the client will understand, appreciate, and be more comfortable with the mediator's role. Third, because the client understands the process, the client will be a better, more helpful participant. Finally, a case is more likely to resolve if the client is fully and completely prepared.

Chapter 8

The Appropriate Mediation Environment

The setting of the mediation — the mediation environment — is also an important aspect to be considered. All parties need to be as comfortable as possible with the setting in order to be comfortable with the process itself.

I would suggest the following factors to create a positive mediation environment:

1. If at all possible, the mediation should occur at a neutral site — typically the mediator's office. The benefit of a neutral site is obvious; no party feels like she is on the other party's home turf. If a mediation takes place in the other side's office, a party may worry whether the environment is truly safe and secure.

2. The mediation setting should have ample rooms for both the initial collective session and the separate caucuses. In certain complex multi-party cases, 30 or more people may attend the session. Participants should not feel cramped or uncomfortable.

3. The temperature at a mediation session should be at a comfortable level. Sometimes parties may feel a room is actually being made very warm as a tactic.

4. The separate caucus rooms should not be contiguous or, if a common wall exists, the wall should be soundproofed. Parties will not talk openly in caucus if they are afraid their words will be heard in the other caucus room.

5. If at all possible, the caucus rooms should have windows or, the party in a windowless room should have access to a windowed office. Sitting in a room with no windows for eight hours can be very uncomfortable for some people.

6. The caucus rooms should contain soft drinks and coffee. Parties need refreshment throughout the process.

7. For long mediations, food or snacks should be brought in to keep up energy levels.

8. Lunch should be delivered to the session. A two-hour lunch break can disrupt the momentum of the process.

9. A designated smoker's room should be provided. A smoker will go absolutely crazy if there is no place for her to smoke during a full day of mediation. Also, non-smokers should not have to suffer by sitting in a room with smokers.

10. Each caucus room should have a writing pad or drawing board to chart the progress of the negotiations.

11. Each caucus room should have a telephone.

12. The mediator should never receive telephone calls during a mediation unless the telephone call relates to the mediation in progress.

13. The parties should not make unrealistic travel plans that may artificially compress the process.

14. Special arrangements should be made for any participant who is handicapped or may need special attention.

The mediation environment is important because the parties must feel as comfortable and secure as possible during the process.

Chapter 9

The Mediation Advocate's Opening Statement

If there is any chapter in this book that you should re-read from time to time, and I do not say this arrogantly, this is the chapter. Permit me to be blunt. With your opening statement, you can do tremendous good for your client, or you can do so much damage that you destroy any chance for a favorable resolution. I have observed exceptional opening statements that have created unbelievable results for the clients. And I have heard opening statements that were so inappropriate and unfortunate that chances for resolution were obliterated with the uttering of those words. In those cases, I have had to spend countless hours in private caucus helping parties get beyond their rage at the words said by opposing counsel. Sometimes, and sadly, it is an impossible task.

Later in this chapter, I will provide you with specific examples (albeit with facts changed to preserve confidentiality) of a best performance and a worst. These examples will breathe life into the points I am about to make. But, preliminarily, you must analyze how your opening statement at mediation is different from your opening at trial and understand what your goals in a mediation opening statement happen to be.

The analysis begins with a simple but critical question. When you represent a party to a mediation and are making your opening statement, who is your jury?

Your jury is not opposing counsel. Opposing counsel has heard your arguments before or, if not, usually has anticipated them. Very few lawyers are ever persuaded "they do not have a case" based on opposing counsel's views. More often than not, a lawyer will redouble his efforts to prove opposing counsel wrong.

Chapter 9
The Mediation Advocate's Opening Statement

Your jury is *the other party*. If you are defense counsel, the other party may be the claimants. If you are plaintiff's counsel, the other party may be the insurance adjuster who will be writing the check. The other party could be the president of a large corporation whom you are trying to persuade to make a good business decision. But unlike a jury of 12 purportedly impartial people, you are speaking to one or two people who are part of the fabric of the dispute and who own the dispute. You, as opposing counsel, are the enemy. You are not to be trusted. You are, most of the time, disliked, sometimes intensely.

What do people who neither like nor trust you do when you speak to them? The answer is simple — *they do not listen*. And you need the other party to listen. More than with a jury who will forgive you (because it is not their dispute), the other party will seize on any word or phrase you say to confirm their pre-existing distrust and dislike for you. And if your words evoke such feelings, you will not persuade them or even get them to listen.

As a litigator, you do everything possible to get *neutral* people to like you, listen to you, and be persuaded by you. Isn't it the ultimate challenge, as the mediation advocate, to get the other party at least to listen if not be persuaded? In a way, your opening statement is both an opening (an introduction) and a closing, in the sense that in the mediation process usually you will have only one extended opportunity to speak to the other side without interruption.

§9.1 Setting Goals

Understanding who your jury is and your jury's state of mind, what are your goals in your opening statement? Your goals and approach should be as follows:

1. To have the other side listen to you.

2. To have the other party respect you.

3. To aspire for the other party's trust, but at least to minimize the degree to which the other party feels threatened.

4. To get the people on the other side to feel that they probably would like you if they met you outside of this litigation.

5. To get the other party to feel you are prepared and professional.

6. To get the other party to feel you are present to listen and have an open mind.

7. To acknowledge to the other party that you understand how he feels, even though as an advocate for the other side you do not agree with him.

8. To acknowledge to the other party he may not agree with what you will say, but that you hope he is open minded enough to listen.

9. To explain to the other party why you believe resolution is in everyone's interests.

10. To persuade the other party that you and your client will work as hard and as long as is necessary to arrive at a fair solution.

11. To explain that a fair solution often requires compromise and re-evaluation.

12. To summarize your case in a way that the other party will understand.

13. At the close of your remarks, to express appreciation that the other party has listened and for his participation in the process.

§9.2 Opening Statement Do Not's

1. Do not refer to the other party by his first name unless the mediator has obtained approval from everyone to do so or unless you have asked permission.

2. Do not look at the mediator when you make your statement. Make eye contact with the other party.

3. Do not move immediately into your position. You must first lay the table as I have outlined above.

Chapter 9
The Mediation Advocate's Opening Statement

---

4. Do not use absolute words or phrases like "never" or "under no circumstances."

5. Do not use inflammatory words like "crook," "stealing," "malingerer," etc.

6. Do not threaten.

7. Do not overstate.

8. Do not use "law talk." Use ordinary words.

9. Do not use a legal concept without explaining it: What is immunity? What is *D'Oenche Duhme*? What is proximate cause?

10. Do not raise your voice.

11. Do not ridicule the other party's counsel.

12. Do not touch on nerves or sensitive spots.

13. Do not discuss money.

14. Do not question the other party's credibility or integrity.

§9.3   Opening Statement Do's

1. Do demonstrate "active listening;" i.e., "I heard you say earlier that . . ."

2. Do make a commitment to listen.

3. Do acknowledge you understand, although do not agree with, how the other party feels.

4. Do state your open-mindedness and commitment to the process.

5. Do express optimism that resolution is possible.

6. Do express compassion, acknowledge pain or distrust, and the like.

7. Do humanize yourself.

Chapter 9
The Mediation Advocate's Opening Statement

8. Do explain your role as an advocate.

9. Do use plain, understandable language.

10. Do demonstrate preparedness and organization.

11. Do express appreciation for the other party's participation.

12. Do acknowledge the professionalism and character of opposing counsel.

You will appreciate, because of confidentiality, why my illustrations are in essence made up stories and purely fictional, but I assure you that the essence of these two diametrically opposite stories is true.

Illustration I

A three-year-old child, who was born with a congenital birth defect and who has a limited life expectancy, is injured in an automobile accident. The claimants, who have sued the manufacturer, take the position the automobile was defective. Although denying liability, the defense counsel has reviewed the medical records and believes that while the child was hurt, he sustained no serious or permanent damage. Defense counsel is aware that the child's parents may believe that an insensitive manufacturer could discount the import of their child's injury because he was born with a congenital birth defect and "didn't have long to live anyway." The child's parents do not want to believe that their child will die and believe instead he will beat the odds. The parents are waiting for defense counsel, either expressly or impliedly, to discuss the life expectancy issue.

The defense counsel, in her opening statement, brilliantly defuses the parents' concerns and attains all of her opening statement goals by taking the following tact: After initially introducing herself, her insurance carrier, and the company representative, defense counsel acknowledges that she feared that the parents might have thought the case would be evaluated on the basis of the life expectancy issue. The defense counsel pledges that at no time did this matter enter into her evaluation, nor would it. The defense counsel then relates that while it is rarely her practice to raise personal issues, she wants the other party to know that she had a sister with a similar birth defect whom she had always loved dearly and specially.

Defense counsel's remarks were not mawkish or theatrical. The remarks came straight from her heart and went straight to the other party's heart. In less than three hours, the case settled on a fair and reasonable basis and to everyone's satisfaction. The sterling mediation advocacy by defense counsel defused a situation that was guaranteed to doom the process and prevent resolution. In terms of litigation cost savings and exposure avoidance, defense counsel represented her client in a superior fashion.

Illustration II

Allegedly because of the negligence of both the hospital and pediatrician, a child is born with permanent brain damage. In his opening statement at mediation, defense counsel for the pediatrician tells the parents that the case has very limited value because their child has a very short life expectancy. The mother of the child breaks down in tears and the child's father becomes livid. Two and a half days of mediation later, the case does in fact settle, but for $500,000 more than it might have.

As stated, the facts have been substantially changed and the events described are purely fictional. But, the gist of the opening statements by both lawyers, albeit also changed, is close to what happened.

My advice for you, the mediation advocate, is to take my suggestions to heart, understand the differences between trial and mediation, and prepare, prepare, prepare.

Mediation advocacy is the litigation art of the future. Those who master the art will be remembered. Those who do not master it will be expendable.

Chapter 10

The Mediation Advocate's Role in Negotiations

For purposes of this chapter, consider mediation as simply a supervised negotiation. The mediator is attempting to encourage the parties to negotiate on a credible basis and to narrow the gap.

The advocate's role in the negotiation process is, quite simply, to assist her client in steering the negotiation to a fair and realistic point in order to maximize the chances for resolution. The mediation advocate must constantly assess whether she is giving away too much too soon, whether the other side's proposals justify a more significant move, and whether the final proposal on the table is in her client's best interests considering the costs of litigation, the time it will take to get the case to trial and through appeal, and the risks associated with the litigation. A mediation advocate does not wish to be either exploited or so unyielding as to prevent a reasonable resolution. A mediation advocate's effectiveness in negotiations is predicated upon proper preparation, anticipation, and the absolute ability to respond to what is going on in the negotiation.

§10.1   Objectively Evaluating Your Case Prior to Mediation

1.   What are the probabilities of a favorable litigation outcome?

2.   What are the costs associated with the litigation?

3.   How long of a delay will there be in obtaining a final decision in the litigation process?

4.   What are your client's interests in obtaining an expeditious resolution at mediation?

5.   What is a reasonable monetary range of the value of the case from your perspective?

---

6. What do you anticipate the other side's range of value to be?

7. Have you checked current jury verdicts or asked a competent, experienced attorney not involved in this case her assessment of value?

§10.2 Preparing a Negotiation Plan

1. Outline several hypothetical negotiations and evaluate the probable outcomes of each negotiation exercise.

2. Who is the negotiator on the other side?

    (1) What is her style?

    (2) What is the most effective way to deal with that style?

3. Adopt a flexible negotiation approach and anticipate probable responses to your proposals along with your anticipated counter-proposals to such responses.

4. Review your negotiation plan with your client prior to the mediation session.

5. Obtain all necessary approval or authority to negotiate as per your plan.

§10.3 Track the Negotiations During Mediation

1. Draw a line and outline each bid. See Appendix B, page 210.

2. Track the length of time it takes to get each new proposal.

3. Determine whether each new proposal is greater or smaller than the proposal that preceded it.

4. Compare each new proposal with your last proposal.

5. Constantly assess how much of a gap remains and how much the gap has been narrowed as a result of the process.

---

6. Determine, based on the size of each new proposal and the time consumed in obtaining it, whether you need to make a more significant move to kick the negotiations into a higher gear and to see whether the other side responds in kind.

7. Do not draw a "line in the sand" too early.

8. Once you draw the line, stick to it within reason; however, do not, out of pride or ego, categorically reject a counter-proposal that, while not meeting your absolute number, comes close to it.

9. Always express appreciation for the other party's good faith proposals.

10. Should the negotiation not end in a resolution, express appreciation to the other side for its efforts. You will probably be negotiating with that other party at some other time in the future.

Your able assistance to your client in the negotiation phase of the mediation will make a substantial impact on the outcome of the negotiation. Planning, patience, and proper analysis of the negotiation are the keys to success.

Chapter 10
The Mediation Advocate's Role in Negotiations

Chapter 11

The Ultimate Question — Why Do I Want To Mediate?

The threshold question a mediation advocate must ask is, "Why do I want to mediate this dispute?" The answer or answers to this question will influence other mediation advocacy decisions, i.e., when to mediate, the selection of the mediator, the format of the pre-mediation submission, the mediation advocate's opening statement, the party's opening statement, and negotiation strategies during the session itself.

This inquiry should go beyond the generally valid reasons to mediate, such as avoiding delay, minimizing risk, reducing expense, etc. The analysis should be case specific and may involve the following sub-questions:

1. What is obstructing settlement in this dispute?

2. What special opportunities will the mediation process provide me?

3. What are my goals at the session?

4. If a communications breakdown has occurred or caused the dispute, how may I restore communications?

5. How may I best motivate the other party? Opposing counsel?

The answer to the "why mediate?" question and the sub-questions will vary from case to case. Regardless, many answers to these questions may center around certain situational patterns. Note that these patterns will apply regardless of whether the advocate is representing the plaintiff or defendant.

Further, I feel obliged as a mediator to state that these patterns contain judgmental words, such as "unreasonable." Obviously, a mediation advocate may perceive a party or opposing counsel to be "unreasonable" and determine the opposite to be true at the session itself. Identifying patterns is not meant to encourage participants to form inflexible judgments about the opponent prior to the session.

1. The Unreasonable Party

A disputant may have or develop unreasonable expectations. For example, a plaintiff may have determined that his case is just like the million dollar recovery he read about in the newspaper; when in fact it is not. Or, an insurance carrier may wholly fail to appreciate the gravity of his company's potential exposure. In such instances, counsel for such a party may be re-enforcing these views or may have failed to persuade the client that his expectations are very unlikely to be met.

A dispute may be mediated because counsel for the unreasonable party needs help in having his client evaluate the dispute more objectively. Or, opposing counsel may suggest mediation in an effort to have the unreasonable party re-evaluate his position.

The unreasonable party situation influences several mediation advocacy decisions and raises the following questions:

A. When should I mediate? The answer, much more often than not, is as soon as is practical. Unreasonable positions tend to become more inflexible over time and with the investment of emotion and expense. Even if an early mediation does not produce a settlement, the session may produce a re-evaluation that triggers a settlement shortly thereafter.

B. Who should mediate the case? You should select a mediator who will be able to communicate with the unreasonable party and to whom the party will listen and respect. In this regard, the mediator's style may be important. Will the unreasonable party respond more favorably to an aggressive mediator or a mediator who will allow the party to ventilate his feelings fully?

C. What should I include in my pre-mediation submission? Beyond the information outlined in Chapter 5, you should explain to the mediator the nature of the party's personality, what you believe that party's underlying interests to be, what you believe will motivate that party, what you think is fueling the dispute, and why you believe the other party is unreasonable. You must understand that the mediator is attempting to develop a communication with a total stranger, someone you have probably deposed and know better. Such information is not designed to prejudice the mediator; rather, you are providing the mediator with information to assist him in communicating with the other party.

D. How should I approach my opening statement? As always, the answer is case-specific and is related to the personality of the party. Remember, your "jury" is the other party. Your goal is to have the other party listen to you and not turn you off. Ask yourself the following questions:

(1) Will an aggressive statement turn off or break down the other party? Most lawyers, especially in unreasonable party situations, are tempted to present strong, reality check statements. In rare instances, such statements are effective. Far more often, these statements close the other party's ears and mind. Keep in mind that you are probably the enemy to the other party. The mediator, because he is not the enemy, has greater ability to reality check. Aggressive opening statements infrequently motivate an unreasonable party.

(2) Will an analysis of the law be helpful? Usually not. However, a brief, concise analysis of the law in plain language may be helpful. An unreasonable party, even one sophisticated in the law, rarely accepts legal arguments. The unreasonable party often believes the law is on his side, his lawyer knows the law better, is ignoring the law, or may think that his case may change "bad law."

(3) Will exhibits or visual aids help? Sometimes, but use them selectively and sparingly. Any videotape presentation should be 10 minutes or less.

(4) What should the length of my opening statement be? Almost always 20 minutes or less. The most persuasive opening statements I have witnessed have been between 10 to 15 minutes, even in complex cases.

(5) Should I have my clients speak to the unreasonable party? Barring highly volatile situations, your client should almost always make a brief statement.

Your client should emphasize his commitment to the process, his willingness to listen, and, when appropriate, an expression of regret may be very helpful.

(6) How should I participate at the session? Consider in advance what negotiation strategy is more likely to be effective with this party. Consider how you may assist the mediator in motivating this party. Outline what you think the mediator should discuss with the party in private caucus.

2. Unreasonable Opposing Counsel

The unreasonable opposing counsel pattern may be broken down into three distinct categories: inexperience/improper analysis, unpreparedness, and greed/ego. Each category involves a different analysis.

A. Inexperience/Improper Analysis

An opposing counsel may be unreasonable because he does not possess the experience to evaluate the case properly. Or, as even the best, more experienced lawyers sometimes do, opposing counsel may not be fully or correctly analyzing his case.

In such situations, the selection of the mediator and your opening statement are the most important mediation advocacy considerations.

In terms of selection, you must identify a mediator whom the opposing counsel will respect. This may involve considerations opposite of what you might expect. You may want a mediator who practiced on opposing counsel's side of the docket. You may want a mediator suggested by opposing counsel and with whom opposing counsel is comfortable. You may want a former judge whom opposing counsel respects. Simply, you want a mediator to whom opposing counsel will listen in caucus.

Regarding you opening statement, educate and do not insult. Do not patronize or appear condescending. Frame your presentation as if opposing counsel knows and understands what you are saying, even if such is not the case; i.e., "As opposing counsel is already aware. . ." Do not intimidate with your superior resources or ostensibly superior knowledge. Do not issue a personal challenge that will guarantee an unnecessary trial. Do not suggest or imply malpractice or unethical behavior.

B. Unpreparedness

Regrettably, certain lawyers are unreasonable because they are unprepared and may have paid little attention to the file.

The most significant mediation advocacy considerations in this situation are when to mediate, whom to select, and your opening statement.

The selection consideration is the same as with the inexperienced/improper analysis situation.

The timing of the mediation in such instances should be very early in the case, otherwise your client may have to pay substantial fees because opposing counsel is paying no attention to the file. A mediation date compels some attention. Lawyers who are unprepared are either too busy, lazy, or incompetent. Such lawyers often are interested in moving the case.

Regarding your opening statement, your most important goal is to demonstrate superior preparedness. Even if opposing counsel does not realize you are far more prepared, his client almost always will recognize such to be true. Of course, specifically pointing to opposing counsel's lack of preparedness is very ill advised.

C. Greed/Ego

The greed issue almost always implies the opposing counsel is putting his interests ahead of the client and is the sole decision maker. Typically the client and lawyer are co-decision makers. Some argue the client should be the sole decision maker and receive only advice and counsel from his attorney.

The greed issue is typically framed in the following two ways: On the defense side, counsel allegedly is obstructing settlement because he has not billed enough on the file or wants the hourly fees derived from trial. On the plaintiff's side, counsel fails to enter into a reasonable settlement because he wants to roll the dice and

Chapter 11
The Ultimate Question — Why Do I Want To Mediate?

try to make larger dollars before a jury. Fortunately, while counsel sometimes perceive this situation to exist, most of the time it does not. Most competent counsel are very interested in fair resolutions for their clients.

In this unfortunate — but rare — situation, your mediation advocacy goal is simple. You must get the client involved. You must hope that the client will become the decision maker. In these instances, the most important mediation advocacy steps are selection and your opening.

You should select a mediator who will involve the other party and whom the other party will respect. And, your opening statement, more than ever, should be directed to the other party.

Finally, a lawyer's ego or personality disputes between lawyers may be obstructing settlement. Your most important consideration in these situations is selection. Usually, you will want someone whom all lawyers highly respect and someone who has the ability to sit the lawyers down and talk realistically to them.

3. Reluctant Lawyer

The reluctant lawyer, as I define it, is the counsel who cannot or will not tell his client what the client needs to hear. Often, the reluctant lawyer is afraid of appearing weak or timid, because he is afraid of losing the client. Such a lawyer may truly fear the negative consequences associated with loss of a client. In these cases, the client may well want to know the entire picture. Or, the reluctant lawyer's fears may be real and the client really doesn't want to know.

Regardless, the problem is that the reluctant lawyer will not be the one to reality check his client. If someone else (the mediator) does it, the reluctant lawyer does not have to be the person bearing bad news and thereby minimizes the perceived risk of losing the client.

If the obstruction to resolution is the reluctant lawyer, you must make several mediation advocacy decisions.

Chapter 11
The Ultimate Question — Why Do I Want To Mediate?

First, you should mediate as soon as practical. After all, your client is paying for the other lawyer's reluctance. You should select a mediator whom the reluctant lawyer's client will respect, probably someone with whom the party will identify. And, in your opening statement, you should praise the preparedness and resolve of the reluctant lawyer. Your goal in that regard is to prevent the reluctant lawyer from obstructing the reality checking during the caucus phase of the session.

4. Party in Need of an Apology

Certain cases do resolve only after an expression of regret or an apology is made at the mediation session. While the party generally still will have to pay money, the apology is a condition precedent to productive negotiations. Lawyers frequently ignore the fact that some people are capable of forgiveness if a sincere apology is made. In litigation, apologies may be converted into admissions of liability. In mediation, apologies meet certain basic human needs.

Many disputes involve unintentional acts; namely, human error. People make mistakes. And, outside of litigation, people often apologize for their mistakes and receive forgiveness. Most people (not all) do not wish to punish for unintentional acts. And, some people are even willing to forgive intentional acts if the expression of regret is sincere.

Apologies are especially significant in instances in which a relationship has existed; i.e., doctor/patient, lawyer/client, business disputes, husband/wife, etc. Apologies suggest concern and caring. Lawsuits sometimes are filed because a party perceived the other party did not care or was unwilling to accept responsibility.

The most important mediation advocacy step involved in such situations is client preparation. By "client preparation" I do not mean creating a slick, insincere presentation. I am suggesting preparing the client to play an active role in the mediation process, something you should do in every case. But, especially important, you should be certain your client understands the value of an apology. Many clients have very much wanted to apologize, but they either have not had the opportunity or thought they could. Some clients have to overcome denial before an apology may be made.

Regardless, you job is to be certain the client understands an expression of regret is permissible. The expression of regret must be in the client's own words.

Expressions of regret do not always have to include an admission of a mistake. Sometimes, an expression of regret for the outcome is enough. Also, an expression that someone did their very best and had no intention of causing harm may be adequate.

In instances in which the disputing parties have no prior relationship, your client, whether an individual or corporation, must be humanized before the apology is made. Apologies are often accepted because of who is making the apology. In situations in which a corporation is involved, the fact that a CEO or executive vice president took the time to attend the session and deliver the apology may be significant.

5. Party on a Mission

Sometimes, parties see their cases in very broad, social terms. In essence, the party's case becomes a social issue; i.e., "I want my case to help warn others," "I will not as a matter of principle pay on such claims," or "I want to send a message to this company." Of course, the dispute may involve a social issue, but far more often, most disputes are not so broad. In many instances, a party, for whatever reason, has created a broader, social issue. While a broader issue may not exist, the party often truly believes it does. And, if not dealt with properly through appropriate mediation advocacy, such a party may not be willing to resolve a dispute. The critical mediation advocacy considerations include your opening statement, listening skills, who should attend the session, your participation during negotiations, and an analysis of possible supplementary non-monetary proposals.

The most critical element of preparation is to engage in active listening. Parties who are on a mission have a dire need to be listened to and understood. You must demonstrate listening, for example, by your demeanor, body language, and attentiveness.

Chapter 11
The Ultimate Question — Why Do I Want To Mediate?

But you will even more effectively demonstrate active listening through your opening statement. Your opening statement should include specific comments that indicate that you both have heard and understood what the other side has said. You should emphasize your commitment throughout the session to listen and understand. But, you should also emphasize that the mediator, all counsel, and the parties may only be able to search for a fair resolution to the dispute involved at the session. You should also add that resolution of the particular lawsuit may do some broader good.

In "mission" cases, the attendance of the true decision maker is both symbolic and helpful. From the plaintiff's perspective, the claimant may wish an audience with the CEO, physician, etc. From the defendant's perspective, the company head or a high-level insurance executive may need to have the plaintiff's case humanized and better understood before considering settlement.

Considering non-monetary supplemental proposals may be very important. For example, a confidentiality agreement may be of interest. Or, a company may consider adding a new safety feature to a product. Such possibilities are limitless. Also, keep in mind that meeting certain non-monetary interests usually impacts economic interests.

6. Angry Party

An angry party also wishes to be listened to and understood. But, to state the obvious, an angry party needs to express anger. In such cases, several mediation advocacy considerations are involved.

First, you must prepare your client to expect that the opponent will express anger and that the expression of such anger may well be a condition precedent to a fair resolution. You should also encourage your client not to respond in kind, unless your client has an equal need to express some anger.

Next, you must be certain that the person with whom the other party is angry attends the session. Many lawyers feel the opposite is true and believe the presence of such a person will exacerbate matters. Much more often than not, however, the angry party needs to express anger to that very person in order to get rid of the anger.

Finally, your opening statement should acknowledge you understand the other party is angry; but, that you are hopeful that through the mediation process everyone will be able to get beyond their anger.

7. Non-Participating Party

Sometimes, a party will attend a mediation session and not speak at all. A party may not be speaking because he is nervous, cautious, or angry, because he is by nature quiet, or because he has been advised not to speak. Of course, many other reasons may explain a party's silence. You may need, however, to engage that party's participation in order to get the dispute resolved.

The mediation advocacy challenge is how are you going to engage and involve such a party?

Beyond demonstrating active listening, the mediation advocate should consider directing non-threatening, open-ended questions to such a party. I am not suggesting that the mediation become a deposition. Rather, through a limited series of open-ended questions, the mediation advocate can show interest in better understanding how a party feels. In many instances, the mediation advocate may wish to request permission to ask a question. In this way, the mediation advocate is not appearing intrusive or intimidating.

If a party, despite such attempts, still does not wish to speak or actively participate, the mediation advocate should discontinue his efforts to engage the party.

8. Parties Who Need to Communicate Directly

In certain instances, a resolution will occur only after the parties have engaged in a direct discussion. Usually, but not always, such parties have had some type of relationship; i.e., employer-employee, doctor-patient, business partners, etc.

The mediation advocate's challenge is to be aware, for purposes of preparation, that there may be a need for such direct communication. While capable mediators will independently recognize such a need, the mediation advocate may assist the process by so advising the mediator early on.

Two primary mediation advocacy steps are involved in such situations. In such cases, you must prepare the client to understand that the dispute may not be resolved unless such direct communication occurs. The client also should understand that some form of dysfunctional communication probably contributed to the dispute.

The other advocacy challenge is to facilitate such direct communication at the session itself. To be sure, the mediator is the facilitator; but, the mediator may want to know that you approve of such a direct communication.

Such direct communication may occur in any number of ways. The mediator may attempt to trigger such a direct communication at the joint session, with all parties and counsel present. Or, the mediator may attempt to get the parties talking with only the parties and the mediator present. In certain instances, the mediator may decide to place the parties in a room with no one else present. The mediator should be attempting to select a setting in which a productive discussion is likely. The mediator must be willing to check his ego at the door and recognize that it is the process that brought the parties together and that the mediator's presence in the room may obstruct a full discussion.

9. Parties in Need of an Explanation

Sometimes, disputes occur because a person feels an inadequate explanation has been given for something that went wrong. The inadequate explanation may have resulted from the absence of time, the heat of the moment, a poor communicator, a feeling no explanation was necessary, a fear of creating liability, or perhaps because no good explanation really existed. Regardless, some people do not believe that things "just happen" and require an explanation before they will be able to resolve a dispute.

A good illustration of such a phenomenon is a medical negligence case. Sometimes, physicians provide a confusing explanation or no explanation. Some physicians believe that lay people will not understand anyway or that their explanation will be misinterpreted or create liability. Some physicians believe that patients or their families may be too upset to really listen. In other instances, an explanation may not be available immediately.

The mediation advocate should focus on client preparation and the opening statement in such instances.

The client must come to appreciate an explanation is necessary, that the explanation may need to come directly from the client, that the explanation must be understandable and clear, and that the client also may have to discuss why no explanation was provided at the time of the event. Sometimes, an explanation implies or suggests a mistake was made. A party may need to hear such a confession before being willing to settle. Some people just need to hear someone admit that something went wrong before they can be conciliatory.

The mediation advocate's opening statement is also important in such instances. The mediation advocate, in tandem with his client, also will be offering an explanation and will acknowledge in his opening his perception that the other party needs an explanation. The advocate's explanation should be clear and not condescending. The explanation should not appear to be a mere convenience. The failure to provide an earlier explanation should itself be explained. And, the advocate should be aware that an explanation direct from the client still may be necessary.

10. Emotionally Damaged Party

On occasion, parties to a dispute may be, in varying degrees, emotionally damaged. A party may believe that the conflict made the subject of the dispute damaged him emotionally or exacerbated pre-existing damage. Or it may be that the emotional damage has nothing whatsoever to do with the dispute. Regardless, emotionally damaged parties make more complicated mediation participants and pose a great challenge to the mediation advocate.

The mediation advocate's goals, in all phases of preparation, is active listening and restraint. The advocate's, and his client's, willingness to listen is critical. More

Chapter 11
The Ultimate Question — Why Do I Want To Mediate?

important, the advocate must prepare his client to be restrained during the session and the advocate must be careful that his opening statement is restrained as well.

The advocate should do whatever possible to make the mediator aware such a situation exists. Ideally, you should advise the mediator of such a situation in your pre-mediation submission. By doing so, you will allow the mediator some time to analyze how best to approach such a party.

At the session itself, the advocate should rely almost exclusively on the mediator to communicate with the party. Far more often than not, the emotionally damaged party will distrust you severely and you will have to rely upon the mediator to bond with the party. In fact, the very reason for mediation may be your belief that only a neutral has any chance to bond with such a party.

11. Disputes That Turn Significantly on Issues of Law

Most disputes are factual in nature or involve mixed issues of fact and law. But, the outcomes of some disputes will depend upon a finding of law. The advocate should consider initially whether mediation, as opposed to some decision-based ADR process, is appropriate.

Assuming mediation is selected, the most important advocacy step is selection of the mediator. Mediation advocates for all parties should identify a mediator whose legal analysis is respected; i.e., someone whom all sides will permit to play devil's advocate with their legal positions.

Conclusion

Mediation advocacy is inherently situational in nature. While the advocacy steps are predictable, the advocate's decisions as to each step are influenced by the type of situation and personalities involved. The situations described above are common ones, but not all-inclusive. You will have to analyze, step by step, what you will have to do to maximize chances for a successful resolution for each particular case.

Chapter 12

Non-monetary Interests

While it is quite true that the mediation of most civil cases results in a monetary resolution, the monetary outcome is often (more often than you might think) influenced by certain non-monetary interests. The litigation process deals with "issues" and "positions" and rarely considers "interests."

The best (and perhaps now overused) example of the difference between issues, positions, and interests is the story of the orange. According to this story, a father is attempting to watch a television program, but he cannot hear a thing because his daughters in the kitchen are engaged in a loud, heated exchange. The father walks into the kitchen, and, without asking any questions, notices his daughters struggling over what must be the last orange in the refrigerator. The father grabs the orange, puts the orange on the table, cuts the orange in half, and gives a half to each daughter. One daughter removes the peel, throws it away, and eats the meat of the orange. The other daughter removes the peel, throws away the meat, and cuts up the peel of the orange for a recipe she is making.

The issue is obvious: Who gets the last orange? The *position* of each daughter is equally obvious: "I get the orange"; "No, I get the orange." But the *interests* of the daughters are very different, and the father never bothers to determine what his daughters' interests in the orange happened to be. As lawyers, we frequently do not ask questions that permit us to explore and identify interests. Our training places us in the universe of issues and positions. And the story of the orange is not a naive suggestion that the determination of interests always results in a "win-win" situation. To be sure though, each daughter, if her interest had been identified, could have received 100% of what she wanted.

But interests are very important in the mediation process. While clients may be concerned with the issues, they frequently are more involved with the interests

Chapter 12
Non-monetary Interests

aspect of the dispute. And as interests are identified and understood, positions often can and do change. I have had countless clients in cases I mediate state, "No one, not even my own lawyer, ever asked me that before or how I feel about that!" These clients are simply reporting that an interests assessment was never done.

I imagine an entire book could be written about interests. But permit me to identify several interests that commonly exist in litigation and their impact on the resolution of a dispute.

1.   **Interest in Being Listened To.** Many litigants simply want an opportunity to be heard. A party sometimes feels that no one has ever been willing to listen. The litigation process usually does not meet this interest; in fact, the litigation process often reinforces a party's view that no one is listening. The mediation process clearly provides a party with the opportunity to be heard.

Mediators prove to parties that they are listening by repeating back what a party has said. Good mediation advocates do the same thing; i.e., repeat key phrases back to the opposing party to demonstrate they have been heard.

2.   **Interest in Being Understood.** Many parties appreciate that the other side will never agree with them, but disagreement may be accepted if the party feels he is understood. Being understood is the step after being heard. A good mediation advocate might say "I understand how you feel" to demonstrate that a party has been understood.

3.   **Interest in an Expression of Regret or Compassion.** Some parties want apologies or expressions of regret. "I'm sorries" often are not offered because they may be misconstrued as admissions of liability. Because of the confidentiality of the mediation process, expressions of regret may be offered. Certain claimants want the other side to appreciate the extent of their loss or injury. Expressions of empathy or compassion meet this interest.

4.   **Relationship Interests.** Many disputes arise out of a relationship — a marriage, a business, a partnership, etc. Such relationships can create a number of interests; i.e., love, economic interest, betrayal, vengeance, vindication, etc.

Chapter 12
Non-monetary Interests

---

5. Future Relationship Interest. Should a current dispute be resolved, the probability of future relationships may exist. The parties may have a real interest in the preservation of such future relationships.

6. Reputational Interest. A party's real interest in a case may be preserving or re-establishing his reputation.

7. Confidentiality Interest. A party may very much have an interest in a dispute remaining private. Obviously, mediation provides for such confidentiality.

8. Public Shaming Interest. A party may want to shame his opposition publicly. Of course, mediation is a private, confidential proceeding. But a party may feel that the public shaming interest is met simply by telling the story to the mediator.

9. Vindication/Principal Interest. A party may desire vindication or have an interest in proving a point. Vindication rarely occurs at the courthouse. Mediation provides a safe forum for the expression of such an interest. Often, once a party's interest in vindication is vented, the dispute becomes more easily resolvable.

10. Political Interest. Resolution may have been obstructed because of a perceived political consequence. Or the dispute may have occurred for a political reason. As sensitive as such interests are, the exploration of political interests may more safely occur in the safe setting of a mediation.

As previously mentioned, the list of interests may be as long as those things that motivate human beings. Of course, a party's interest may be purely monetary, less benignly referred to as greed. But, surprisingly, interests such as those described above are often very important to parties, and frequently influence monetary outcomes. If a party's non-monetary interests are met, he is often more flexible, more reasonable, and more willing to negotiate.

Mediators constantly are searching for the non-monetary interests in a dispute and find them to be helpful keys to resolution. Mediation advocates should also

Chapter 12
Non-monetary Interests

---

seek to identify the other party's interests and to consider how such interests might affect the negotiations.

Chapter 13

Mediation Exhibits and
Demonstrative Aids

Mediation advocates obviously do not offer, introduce, or object to evidence at the session itself. But the use of demonstrative evidence, charts, and exhibits may be as persuasive to the other decision-maker as it might be to a jury. The difference in presenting demonstrative evidence at a mediation is that the mediation advocate should more selectively determine what demonstrative evidence to present.

I have observed the following demonstrative evidence to have been helpful in mediation:

1. Blow-ups of the essential documents (i.e., the contract, a letter, etc.), critical deposition or expert witness report excerpts, photographs, diagrams, etc.

2. A chronology of key dates, times, and events. Chronologies are almost essential in medical malpractice/hospital liability mediations.

3. Concise videotape presentations. For example, portions of a well-done "day in the life" video may be helpful in a personal injury case mediation. A videotape showing a piece of property may be helpful in a case in which the issue involves the property's value.

4. Copies of all medical bills and wage loss statements should always be brought to the mediation session.

5. Financial statements, tax returns, and other supporting documents should be brought to a mediation in a case in which solvency will be an issue.

6. Proposed structural settlements are particularly helpful at a mediation session.

Chapter 13
Mediation Exhibits and Demonstrative Aids

---

7.   Models demonstrating design or manufacturing defects may be useful in the mediation of a products liability case.

Again, the mediation session should not become cluttered with every piece of documentary or demonstrative evidence you might be offering into evidence at trial. But the selective use of demonstrative evidence at mediation may permit the decision-maker on the other side to get a much better feel for your position and what the jury may see at trial.

Chapter 14

Impasse-Breaking Techniques

"This is our bottom line, take it or leave it offer. We really mean it."
— Anonymous

"The line is drawn in the sand. It's time to fish or cut bait."
— Anonymous

"We're ready to leave. Tell them we're packing our briefcases."
— Anonymous

"Between a rock and a hard place."
— Mick Jagger

§14.1 What an Impasse Is

In teaching mediation to prospective neutrals, I tell them to look forward to impasses, but teach them how to prevent impasses from occurring at all.

In mediation and negotiation circles, "impasse" is an often used word, but "impasse" is rarely defined. *Webster's Dictionary* defines "impasse" as a "predicament affording no obvious escape; a deadlock." But, as you will readily conclude, "impasse" has a strong subjective component.

Who thinks that an impasse exists? The parties? The lawyers? The mediator? And how and when does one conclude that a "deadlock" has occurred and that all "less than obvious escapes" have been explored? A declaration of impasse by a party may in fact be a thinly disguised negotiating strategy.

Nonetheless, new mediators, in varying degrees, fear an impasse occurring despite their passionate belief in the mediation process. Mediators wonder, "What do I do when things get stuck? How do I keep things moving and get the negotia-

Chapter 14
Impasse-Breaking Techniques

tions back on track?" The feeling, more candidly stated, is best described by one word: "Help!"

In my view, mediators must become skilled at impasse avoidance techniques and must emotionally and mentally look forward to impasse situations. A mediator's art is in part defined by the ability to work parties out of ostensible impasses.

This chapter was written both for the mediator and the counsel for a party (or the party) in a mediation. If you are either counsel for a party or a party in a mediation, you may in separate caucus wish to suggest any of these techniques to your mediator in an impasse situation.

But I would like to provide a word of warning: Each mediation is different and unique. Each mediation has its own feel, its own players, and its own tempo. Some of the impasse breaking or avoidance techniques I have listed below may be perfect for a particular mediation, but wholly inappropriate in a different one. This is an attempt to provide you with an extensive laundry list of options for impasse situations or impasse avoidance. The designation (C) after a listed item is my suggestion that the technique be used only in the separate caucus.

§14.2 Impasse Prevention

Obviously, the ideal situation is to prevent an impasse from occurring at all. And while recognizing that prevention is not always successful, the following list culled from previous chapters is useful in helping avoid impasses.

1. **Teach negotiation in the caucuses (C).** A mediation, in a way, is a supervised negotiation. And, unfortunately, many lawyers have not had much training in negotiation or have limited negotiation skills. Parties in each room have to consider that they must accept responsibility for the proposals they make; that is, a party's proposal will likely trigger a similar counter-proposal from the party in the other room. More mechanically, you should consider the following:

(1) Who is the decision-maker in the room? The party? The lawyer? Both? Or, heaven help you, someone who is not even there?

(2) What is the negotiating style of the decision-maker? Fast? Slow? Mid-range?

(3) Are the negotiating styles of the parties in the different rooms similar or divergent?

(4) If the styles are similar, you must adjust the negotiation "music" to suit the similar styles.

(5) If the styles are divergent (a fast, cut to the chase negotiator vs. a slow, analytical, let's not rush negotiator), you must specifically get the parties to acknowledge and accept their stylistic differences early in the mediation or the parties will become very frustrated. The stylistic differences, not the issues, may create impasses.

(6) Explain basic negotiating theory — the importance of the first credible proposal, anchoring, the winner's curse, the Harvard theory, etc.

(7) Help the party keep track of the negotiations on a board or a drawing pad. Parties will forget the progress made if you don't remind them. Also, the drawing is a constant visual reminder that the gap is narrowing. The drawing permits comparison; for instance, a $150,000 gap four hours ago is only $40,000 now. I find the "negotiating line" method a superb way both to avoid impasses and to break them. In the heat of the moment, a party may forget where he has been and where he may be going.

2. Case evaluation (C). Case evaluation (strength/weakness analysis), at least for me, begins before the very first caucus with the preparation of the confidential pre-mediation submissions. As explained in Chapter 4, the purpose of the submissions is to have the parties focus on the issues prior to the mediation and to educate the mediator for purposes of the caucus strength/weakness analysis. Case evaluation helps avoid impasses and to break impasses when they occur. Case evaluation is not a judgment of who will win or lose or the imposition of the mediator's opinion. Case evaluation is simply issue raising and discussion. The party draws his own conclusion as to whether something is a strength or a weakness. During the case evaluation process you may discover any of the following:

(1) A perceived weakness may not have been considered previously.

(2) Counsel for a party may have identified and discussed a weakness with the client, but the client may not have paid attention to it.

(3) Counsel for a party and the party may have very different views about the case. For example, counsel may have advised the client that a case has a certain value, but the client may not understand or believe that the attorney is correct.

(4) A party may not acknowledge a weakness early in a mediation, but may acknowledge one later on in the process.

(5) A party may not ever acknowledge a weakness to the mediator in caucus, but will do so with counsel when the mediator leaves the caucus. The mediator must always be aware that a discussion and evaluation occurs every time the mediator leaves the caucus room.

3. Control. The mediator must gain control of the proceedings from the onset and keep control.

4. Preparation. The mediator, the parties, and counsel must be prepared for the mediation session. Preparation for mediation is every bit as important as preparation for trial. Pre-mediation submissions and client pre-mediation preparation are, in my opinion, essential.

5. Authority to settle. Authority to settle issues *must* be resolved prior to the mediation. An authority to settle issue that surfaces during a mediation will probably create fatal impasse, or worse, further polarize the parties.

6. Constructive participation. During the mediation itself, the parties should commit to constructive participation in the process. I am *not* suggesting that the parties promise to settle, but rather that they promise to give the process a chance.

7. Interest identification. The mediator must identify the interests of the parties early on. Some interests are obvious. Other interests are not.

8. Appropriate environment. The mediation environment must be appropriate. Pre-arrangement for adequate rooms and food must be made. Further, everyone must plan to allocate adequate time for the process.

9. Listening. The parties and their counsel should be encouraged to listen. The mediator, as much as anyone, must listen.

10. Flexibility. The parties, in separate caucus, should be discouraged from using "bottom line" language. Flexibility is the key to success.

§14.3 Impasse Breaking and Impasse Avoidance

1. People moving. Mediators are in the people-moving business. Sometimes you may have the wrong people together. Sometimes new and different combinations of people produce a better chemistry, which generates intriguing options. The mere physical act of motion suggests progress. New combinations create the perception that a new chapter is being started and renews hope. In his introduction, the mediator should preview and explain the possibility of people involved in the mediation being put together in different combinations. As a result, parties will be less intimidated when it happens and perceive such changes as part of the process.

2. Change the scenery. Mediators lose sight of the fact, particularly in the separate caucus phase, that parties may feel stuck or claustrophobic in their room. Sometimes, especially in an impasse situation, I may take one room "for a walk," usually to my office. My office is a happy place, full of my children's drawings, pictures, and the like. I sense an immediate mood shift during such a "tour." People get to move their legs, look out the window, and feel more energized. In several mediations, I have taken one room outside and caucused with them on a park bench. Be

Chapter 14
Impasse-Breaking Techniques

---

especially vigilant of this if your caucus rooms don't have windows. Imagine how you would feel after eight hours in such a room.

3. **Food.** If an impasse occurs at, for example, 4:00 p.m., I often send out for snacks. Food changes moods. Food energizes. Food keeps people going. Food is something new and different. Food implies we are going to continue to work. Many people can't think if they are hungry. Some people, in this non-smoking age, use food to relax. For whatever reason, people become more agreeable when they are eating. As an interesting side note, observe (when you bring in lunch) who is eating and who is not eating. You can get a good read on the participants' temperatures through such an observation.

4. **Humor — please be careful.** Something you think might be terribly funny may be terribly unfunny to the listener or perceived as demeaning. On the other hand, I have used humor to break tense moments, which has served on several occasions to break an impasse. The safest form of humor is self-deprecating humor. If you can demonstrate that you don't take yourself all that seriously and can laugh at yourself, perhaps the listeners may begin not to take themselves so seriously.

5. **Lawyer caucus.** When things get stuck, I sometimes find it useful to call a lawyer caucus. In my introduction, I advise the parties and their counsel that I may do so. Lawyer caucuses are useful when issues of law continue to be an impediment to resolution or where new issues have arisen since the initial group meeting. Such caucuses may be particularly effective in cases in which the lawyers involved enjoy a positive, professional working relationship. Out of discretion, a lawyer may have been reluctant to point out a weakness aggressively in the presence of the other lawyer's client. A lawyer's caucus permits such candid discussion and may be a real impasse breaker.

6. **Recess.** Most mediators, myself included, believe that progress made in a mediation is cumulative and that momentum towards resolution is created. However, in certain situations, the parties may be too tired to continue or need some time to reflect. A party may also feel pressured. Fatigue or feeling pressured should

never become a basis of a fatal impasse. A mediator should consider calling a recess and setting up a time to continue the mediation.

7. **Reconvene the group.** The impasse may suggest the parties need more direct interaction. A feeling may need to be expressed. The parties may be more inclined to talk later in the day than they were at the beginning of the mediation. Additionally, the mediator is more aware of the interests and feelings at this point and may be in a better position to facilitate the discussion.

8. **Confess being stuck.** Mediators must be willing to check their egos at the door. At some later phase of the mediation, a mediator may need to advise the parties that he has "run out of ideas" and that if the matter is to be resolved the parties should consider providing him with some ideas. Parties develop a great deal of trust and confidence in a mediator and are very aware the mediator is working hard. Much more often than not, an honest confession by the mediator will be well received by the parties. Also, in the wake of such a confession, the parties may come up with some excellent ideas.

9. **Suggest the possibility of fatal impasse.** The mediator's confidence and belief that resolution will happen is critical. If the mediator does not believe in resolution, no one else will. But late in a mediation, the mediator may suggest that unless some progress occurs, a fatal impasse may result. Most parties do not want a fatal impasse and will work to overcome the possibility.

10. **Re-review litigation costs.** Undoubtedly, the mediator has discussed costs in the group session and initial caucus. But in the heat of a mediation, parties may forget. Review the future costs again, but not in a coercive manner.

11. **Re-review risks (C).** Again, the mediator has already discussed risk in the initial caucus. But re-assessing risk late in a mediation may be very effective. As always, re-assessment of risk should not be coercive or heavy-handed.

12. **The value of today.** Most parties want to achieve closure. In most matters, the trial date (even when set) is uncertain and the possibility of appeal may exist. The problem may not be resolved for two to four years. The parties have a

window of opportunity to resolve their problems today. As I've come to learn, "today" has a great deal of value.

13. **Re-trace the parties' progress.** After five or six hours, the parties may have forgotten the progress that has been made. The mediator must remind the parties of where each was at the beginning of the mediation and where they are now.

14. **Solicit disagreement by the party's counsel (C).** In a separate caucus, ask the party's counsel whether he seriously disagrees with an identified weakness in the other party's position. The party may need to hear that his lawyer disagrees with him. The mediator, however, must never come between the party and his counsel or humiliate the party's counsel. To do so would be unethical, coercive, and just plain wrong.

15. **Review the party's initial goals.** During the first caucus, the parties should have identified their goals and interests. But during the mediation, a party may have changed his goals. If so, the mediator should review with the party his initial goals and discuss whether these goals have changed and why.

16. **Declare a goal unattainable (C).** While it is not appropriate for the mediator to criticize a party's goals, it may become apparent during the mediation that the other side simply will not meet one of the party's goals — and the mediator may choose to make this declaration. Certainly such a declaration risks fatal impasse, but much more often, a party may welcome knowing what is not possible.

17. **Focus on future relationships.** When the parties may have future relationships beyond the particular problem, the mediator should discuss with the parties how the resolution of this problem will affect future relationships or the possibility of future relationships.

18. **Acknowledge that everyone is trying.** While the mediator must never be coercive, he may occasionally need to be a "cheerleader" for resolution. The parties may need to be reminded that while a log jam exists, everyone is trying hard to work through it.

Chapter 14
Impasse-Breaking Techniques

---

19.   Have the party's lawyer describe what will happen at trial (C). Sometimes a party may need to hear what the trial will be like, the nature of cross-examination, and what issues may be covered in cross-examination.

Of course, these techniques are not an exclusive list and, as I have said, one may be very effective in a particular case and terribly wrong in another. We are constantly learning and revising techniques to break an impasse.

Chapter 15

Special Factors in Mediating
Family Law Cases

This chapter begins a series of chapters designed to point out special factors that exist in the mediation of certain kinds of cases. General mediation principles and mediation advocacy concepts still apply, but certain unique issues seem to arise in certain kinds of cases and the mediation advocate must consider such matters.

Family law, as you well know, is among the most emotionally charged and volatile practice areas. Disputes involving the parent-child relationship, property, or both are fueled by the emotional upheaval associated with the break-up of a marriage. Divorcing parties are asked to make good decisions at a time when they are least emotionally able to. Often, communication between parties is either non-existent or antagonistic. The trust level between the parties may be non-existent.

The divorce process itself tends to take on a life of its own. Even well-intentioned parties, who are focusing on the needs of children, have difficulty making decisions. Divorce is usually a severe and painful loss of many things — the marriage itself, contact with children, property, extended family, etc. The parties are in a grieving process, and they may desperately need closure for the healing process to begin. Divorce litigation, although necessary in certain instances, usually obliterates communication. Mediation may, in certain instances, provide necessary closure and restore the parties' future ability to communicate on an acceptable basis. When children are involved, such restoration may be critical.

Perhaps the most unique factor in family law mediation is the imbalance of power issue. Typically, the wife feels that the husband is controlling, perhaps better able to wage war, and has a power advantage. The wife, through her counsel, may feel compelled to react in such a way as to equalize power. Such efforts often result in antagonizing the husband and escalating the conflict.

Chapter 15
Special Factors in Mediating Family Law Cases

Also, well-intentioned friends on both sides provide "advice" that may escalate the conflict. The wife's friends may suggest she must not be taken advantage of. The husband's friends may suggest he not take a beating.

Additionally, special emotionally charged factors may exist because of an extra-marital relationship, alleged physical abuse of the spouse or child, or alleged sexual abuse of a child. Such factors serve to minimize communication at a time when it is perhaps most needed.

It should be pointed out that family law has often been singled out for being most suitable for mediation. As a result, family lawyers may be sensitive to the idea that mediation in itself may be coercive. A family lawyer may believe her client will "do better" in court than she might do by way of compromise. Some family lawyers believe that the trial itself is the only true way to purge conflict, thinking that even if the parties enter an agreed settlement, a future battle, in terms of a modification, is more likely to occur if the parties haven't had their fight.

This chapter is not intended to suggest solutions to such global issues. The truth is that many family law cases are mediated successfully, and that the mediation advocate must be prepared for those special things that may arise. The following guidelines are neither an all-inclusive list nor do they all apply to every case, save and except for the first item listed.

1. **Counsel.** At the risk of beginning on a controversial note, the parties should never attend the mediation session without counsel. A recent study suggests that women who are not represented by counsel at mediation do poorly and often feel coerced. The mediation process was not designed to be coercive or to take advantage of either party. Further, during the mediation process, a party may often have a legal question that must be answered or a question about whether a proposal is "fair." A mediator must not dispense legal advice, and the fairness of a proposal should be an attorney-client matter. Further, because of the very real balance of power issues, a mediator may appear coercive to a party not aided by counsel. As a result, the process may be unnecessarily obstructed because such party does not trust or feels intimidated by the mediator.

Chapter 15
Special Factors in Mediating Family Law Cases

---

2. Hostility toward opposing counsel. On the other hand, the attorney's role in a family law mediation may be somewhat different than an attorney's role in other civil litigation matters that are mediated. Because of the emotion inherent in family law, it is not uncommon for a party to develop intense, negative feelings for her spouse's counsel. A party may see her spouse's lawyer as the problem and the primary obstruction to a fair resolution. The attorney's presence may exacerbate negative feelings and obstruct resolution. In such instances, the following framework may work well and still permit counsel to participate actively in the mediation process:

(1) Counsel should be *especially cautious* about the content of her opening statement. If the goal of the mediation is resolution, counsel should make a low-key, restrained presentation. Threats, accusations, and name-calling are ineffective and damaging.

(2) Counsel may suggest that once the parties split into separate caucuses, the mediator work privately with the parties. Prior to any final decisions being made, the parties may at any time privately caucus with their counsel. This prevents the disliked-lawyer factor from harming the process, but at the same time gives the parties the security of knowing their counsel are close by and available for consultation.

3. Opening statement. Even in cases in which a "lawyer dislike" problem does not exist, care in the opening statement is necessary and often critical in terms of the chances for resolution. Counsel's opening statements should be well set out, conciliatory, and non-threatening. Counsel should be reminded that her jury is the spouse on the other side.

4. Parties' tolerance levels. Special attention should be given to how the parties are emotionally tolerating the process. If either party appears overwhelmed or unduly tired, the mediator should consider calling a recess and resuming the mediation the next day or later in the week.

Chapter 15
Special Factors in Mediating Family Law Cases

---

5. Co-mediation. Certain cases may require a co-mediation team consisting of an attorney mediator and a psychologist/counselor mediator.

6. Mediator's gender. Gender considerations may enter into the mediator selection process. Would a male or female mediator be better? What about a co-mediation team consisting of a male and female mediator?

7. Issue clarity. The issues to be mediated should be clearly delineated prior to the session; for example, property division, custody, support, etc.

8. Experts. If property values and the like are in issue, counsel might elect to bring their experts to the session.

9. Reflection time. If a resolution is reached, the parties should be permitted adequate time to reflect on whether the resolution reached is fair. There is no point in having an agreement that will fall apart after the session.

In my opinion, the area of family law mediation, perhaps more than any other, requires specialized mediator training and should be recognized as a sub-specialty. A mediator who mediates personal injury or commercial cases may have a very difficult time dealing with the special and highly sensitive issues associated with a family case.

Chapter 16

Special Factors in Mediating Medical Negligence Cases

More than 100 of the first 700 cases I mediated were medical negligence cases. For reasons I will explain, mediation works particularly well in such cases; in fact, all but two of the medical negligence cases I have mediated have resolved, and have done so on a basis satisfying to all parties.

Every medical negligence case requires proof of three basic elements: negligence, causation, and damages. But, as those who specialize in medical negligence litigation will tell you, most medical negligence cases turn on the issue of causation — assuming the physician or hospital or nurse made a mistake, did the mistake cause the claimed injury or death? Expert witnesses are easily found on both sides of the claim on the issue of causation, in large part because medicine is not an exact science and, as such, a multiplicity of causes (based on reasonable medical probability) may be offered to explain an injury or death. Of course, negligence is not usually conceded, both sides will have an array of experts on the standard of care issue, and the damages assessments are also in conflict. Nonetheless, causation is usually the most debated point during a medical negligence mediation.

§16.1 Why the Suit was Filed

In order to understand the special factors involved in medical negligence cases, one must also understand how the majority of these lawsuits arise. I have heard the story of "why I filed this lawsuit" time after time in caucus, and the categories of stories are quite consistent. Of course, the explanations always begin with the injury or death, but the explanations almost always include any of the following factors:

1.   The physician, hospital, or nurse didn't seem to care. The claimant perceived the health care provider as aloof, indifferent, cold, uncaring, etc.

2.   The physician, hospital, or nurse failed to express regret about what occurred. Of course, such expressions as "I'm sorry" could be converted into purported admissions of liability if a lawsuit is filed. But many claimants report feeling angry, astonished, or hurt that the health care provider failed to express regret.

3.   The health care provider failed to explain *at all* what had occurred. Many claimants report their feeling that no explanation or information was ever provided. Of course, because of the high emotions that typically occur during medical emergencies, an explanation may have been offered that the claimant did not really hear.

4.   No information was provided during the crisis itself or even shortly thereafter. The information or explanation was provided well after the event. This is a timing issue. The claimant's feeling is that being kept posted during the event would have been preferable and the explanation would, as a result, have been more credible. Impliedly, an explanation offered after the event is deemed not to be credible. From the health care provider's perspective, however, maintaining the flow of information while a crisis is occurring may be extremely difficult.

5.   The explanation offered was confusing, made no sense, or was perceived as an obvious lie. Great variation exists in this area. Some claimants report that the explanation offered was presented in words that they did not understand or that "went over their heads." Some physicians, as with any professional group, are poor communicators and use jargon that lay people just don't understand. Other claimants report that they understood the actual words used, but the explanation made no sense to them. These claimants felt that they still did not understand why things happened as they did. Finally, certain claimants report they felt that the health care provider was just lying. Usually, the physician's demeanor is the primary factor in the development of such a feeling.

6.   The physical appearance of the physician is sometimes a factor. Certain claimants report that the physician appeared "intoxicated." Other claimants report the physician appeared "exhausted" or "out of it." Again, explanations from the health care side often exist, but I am simply reporting the perceptions of such claimants.

7.   The absence of the primary caretaking physician is sometimes a factor. Such situations usually break down into two categories: the primary caretaking physician is on call, but is nowhere to be found or is found too late; or the primary caretaking physician is not on call, efforts are made to locate him, but such efforts are unsuccessful. The claimant's general view is that if the primary caretaking physician (who was fully aware of the patient's history) had been present, the incident would not have occurred.

8.   Some claimants report overhearing critical or negative remarks of other on-the-scene health care providers: "I heard the nurses talking in the hall and one nurse said to the other that Dr. Jones screwed up again."

9.   Some claimants report that in instances in which an obvious, inexcusable mistake was made, an explanation was nonetheless offered, which, according to the claimant, was a clear effort to cover up or distort the truth.

10.   Many claimants express anger that they requested to see the actual medical records and the records were either not provided at all or not timely provided. In such situations, claimants believe that an attempt to cover up is being made.

11.   Certain claimants report that medical records were provided, but that the records appeared to be altered or changed, or were not in fact the correct records.

12.   Finally, certain claimants report that after the incident, attempts were made to have them execute releases or to settle the matter, which they deemed to be either coercive or a virtual admission of liability. Most of these claimants report that such attempts were made at a time when they were still grieving, upset, or confused.

This list is important in several regards. In some instances, if these situations had not occurred, a lawsuit might not have been filed at all. But perhaps more important, the motivations for filing a claim help identify non-monetary interests on the claimant's side that may, or must, be met if resolution is to occur in mediation. The claimant's mediation advocate, however, must be aware that the health care provider has an array of non-monetary interests as well.

Chapter 16
Special Factors in Mediating Medical Negligence Cases

As you are aware, throughout this work I am attempting in a specific way to assist the mediation advocate on both sides of the case. As a result, whether you are representing the claimant or the hospital/physician, you will not be able to represent your client effectively at mediation unless you identify and understand this type of non-monetary interests and format your presentation and approach at mediation accordingly. In some instances, the mediation advocate understands such interests before the session itself. But in many cases, the mediation advocate may identify such interests for the first time at the session itself and must be able to react at that moment. As repeatedly stated in the chapters on mediation advocacy, preparation is always the key. A mediation advocate can, with proper preparation and interviewing, anticipate what such interests might be — even when such interests have never been specifically expressed in discovery or otherwise.

§16.2 The Claimant's Interests

This is a comprehensive list of interests that the claimant may have in a medical negligence case. Usually, several of these interests exist, although the claimant may prioritize or give greater weight to certain interests.

1. **Monetary interest.** The party's monetary interest may take several forms. In cases of clear negligence, it may be the need to meet past, present, and future obligations. For example, in a brain-damaged baby case, the interest may be in meeting medical needs, providing care, providing proper therapy and facilities, and compensation for suffering and anguish. The monetary interest may in part reflect a need to punish or teach the health care provider a lesson, or it may reflect an unrealistic desire to obtain a windfall. The point is that there are often needs that must be ferreted out to understand the nature of the monetary interest.

2. **Expression of regret interest.** A claimant often feels like, and may well be, a victim. A claimant is often attempting to deal with a tragedy. An expression of regret or apology, if sincere, may not and perhaps should not result in a dismissal of a lawsuit. But in appropriate cases, the claimant may have to hear such actual words before he will be emotionally prepared or able to resolve the dispute.

Chapter 16
Special Factors in Mediating Medical Negligence Cases

---

3. Full and understandable explanation interest. Certain claimants will not be able to resolve a dispute unless they understand why things happened as they did — especially if no information or confusing information was provided.

4. Interest in preventing future incidents. Some claimants feel that their lawsuit will prevent a physician, hospital, or nurse from making "similar mistakes" in the future. Beyond the claimant's loss, the claimant feels a larger, social cause exists.

5. Interest in public shaming. Some claimants are so angry, rightfully or wrongfully, that they have a real interest in exposing the health care provider to ridicule and criticism, among his peers, the public, or both.

6. Grief interest. For certain claimants, the claim becomes part of the grieving process. The claimant may not have yet come to terms with the loss or injury, and the lawsuit itself becomes a method of coping or dealing with it.

7. Closure interest. Conversely, many claimants have a great interest in resolving the dispute to obtain closure — the claimant has a fundamental need to put the dispute at an end in order to get the problem behind him.

8. Denial interest. In certain cases, and these are exceedingly sensitive, the claimant's own conduct has played a part in the injury or loss. Human nature being what it is, many claimants engage in denial, and the lawsuit is part of the denial process. In my view, defense counsel should never confront such contributory negligence but, rather, should advise the mediator of this issue in separate caucus and authorize the mediator to deal with the issue sensitively in the other separate caucus. A mediator may feel that the issue should not be confronted, even in caucus, until it is obvious that the case may not resolve without the issue being addressed. In certain instances, the claimant may never be able to accept any responsibility and any effort, no matter how sensitive, to confront such issue will only make the claimant further entrenched.

Chapter 16
Special Factors in Mediating Medical Negligence Cases

§16.3 Health Provider's Interests

From the health care provider's perspective, any of the following interests may exist in a medical negligence dispute:

1. **Reputational interest.** Physicians, hospitals, and nurses, like any other professionals, are passionately concerned about their reputations. A physician may feel a claim to be an insult to his reputation. Or, a physician may feel that settlement, regardless of the denial of liability in the release documents, is a tacit admission and will damage his reputation. The delivery of hospital services is a very competitive business. A hospital may have a keen interest in avoiding adverse publicity in a very competitive environment — especially in a possible gross negligence case that might bring terrible press.

2. **Denial interest.** In my opinion, the denial factor is the single greatest obstacle in resolving medical negligence factors. Certainly, the physician's denial may be very valid — nothing wrong may have actually occurred. Most responsible health care providers are extremely concerned about their patients. While most acknowledge their humanity and the possibility of human error, many find it exceedingly difficult to believe their own human error could have caused a profound injury or death. For such professionals, who they are is what they do. And when mistakes occur in this realm, the results may often be catastrophic and difficult to accept responsibility for. Many physicians or nurses may never be able to admit they made a mistake that caused real harm. However, in mediation, a physician may be able to admit he is human and that human beings sometimes, despite their best efforts, make mistakes.

3. **Confidentiality interest.** Many physicians and hospitals that consent and determine to settle will do so in order to keep the matter private. Physicians may, depending upon the settlement amount, be reported to the National Data Base, but the interest is in preventing the story from being reported in the press or from person to person in the community at large. This interest, of course, is related to the reputational interest. In certain cases, the physician's or hospital's willingness to settle will be tied to a confidentiality agreement.

Chapter 16
Special Factors in Mediating Medical Negligence Cases

4. Vindication interest. Some physicians feel that the majority of medical negligence cases are brought wrongfully by "greedy plaintiff's lawyers." In reality, some lawsuits are brought wrongfully and some are based on unequivocal negligence. Of course, another class of cases falls in the realm of an honest (or not so honest, depending upon which side you are talking to) difference of opinion of experts. As I see it, experts are either saints or (as they are called to me) "whores," depending again upon which side is offering the opinion. Regardless, some physicians feel that they are victims of the medical negligence crisis and have a real interest in vindicating what they perceive to be a wrong.

5. Spreading the blame or casting the blame elsewhere interest. In certain instances, the physician or hospital feels the responsibility for the incident lies elsewhere or is a shared responsibility; sometimes the feeling is based on reality, sometimes it is not. Regardless of whether this interest is or is not born in reality, it must be dealt with as part of the denial interest.

6. Privileges interest. Some physicians feel that a settlement may adversely affect their hospital privileges. Such privileges may be a condition precedent to the physician's economic survival.

7. Insurance interest. Some physicians, especially with a prior claims history, may fear that settlement will result in cancellation of their coverage or significantly higher premiums.

8. Economic interest. In certain instances, a physician's potential exposure may exceed his insurance coverage and he may possess non-exempt assets that would satisfy all or part of a judgment.

§16.4 Opening Statements

The general guidelines regarding opening statements, which are set out in Chapter 9, pages 75-80, apply in medical negligence mediations, but the mediation advocate in these cases must be especially vigilant of the interests described above. Because of these special interests, a mediation advocate may either fatally damage the prospects for settlement or greatly improve the chances for resolution with his opening statement. Now, thinking in terms of these interests, you may consider the following list of do's and don'ts for opening presentation.

1. Do's

(1) Because medical terms are involved, speak in plain, clear language that the adjuster or claimant will understand.

(2) Demonstrate preparedness. Blow-ups of records, charts, or a prepared chronology shows you are prepared and organized.

(3) Express compassion and understanding. You are not admitting liability or being sympathetic to a physician. Rather, you are acknowledging how someone feels — even if you do not agree with the position a party is taking.

(4) Express regret when appropriate. A defense counsel may express regret about a death or a profound injury. A plaintiff's counsel may express regret to a physician that he feels attacked by the lawsuit.

(5) Express your view that your opposing counsel is competent.

(6) Outline objectively, clearly, and concisely your view of the case.

(7) Acknowledge that risk exists for everyone.

(8) State that you hope the process will result in a fair resolution for all concerned.

(9) Express appreciation for the other party's participation in the process.

2. Don'ts (much more important)

(1) Never engage in a personal attack on a party or his counsel — even if you think it is warranted.

(2) Never express your view that the outcome at trial is absolutely certain and will be favorable to you.

(3) Never attempt to have a party accept or declare responsibility. The denial process is too strong and the party will only entrench.

(4) Never raise a particularly sensitive or personal issue in your opening statement. Save it for the separate caucus and permit the mediator to deal with it.

(5) From the defense side, never obliquely suggest that despite the negligence of the health care provider, the death or injury would have happened anyway. You may win on causation at trial, but in mediation the claimant will never believe that is true and will consider such a statement to be callous, a rationalization, or flat-out lying. Handle your causation defense gingerly and permit the mediator to deal more directly with the issue in caucus.

(6) From the plaintiff's perspective, never engage in a reputational assault of a physician or hospital.

(7) Never threaten adverse publicity. Such things are already known and do not need to be stated.

(8) Never insult the other side's experts. However, you may criticize their findings and conclusions and credentials.

(9) Never use absolute words such as never, always, etc.

(10) Never discuss money. Leave monetary discussion for the caucus.

§16.5 The Role of the Physician/Hospital Representative/Nurse

On occasion, I am asked whether the physician himself should attend the mediation session. My answer is routinely "yes." Permit me to explain why and the role the health care provider should play.

As stated above, claimants often feel that the health care provider does not care, communicated poorly, or, in more extreme instances, made up a story about what occurred. The failure of the physician to attend the session will serve only to re-enforce the claimant's feeling that the physician is indifferent or uncaring.

Chapter 16
Special Factors in Mediating Medical Negligence Cases

The physician often feels powerless in the litigation process, feels that he has been afforded no opportunity to explain what occurred, and may also have no real understanding of the nature of the claim asserted against him. As a result, the physician needs to be a participant in the mediation process. The physician also needs to be present in order to hear directly the claims asserted against him in order to understand fully the nature of his exposure.

Assuming the physician will be an active participant in the mediation process, what should the physician's role be? I would suggest the following:

1. **Talk.** In almost every instance, the physician should make a brief, clear presentation to the claimant in language that the claimant will understand. The presentation should explain what occurred and why it occurred, and, most important, express his acknowledgement of how the claimant feels about the loss or injury.

2. **Listen.** The physician should make a determined effort to listen to the other side's presentation for purposes of evaluation.

3. **Assist.** In the separate caucus, the physician should assist his counsel and the mediator in understanding both the strengths and weaknesses of the claims that are asserted.

4. **Consent to settle.** Finally, the physician should consent to a settlement, if at all possible, prior to the mediation session. As you are aware, many medical malpractice insurance policies provide that the physician must consent to settlement. Medical negligence mediations in which the physician has not previously consented to settlement are more rigorous and time consuming, in large part because the consent issue must be resolved before any meaningful negotiations may commence.

§16.6 The Insurance Representative's Role

In medical negligence cases, the insurance representative's role is critical and the representative should actively participate. The question, as always, is the nature of the representative's participation.

Chapter 16
Special Factors in Mediating Medical Negligence Cases

In essence, the representative's role at mediation has two key components: engaging in active listening and evaluation, and interacting with the claimant. In these regards, the representative's effective participation may be a real key to resolution of the dispute.

In terms of active listening, the representative must demonstrate to the claimant that he is making a sincere effort to hear and understand the claimant's position. Prior to the session the claimant may feel that the insurance carrier does not care or is not willing to listen. Active listening may be demonstrated in a number of ways. First, the representative's body language provides an indication of active listening. The representative should be looking at the claimant's counsel or the claimant whenever they are speaking. Note-taking also demonstrates active listening.

But body language alone does not always confirm active listening. The representative should make an effort to repeat back key points raised by the claimant or claimant's counsel to demonstrate that the representative has in fact listened. Additionally, the representative should ask questions (not conduct a cross-examination) to establish both listening and interest.

The representative, by asking questions, also demonstrates that the representative is present to evaluate and re-evaluate the claim. Effective questioning demonstrates open-mindedness and a willingness to understand. The questions should not be leading (i.e., "isn't it true that . . ."), threatening, or accusatory. Rather, the questions should be open-ended and intended to help the representative better understand the claimant's position.

In terms of the representative's interaction with the claimant, the representative must demonstrate the same sensitivity, compassion, and humanity that defense counsel must exhibit. By doing so, the representative humanizes his company. As a result, the negotiation is no longer between the claimant and a large, uncaring company; rather, the negotiation is between the claimant and a living, breathing human being.

I have observed representatives establish a sincere, honest, and candid bond with claimants. When such a bond is created, the chances for resolution are greatly enhanced.

§16.7 Multi-Defendant Factors

Many medical negligence cases involve multiple defendants: possibly several physicians, a nurse, the hospital, etc. Most physicians carry malpractice insurance policies, although policy limits vary. Some nurses carry malpractice insurance, but others do not. Hospitals either are self-insured or have malpractice insurance, usually with very high policy limits.

In some medical negligence cases, the defendants, while ostensibly aligned to defeat the plaintiff's claims, are in reality antagonistic for settlement purposes — who is going to contribute what to the settlement pot? For example, assume that as a result of mediation the claimant reduces his demand to a number that all defendants agree is a fair figure. Then the real fight begins regarding the level of each defendant's contribution. In essence, two mediations are occurring — the mediation between the plaintiff and the defendants, and the mediation between the defendants. Of course, if the defendants cannot as a group wholly settle with the plaintiff, certain defendants may wish to settle independently with the plaintiff.

While every case varies, many cases involve a conflict between the hospital and the physician or physicians. In many instances, the carrier for the physicians wants the hospital to pick up a greater portion of the settlement pot. Conversely, the hospital often wants the physicians to exhaust their policy limits before making up the difference. Such a situation may result in a real stand-off — especially when the strength of the liability theories may vary from defendant to defendant.

On occasion, defendants as part of their first offer may attempt to agree initially on the pro rata contribution from each defendant. Often defendants are unwilling to make the pro rata commitment early on in the negotiation or, if they do, the defendants can get "locked in" and obstruct the negotiation with the claimant. Further, if the defendants cannot agree initially upon the levels of their attendant contributions,

Chapter 16
Special Factors in Mediating Medical Negligence Cases

the defendants may not be able to respond to what they perceive to be a reasonable proposal from the claimant.

Of course, no bullet-proof solution exists, but a solution is for the mediator to deal with the problem in the initial caucus and attempt to create some consensus. Initially, the mediator may obtain consensus from all defendants regarding what would be a fair settlement range generally on the case; e.g., if the plaintiff gets to $500,000-$650,000, such a range would be a fair settlement. Next, the mediator should obtain each party's willingness to put up an initial contribution, without looking into a formula, to make preliminary offers to test whether the plaintiff is likely to get within such a range. Should the plaintiff enter a perceived reasonable range, the mediator then only has to deal with whatever the monetary gap is to meet the offer. The discussion regarding percentage contribution should center on an objective exposure ranking. Such discussion may occur only by breaking up the defendants and separately caucusing, for case evaluation purpose, with each defendant.

Such situations protract the length of the mediation and make obtaining resolution more difficult. Further, such situations create delays in responding to the plaintiff's proposals, which may, if not properly dealt with, frustrate the plaintiff. The mediator should obtain authority from all defendants to let the plaintiff know that disagreement exists regarding the extent of each defendant's contribution and, as a result, the process may take longer. Fortunately, the plaintiff's willingness to move to a perceived reasonable range often provides the incentive for the defendants to resolve their conflict regarding the extent of contribution.

§16.8 When to Mediate

In Chapter 2, pages 6-7, we discussed the issue of when to mediate. The guiding principle generally is that mediation should occur as soon as is practical and a reasonable preliminary evaluation of the case is possible.

In medical negligence cases, the guiding principle remains applicable, but given the special interests described above, such cases seem to resolve more consistently

Chapter 16
Special Factors in Mediating Medical Negligence Cases

if the mediation occurs very early in the case. Claimants' negative feelings towards the physician or hospital harden over time. Conversely, physicians' denial matrices seem to become more hardened as more time passes from the incident itself. Both parties seem to have a greater ability to communicate and listen early in the dispute. Finally, the handling of a medical negligence case is a very expensive proposition on both sides. As a result, the significant cost basis in itself may create a real obstruction to resolution.

Chapter 17

Special Factors in Mediating
Consumer Cases

A couple buys a home and discovers the foundation is cracked six months after they move in. A lawsuit is brought against the seller and builder. A consumer buys a new car that has to be brought in 12 times for repairs in the first six months. Ultimately, the consumer files a lawsuit against the car dealer. A business person alleges that a bank expressly promised to make a loan so that she could acquire a piece of property. The bank decides not to fund the loan and the business person files a lawsuit against the bank. Such cases are consumer cases. And while they are perfect candidates for mediation, consumer cases involve special interests and factors that must be dealt with in the mediation process. Not surprisingly, emotions run high in consumer cases, and the mediator must be prepared to manage the volatile feelings that often arise during their mediation.

§17.1 Consumer's Special Interests

From the consumer's perspective, any of the following interests may form the basis of the dispute:

    1. Economic interests. For many consumers, the item purchased (a house, a car) is one of the most costly items acquired by the consumer. As a result, repair or replacement of the item often involves a significant expense.

    2. Betrayal/trust interests. Consumers often feel that they have been lied to, misled, or cheated. Consumers typically feel their trust and confidence has been breached.

    3. Vindication/cause interests. Because the consumer feels lied to, she has an interest in vindicating this wrong. On occasion, the consumer feels her claim may prevent others from being victimized. As such, the incident itself becomes a larger cause.

§17.2 Seller's/Business' Special Interests

From the seller's/business' prospective, any of the following interests may exist:

1.   **Reputation interest.** Very often, the business (car dealership, real estate company, etc.) feels the lawsuit is an attack on its reputation. To resolve the suit, regardless of the non-admission of liability language in the settlement documents, would be an admission of liability and would harm its reputation. Of course, if the claimant's allegations are true, a public trial will cause the business more significant harm.

2.   **Economic interest.** Businesses are in business to make money. Repair, replacement, return, cancellation, and attorneys' fees all have an economic value and cost. Additionally, in more serious cases, the rendition of a large jury verdict might disable or do substantial harm to the business.

3.   **Confidentiality interest.** Because of the reputation interest, the business may have a significant interest in keeping the matter out of the public eye. The business may fear publicity will spawn additional lawsuits or, because of damage to its reputation, result in decreased sales. Not surprisingly, a business' willingness to resolve a dispute may be absolutely conditioned upon the claimant's execution of a confidentiality agreement.

4.   **Frivolous lawsuit policy interest.** Many businesses feel that a lawsuit crisis exists in our country and that frivolous suits often are filed. Such businesses feel that the suit itself is a form of "blackmail," and may have developed a general policy not to settle such suits as a matter of principle. Of course, the dispute in question may or may not be frivolous. On occasion, such a general policy not to settle blinds the business from objectively analyzing this case in particular, and this case in particular may create substantial exposure. Further, while frivolous suits may be filed, certain cases may be perceived as frivolous but have a foundation based on operative law or the facts.

Chapter 17
Special Factors in Mediating Consumer Cases

---

5. Domino effect avoidance interest. A business may feel that the successful defense of a dispute is critical in avoiding a multiplicity of other lawsuits. The fear is that word will get around that the business settles cases and is afraid to go to trial. As a result, the business, regardless of exposure, may feel it is important to show the claimant's lawyers that the business is not afraid to go to trial and that the claimant's lawyer must work for her money.

6. Matter of principle interest. Mediators often hear corporate executives state in the separate caucus, "I will not pay the claimant anything as a matter of principle." Principle may be the perception that the lawsuit is frivolous. Principle may relate to reputation. Principle may specifically relate to an executive's feeling that she did nothing wrong or bent over backwards to help the claimant. The principle interest is usually generally stated.

7. Future relationship interest. The claimant may have had a long-standing relationship with the business, and the business may have a real interest in resolving the dispute to leave open the possibility of a future relationship.

§17.3 Apply Special Interests in the Opening Statement

The mediation advocate, as always, must be aware of the interests that exist beneath the dispute itself in order to fashion an effective opening statement. The failure to consider such interests may result in an opening statement that makes a party become even more entrenched and inflexible. This is not to suggest that the mediation advocate must make an insincere statement or fail to communicate fully the integrity of her client's position. The critical point is the manner in which that message is communicated and the avoidance of statements that will make the other party (who is, you'll remember, your jury) not listen and not be willing to re-evaluate.

1. Consumer's side.

(1) Avoid words like "crook," "thief," "lie," "steal," "cheat." Personal attacks and threats never work; in fact, such attacks virtually extinguish the possibility of resolution. In many instances "fraud" is too strong a word.

(2) Never threaten adverse publicity. The mediator will discuss the publicity issue with the other side in caucus. Because the mediator is neutral, she can discuss such matters. You cannot.

(3) Avoid references to an existing "bad reputation" or an innuendo that your case may ruin or damage a reputation.

(4) Avoid references to the possibility of other lawsuits or other claimants.

2. **Defense side.**

(1) Avoid describing the claimant's lawsuit as "frivolous."

(2) Avoid personal attacks on either the claimant or her counsel.

(3) Avoid words like "extort," "blackmail," etc.

(4) Avoid declarations of absolutes such as, "We will never . . ."

Obviously, you must condition your client in advance of the session that your decision to avoid such references is not a result of an absence of conviction, but rather because your goal as a mediation advocate is to keep the lines of communication open, as opposed to severing them. Further, you must prevent your client from making such references in the collaborative joint session.

But what about the value of "venting?" Doesn't the consumer need to call the car dealer a crook before she will be able to settle? Doesn't the car dealer need to tell the consumer her lawsuit is bogus? In consumer mediation, the answer to these questions is "no." Each side may vent in the private caucus, but human nature controls the answers to these questions. A business person who has been called a liar, cheat, or thief, even if it is true, will not be inclined to listen or attempt to understand the consumer's position. Such verbal assaults may be vindicated only by winning at trial. Similarly, a consumer who is advised that her claims are frivolous, even if that is true, may be inclined to do whatever it takes to demonstrate that the claims were warranted.

Chapter 18

Special Factors in Claims Against or Involving Governmental Entities

Mediation may successfully resolve claims involving governmental entities, but, as in every area, several special factors must be considered. There are two special factors, however, that *must* be carefully considered prior to the mediation session: Who has the authority to settle and what the funding or budgetary limitations are.

§18.1 Authority to Settle

As stated in Chapter 6, pages 61-68, the mediation process works best when the person or persons fully authorized to make the decision are *present at the session itself.* In suits involving governmental entities (cities, counties, states, etc.), one person is rarely singularly authorized to make a final decision. Often a city council, the county commissioners, or even the governor must approve and bless a decision before it becomes truly final. And, applying a rule of reason, it is often simply neither practical or possible to have the entire city council, for example, attend the mediation session.

Assuming, therefore, that most "resolutions" produced through mediation will be "subject to approval" agreements, what steps should be taken to maximize such a resolution becoming truly final? You should consider the following:

1. **Who will attend.** Who will attend *must* be fully discussed between all counsel prior to the session itself. This issue *cannot* be resolved on the day of the session.

2. **Comfort level.** All parties should feel comfortable with the representatives who will attend. If all counsel *cannot* agree upon the representative or representatives, the mediator, via telephone conference call, should be brought in to

assist with the resolution of this issue, but not on the day before or, worse yet, the morning of the session.

3. **Pre-approved authority.** The government's representative or representatives should, if at all possible, have some pre-approved authority to settle — even if final approval will require someone else's signature or a resolution.

4. **Likely approval.** The representative or representatives should be a person or persons whose recommendation will be strongly considered and likely approved. For example, assume that before the mediation the city council determined that $500,000 would be a fair basis to settle a claim. Assume further that two members of the city council who attend the mediation determine, as a result of the session, that the city's exposure is much greater than previously thought and enter into a "subject to" resolution with the city paying $850,000. Those representatives sent to attend the session must have absolute credibility with the non-attending members who have not had the opportunity to be a part of the process itself.

5. **Availability by telephone.** If at all possible (and sometimes it is not), the absent decision-makers should be available by telephone *during the session itself.* As a result, the attending representatives may be able to receive a preliminary indication that their recommendation will be approved.

Again, the most important step is to resolve the authority to settle issue fully *prior to* the session. Nothing can be more destructive than having participants arrive at the session only to have a vehement, and usually incurable, dispute over who is present, as opposed to attempting to resolve the real dispute in issue.

§18.2 Funding/Budgetary Issues

In certain instances, the governmental entity being sued has certain budgetary constraints. As a result, a state agency, for example, may have only so many available dollars to settle a lawsuit and no ability in a given fiscal year to obtain additional funding. Also, the agency may have the ability to request funding for a settlement in the next fiscal year, but may not be able to predict whether such funding will be approved.

Chapter 18
Special Factors in Claims Against or Involving Governmental Entities

Regardless, if a funding or budgetary limitation in fact exists, counsel for the governmental entity should disclose this limitation to the plaintiff's counsel before the session.

Assume hypothetically that the plaintiff's demand before the session is $500,000, but that a budgetary limitation will limit any settlement offers to a maximum of $100,000. Even if the claimant is willing to settle for $200,000 as a result of mediation, the issue cannot be resolved. Further, at the session itself, the plaintiff's counsel cannot assess whether a budgetary limitation is in fact real, or whether it is simply a negotiation tactic. Regardless, any budgetary cap or limit should be discussed in advance and a determination made, based on such disclosure, whether the mediation should proceed.

§18.3 Political Interests

Suits against governmental entities frequently have political implications for those within the governmental entity itself. Re-election may either hinge on or be somewhat affected by the outcome of a significant and widely publicized piece of litigation. Because the matter often is one of public interest, the terms of any settlement can rarely be kept confidential. Such political factors may therefore be the primary obstruction to resolution and can be exceedingly difficult to deal with.

A politician may feel that it would be less damaging to her politically for a lawsuit against the entity to which she is elected to go to trial, sustain a terrible jury verdict, and then blame the result on the jury or our legal system. Or sometimes a politician will determine that a public trial would be more damaging politically because it could make her look bad in the media.

From the mediator's perspective, once such political interests are identified, the challenge may well be to determine whether there is some way to structure a resolution or settlement in such a way as to minimize potential political harm. Or the mediator may well have to ask a politician in caucus whether he would put his political interest over the citizens he is sworn to represent and protect. Attitudes regard-

Chapter 18
Special Factors in Claims Against or Involving Governmental Entities

ing resolution may also be influenced by a politician's assessment of the political impact of a settlement on a fellow politician's career.

§18.4 Absolute Defensive Bars

In many lawsuits involving governmental entities, the entity will assert governmental immunity as an absolute bar to any recovery by the plaintiff. Typically, counsel for the governmental entity will file a motion for summary judgment attempting to have the claim dismissed.

Mediation may work effectively even in instances in which such an absolute defensive bar is asserted. The question remains just how solid the absolute defensive bar is and, if the claimant gets past such a bar, what the potential exposure is.

Nonetheless, counsel for both sides might consider a combination of ADR mechanisms to deal with such a situation. As you are aware, a mediator will not render an opinion as to whether the absolute defensive bar will prevail. But both sides may need such an opinion before productive negotiations may commence. If that is the case, counsel should consider submitting the immunity issue to an arbitration panel. Ultimately, in an abbreviated and cost-effective proceeding, the panel will render (depending upon the written agreement of the parties) either a binding or non-binding decision as to whether the immunity defense will succeed or fail.

Based on such a decision, counsel may attempt to negotiate a resolution independently, and failing that, submit the matter for mediation. The chances for resolution at mediation will be greatly enhanced with the defensive bar issue already resolved and decided by an arbitration panel.

Chapter 19

Special Factors in the Mediation of Miscellaneous Substantive Areas

In this chapter, I will attempt to outline in an abbreviated form those special factors and issues that may exist in a variety of substantive disputes. The fact that these substantive areas are given a more concise treatment certainly does not mean that they are not conducive to mediation. In fact, the contrary is true, but general mediation principles apply well to all of these substantive areas along with the few important differences I will mention for each area.

§19.1 Vehicular Collisions

Vehicular collisions make up a significant portion of any mediator's docket. Such cases involve three critical issues: whether there was negligence; whether the negligence caused the harm; and the nature and extent of the injuries.

1. Categories. Typically, vehicular collision mediations fall into one of the following categories:

(1) Liability *and* damages in dispute.

(2) Liability disputed, but damages, subject to some range, conceded.

(3) Liability virtually conceded, but damages in dispute.

Such cases are further complicated if the contention is that one or more parties, including the claimant, were negligent. In my experience, about 65% of the vehicular collision mediations involve situations in which liability is virtually admitted and damages are in dispute, with the remainder of the cases falling equally into the other two categories listed above.

2. Enhancing mediation. The chances of a successful mediation of a vehicular collision case are enhanced under the following conditions:

Chapter 19
Special Factors in the Mediation of Miscellaneous Substantive Areas

---

(1) If liability is disputed, both plaintiff and defense counsel should bring all liability evidence to the session. Such evidence might include police reports, photographs, diagrams of the accident scene, accident reconstruction charts or models, etc.

(2) To support the damages claims, plaintiff's counsel should bring any of the following to the session:

(a) Medical records

(b) Expert reports

(c) Copies of all medical bills

(d) Videotapes

(e) Excerpts from key depositions

(f) Wage loss statements

(g) Economist reports

(3) Almost always, plaintiff's counsel should make a demand prior to the session. In this way, the carrier will know in advance what level of authority to anticipate in designating a representative to attend the session.

(4) Both the claimant and the insured should attend the session. Often the insurance carrier comes to the session without the insured. The insured is often a meaningful participant.

(5) Certain interests that may exist in other cases rarely exist in vehicular collision cases. Typically, the claimant and the insured are total strangers and future relationship interests do not exist. The exception would be when a passenger makes claims against a driver with whom he has some type of relationship.

(6) From the defense viewpoint, issues of secondary gain, malingering, and the like are often present. The defense should discuss such matters with the

mediator in private caucus and have the mediator deal with them. Calling the claimant a malingerer in the defense opening statement is rarely helpful.

(7) Usually, the claimant's interests are largely economic. But what are the needs underlying the economic interests? The claimant may be concerned about her ability to obtain future insurance. Or the claimant may not be able to obtain insurance to meet certain medical needs.

(8) The exception to the above are cases in which the defendant was intoxicated at the time of the accident. In such instances, claimants, beyond their economic interests, may have a social interest in getting intoxicated drivers off the road.

§19.2 Business Disputes

Under the category of business disputes, I would include partnership disputes, contract claims, and the like. Partnership disputes, in many instances, resemble marriage dissolutions more than commercial disputes, and contractual claims between competing businesses may be equally venomous. Because the interests, while overlapping, are somewhat different between partnership and contractual disputes, I will break them up into two distinct categories.

1. Partnership disputes. In many instances, a personal relationship exists between partners who have entered into some type of business venture. Often, the personal relationship long pre-dated the business relationship. Of course, situations do exist in which the parties had no personal relationship prior to the business partnership and the relationship was created solely for economic purposes; in these cases, personal relationship interests are of little consequence.

(1) Personal relationship exists. Partnership disputes in which the parties have enjoyed a personal relationship are often fraught with emotion. Often, the partners feel betrayed, disappointed, or perhaps even cheated. Beyond the business dispute itself, partners often are grieving the loss of a personal relationship that, at one time, was greatly valued. Or a partner may be questioning her judgment in ever placing confidence in her partner. Regrettably, a written partnership agreement

---

sometimes does not exist or, if it does exist, may have been hastily drafted. Additionally, the partnership's business may be failing or have failed. Not surprisingly, allegations of self-dealing, fraud, or misappropriation of funds are common. Further, a partner may have found her friend may have made a better friend than a business partner. Often, one partner may feel her partner has not met his obligations.

While the economic interest in such disputes is very real, the potential for resolution on an objective/business decision basis is often only possible if these other interests are identified and met. The partners may have a real need to vent, to express their disappointment, or to receive an apology before a business settlement may be reached. The personal relationship, which creates some of the impediments to resolution, may also be the glue necessary to put together an accord. The personal relationship, despite the business dispute, may not be hopelessly lost and may still be of great value to the partners. Because of this, the future personal relationship may be the key to resolution.

Finally, the possibility of future business relationships outside and after the partnership may be of importance to the parties. Destructive litigation often eviscerates the chances of such future business dealings.

(2) **Personal relationship does not exist.** By way of contrast, partnership disputes in which no personal relationship was pre-existing tend to involve largely economic interests. The parties are not grieving the loss of what they never had personally, nor are the parties typically interested in any future business relationship. In such cases, the parties may be equally angry and outraged, but forgiveness and conciliation born out of a long-standing personal relationship does not exist. Often such parties may want vindication by exposing an allegedly corrupt partner through a public trial. In such instances, the mediator must constantly remind the parties that an objective business decision is in everybody's best interest, and that substantial litigation costs serve no one's purposes.

2. **Contractual disputes between businesses.** These cases may vary from a dispute over whether defective goods were delivered to allegations of tortious inter-

Chapter 19
Special Factors in the Mediation of Miscellaneous Substantive Areas

ference with an existing contract. While such cases obviously involve an economic interest, any or all of the following interests may exist:

(1) **Reputation interest.** A business may perceive the claim to be an assault upon its reputation and may feel that a settlement, regardless of the language of the settlement documents, is an implied admission of wrongdoing.

(2) **Confidentiality interest.** A business may feel that a public trial may be more economically damaging than a private resolution.

(3) **Principle interest.** A business may feel that a fundamental principle must be vindicated by an aggressive pursuit or defense of a claim.

(4) **Future business relationship interest.** An amiable resolution of the dispute may leave open opportunities for future, profitable business relationships.

(5) **Competition interest.** A business may feel a successful trial outcome may be so devastating that the competing business may be fatally damaged.

(6) **Third-party/shareholder interest.** Pursuit of a claim or resolution may be influenced by the business' fiduciary obligations to its shareholders or third parties.

(7) **Integrity of contract interest.** A business may feel that a resolution that forgives a breach of a carefully drafted contract will expose the business to even greater potential harm. The business may feel an important contract clause must be validated.

While each case varies and any one of these interests may be dominant in a particular case, the future business relationship interest is often the key to resolution. Unlike litigation, a consensual resolution, because it is mutually agreed to, leaves open the real chance for rewarding and profitable future ventures.

Chapter 19
Special Factors in the Mediation of Miscellaneous Substantive Areas

§19.3 Borrower-Lender Disputes

In many borrower-lender cases, a borrower has allegedly defaulted on an obligation and a deficiency remains after foreclosure. In response to a deficiency lawsuit, the borrower usually will assert various counterclaims along with defenses to the claimed deficiency. Because of the federally legislated "super-power" defenses and case law construing them, institutions that have been taken over by the federal government rarely feel vulnerable to counterclaims or at risk to any defenses asserted. Of course, many cases do involve borrower-initiated lawsuits against a lender; i.e., usury, breach of a loan agreement, breach of the duty of good faith and fair dealing, deceptive trade practices, etc.

1. **FDIC/RTC special factors.** While borrower-lender disputes may take many forms, the class of disputes in which the lender has been taken over by the FDIC or RTC has its own special factors. In almost all FDIC/RTC lending institution cases, the FDIC/RTC is attempting to recover a deficiency or is asserting a claim for recovery against third parties — a law firm that represented the lending institution, for example.

In deficiency suits, the borrower often asserts various defenses or counterclaims, but as mentioned above, such defenses and claims often fail because of the "super-power" rights and defenses conferred upon the FDIC/RTC.

The borrower's goal, more often than not, is either to escape the deficiency completely or to negotiate a reduction of the deficiency (with or without an extended pay-out). In certain instances, a borrower may have defenses or claims that are not barred. These defenses and claims create negotiating leverage for the borrower. Far more often, the only leverage a borrower may have is insolvency or inability to pay. While the FDIC/RTC may in fact obtain a large judgment with little difficulty, the collection of such a judgment may be difficult to impossible.

Two special factors, one on the FDIC/RTC side and the other on the borrower's side, are critical to the resolution of such deficiency claims. Fortunately, as of this writing, both the FDIC/RTC and counsel for borrowers have made good faith strides as to both these factors.

(1) On the FDIC/RTC side, the FDIC/RTC must be provided with reliable financial information well in advance of the mediation session in order to evaluate the solvency of the borrower. The mediation session should never become a deposition, but if the appropriate financial information is provided in advance, the session itself may become an information exchange that will clarify the data provided. Further, the tendering of such information in advance may permit FDIC/RTC representatives to secure in advance necessary approval and authority to settle on some discounted basis. The tendering of the information for the first time at the session is rarely successful. The FDIC/RTC representatives will not feel they have the time or ability to evaluate the financial data fully.

(2) On the borrower's side, the critical factor is that the FDIC/RTC representatives sent to the session are fully authorized to make a decision to settle the dispute. Alternatively, the decision-maker, if she is not in attendance, must be available by telephone throughout the session. A mediation with a representative who knows little about the file or who has little influence with the true decision-maker will be a waste of time.

When the FDIC/RTC are suing a third party (such as a law firm) on behalf of a failed institution, the true decision-makers for the FDIC/RTC must be present at the session. In such instances, the third party will likely fully explain various defensive theories during the mediation session. The true decision-makers must be present to evaluate such defensive positions.

If the two special factors are met, mediation works very well in FDIC/RTC cases. Additionally, an important and broader social goal is met. Expeditious resolution of such disputes minimizes what can be substantial litigation costs, which obviously has an impact on the net return to the federal government and all taxpayers.

Chapter 19
Special Factors in the Mediation of Miscellaneous Substantive Areas

---

2. Borrower/lender special factors. While the factors listed above also may apply to a borrower/lender situation in which the FDIC/RTC is not involved, additional factors apply because the borrower may have broader defensive and offensive theories. Beyond escaping liability for an alleged deficiency, a borrower may have a claim that could create great exposure for the lending institution.

Such disputes frequently are volatile, with the borrower feeling deceived or abused by an allegedly uncaring lending institution. Typically, such feelings are exacerbated by the existence of a long-term banking relationship and a personal relationship with a bank officer. The primary interest, to be sure, is economic. But counsel on both sides should be aware that pre-existing relationships and the possibility of future business relationships are also important issues. Adverse publicity, especially in a highly competitive banking industry, may also be an important interest of the institution's.

§19.4 Employment Disputes

In an uncertain economy, employment retention is of vital concern to most Americans. As a result, employment law is likely to be one of the most explosive practice growth areas over the next decade. Large corporations are already developing internal conflict resolution mechanisms. Many corporations are training their employees to become peer mediators in order to help resolve problems before they rise to the level of a lawsuit.

Employer-employee problems adversely affect morale and reduce productivity. Further, employer-employee disputes that escalate to a lawsuit result in substantial litigation cost and are a drain on management time. While employer-employee disputes may take many forms, three types of disputes are particularly suitable for mediation: sexual harassment claims; discrimination (age, race, sex) claims; and wrongful discharge claims. The remainder of this chapter will be devoted to the special mediation factors for each type of dispute.

1. Special factors in mediating sexual harassment claims. Undoubtedly, sexual harassment claims are among the most volatile and sensitive employment

Chapter 19
Special Factors in the Mediation of Miscellaneous Substantive Areas

---

law disputes. The claimant, sometimes at great risk, reports an incident or incidents. The claims are often vehemently denied by the alleged offender. In certain instances, the alleged offender characterizes the claims as fabrications, or as misinterpretations by the claimant of purely innocent conduct. While many corporations, to their credit, have sponsored internal seminars on sexual harassment for their employees, a clear understanding of what is and is not sexual harassment sometimes does not exist.

(1) **Claimant's interests.** In a case of probable sexual harassment, the victim has to make many difficult choices. Often the offender is in a position of power and control. Not surprisingly, the victim fears that reporting the harassment might result in loss of job, humiliation, isolation, and impairment of future career development or earning capacity. In the American work place, many sexual harassment victims do not make reports in order to avoid such potential consequences.

On the other hand, sexual harassment claims are sometimes made that are not supportable either because the conduct does not meet the elements of sexual harassment or because the conduct did not occur. The concept of a pure fabrication is a sensitive issue. We all recall, prior to the legislative changes in our rape laws, that many rape victims did not report such incidents because they feared they would be humiliated, accused of lying, or accused of "asking for it." Regrettably, many incidents of rape are still not reported even today for these reasons. Nonetheless, fabricated complaints are sometimes made, which puts the alleged offender in the position of proving a negative.

Obviously, rape and sexual harassment are different things, but they are similar in the sense that both involve coercion, the absence of consent, and un-wanted conduct.

In the work place, peer pressure functions in many ways. Certain female co-employees, out of a desire to fit into a male controlled work place, may be highly critical of the claimant. Such female co-employees' reactions may vary from "she just can't take a joke" to "she brought it on herself and asked for it" to "she is just lying." Female co-employees may criticize the claimant's choice of clothes (her dress was too short), the claimant's verbal language, or the claimant's body language around the alleged offender. Most office managers are well aware of the office rumor mill.

Further, co-employees may seize on remarks made by the complainant regarding her personal life that have nothing to do with the reported incident.

The point is that the claimant may have a legitimate fear of isolation from her co-employees. To be sure, many co-employees will be sympathetic and supportive, but the claimant will undoubtedly suffer some isolation and will be aware that she is being talked about in certain peer circles.

The claimant's fears regarding management response are more obvious. The claimant fears management will discount or disbelieve her report, that reprisal is likely, and that even if her report is validated that her future growth within the business will be limited.

(2) **Alleged offenders and their interests.** Three classes of alleged offenders exist: the true offender who intentionally engaged in the conduct; the alleged offender who did not understand that his conduct was unappreciated, harmful, and actionable; and the innocent alleged offender whose conduct was either not actionable or who engaged in no harassment at all.

The true offender has a multiplicity of fears and interests. The true offender will be concerned about job retention and future growth within the business. He will fear that such a black mark will affect his employability outside the business. He will be concerned about his personal exposure, and will fear isolation and disapproval within the work place. The true offender, especially if he is married, will fear the impact of the claim on his personal life away from the office.

The offender who did not appreciate that his conduct was unwanted or actionable fears all of the above, but his interests and responses to the claim are to some extent different than the true offender. Many offenders within this class are sincerely apologetic and startled to learn that their conduct was either wrong or harmful to the claimant. Such offenders often want to "make things right," apologize, indicate they have learned an important lesson, and request forgiveness. On the other hand, many offenders within this group, because they did not understand their conduct was wrongful, engage in denial. Such offenders often either take the position that nothing happened or that the claimant either misunderstood or is lying. The fear of an adverse management response or a devastating personal consequence enforces the denial mechanism.

The third class of alleged offender, the truly innocent, while also fearing all of the above, is the most difficult to deal with. Not surprisingly, the truly innocent accused's primary interest is exoneration and vindication. Such individual wants to suffer no consequence because of the invalid report. He wants to experience no harm to his employment situation or personal life. A truly innocent accused is often angry, profoundly upset, and interested in not only exoneration, but also vindication.

In light of these three classes, management may respond differently.

(3) **Management response to the true offender.** For the true offender, a proper management response would be any or all of the following:

(a) Termination, both as a sanction for the offender and as evidence of management's enforcement of a no sexual harassment policy.

(b) Additional internal education to minimize future occurrences.

(c) Support, assistance, and counseling for the victim.

(4) **Proper management response to the "unintentional" offender.**

(a) Some sanction, including demotion, termination, transfer, suspension, etc.

(b) Additional internal education and specific education for the offender.

(c) Support, assistance, and counseling for the victim.

(5) Proper management response to the innocent accused.

(a) Recorded and written exoneration.

(b) Support, assistance, and counseling for the accused.

(c) Some sanction, including demotion, termination, transfer, or suspension for the claimant.

From a mediation vantage point, the interests described above must be identified to attain resolution. But perhaps more importantly, a mediator, as a result of the process, should attempt to identify what class of sexual harassment case she is dealing with. Depending upon the class of case, the options for resolution may be very different.

As with family law cases, the imbalance of power issue is very real in mediating sexual harassment cases and the mediator must be very aware of this. By "aware," I mean the mediator cannot lose neutrality by overcompensating to "even out" the imbalance. Rather, the mediator should recognize that a perceived imbalance exists and that the process itself should never be perceived as coercive.

In conclusion, mediation is highly appropriate for sexual harassment cases. Mediation permits necessary venting of deep feelings and emotions in such cases, but also permits creative options and solutions. Equally important, mediation can help accomplish the desirable goals of saving on litigation costs and giving the parties closure on a problem that has adversely affected their morale and productivity.

2. Special factors in mediating discrimination claims. General mediation principles apply to the mediation of discrimination claims, as do many of the special factors that apply to the mediation of sexual harassment claims. Discrimination claims, of course, may be based upon race, age, and gender.

A few special factors appear to be unique to this class of cases, however, and they are as follows:

Chapter 19
Special Factors in the Mediation of Miscellaneous Substantive Areas

---

(1) **A cause interest.** Beyond the relief she is seeking, the claimant often sees her claim as being part of the larger cause of eliminating or calling attention to racial, age, or sex discrimination. Discrimination, when it occurs, is a pernicious societal problem, and bringing a proper claim is but one way to address it. However, the successful mediation of a discrimination claim must necessarily focus on this case in particular.

(2) **Policy interest.** The employer likely has an internal policy prohibiting discrimination and may perceive the claim to be an affront upon the policy, which is in fact enforced. As such, the defense of the claim can become the defense of the policy.

(3) **Confidentiality interest.** The employer, for a variety of reasons, may have a keen interest in avoiding publicity regarding alleged discriminatory practices.

Because of societal disapproval of discrimination, employers generally are prone to deny any discrimination occurred. Of course the employer may be right — no discrimination did take place in this instance.

Discrimination cases are both difficult to prove and difficult to defend. Typically, such cases are very labor and cost intensive, and the interests described above often make a confidential settlement good for both sides of the dispute.

3. **Special factors in mediating wrongful discharge cases.** This class of employment dispute, while including certain non-monetary interests, usually focuses on economic interests. The claimant, of course, is often interested in being compensated for the loss of income for a specified term of employment, but in many instances the claimant may also see the termination as a real obstacle to future employment and earning capacity. Claimants almost always feel this way when they have left long-standing secure jobs (usually later in their careers) and relocated geographically to take what they believed to be career-advancing positions.

Chapter 19
Special Factors in the Mediation of Miscellaneous Substantive Areas

---

The defense of a wrongful discharge usually involves assertions that the termination was warranted and that the claimant has made no effort to mitigate damages by finding new employment since the discharge.

Beyond economic interests, therefore, reputational/employability interests are often important issues in the mediation of such disputes.

Rather than additional special factors, I have listed here options beyond economic solutions that may help to meet these interests described above.

(1) The claimant may have a very real interest in obtaining a letter of reference that is at least neutral. Such a letter meets the interest of future employability.

(2) The claimant may need assistance in finding new employment. An employer may have an internal mechanism to provide assistance or may be willing to pay for an external support service.

(3) While also economic, the claimant may need help with relocation, either back to where she came from or to a new job destination.

(4) The claimant may have a real interest in having her employment record corrected if in fact there are inaccuracies.

(5) The claimant may have an interest in being released from a non-compete agreement that was executed as a condition of employment.

(6) The claimant may have an interest in an expression of regret.

As stated in an earlier chapter, identifying and meeting non-monetary interests are not only keys to resolution, but also affect monetary interests and settlement outcomes.

Mediation does work favorably in almost any employment dispute situation, but these cases seem to do much better *very early* in the litigation process. As always, attitudes harden over time and the litigation costs themselves may become an impediment to a consensual resolution.

Chapter 20

Using Multiple ADR Procedures

One of the initial premises of this book is that mediation as a form of alternative dispute resolution, no matter how effective, was never designed or intended to replace our trial system. Certain cases will always have to be tried, regardless of whether an ADR procedure is used. Further, because mediation is by far the most favored ADR form, this book is intended to help you as a lawyer understand that process and to assist you in translating your legal experience most effectively into the mediation setting.

Mediation, as you now understand it, is not a decision-rendering ADR process. While the mediator in separate caucus may go through a rigorous strength/weakness analysis with each party and assist the parties in objectively evaluating the case, the mediator will never suggest who wins or loses on a particular issue or the entire case. But there are cases in which a non-binding decision would be helpful — either to assist the parties in their direct negotiations or to permit a more effective mediation if such independent negotiations fail.

§20.1 Using ADR Tools

My first hope is that you will appreciate that ADR, along with litigation, independent negotiations, and informal settlement conferences, is a tool that is part of a much larger problem-solving toolbox. No process is perfect or beyond question. No process is a panacea. Your goal, on behalf of your client, is to obtain a fair, cost-effective, and timely solution to your client's problem. The only difference today, as opposed to five years ago, is that you have a wider variety of conflict resolution tools at your fingertips. You should also recall that ADR was intended to obtain more cost-effective resolutions of disputes — not to escalate costs. As often as ADR may be successful, the reality is that ADR may not be appropriate for a particular case. The parties to whom the dispute belongs have an unalienable right to decide to go to trial. The ardent proponents of ADR must never lose sight of that important truth.

Before continuing, I need to summarize briefly the remaining four ADR procedures (and a fifth unofficial form). All of the remaining forms are procedures in which a *non-binding* decision is rendered, save and except for arbitration, in which the parties may stipulate in writing in advance to be bound by the award. Otherwise, arbitration awards are non-binding as well.

1. **Arbitration.** Arbitration is a process in which a lone arbitrator or three-person arbitration panel hears an abbreviated summary of the evidence and renders an award on liability, damages, or both. Evidence is typically presented in narrative form by each counsel, although witnesses may be sworn and an abbreviated direct and cross-examination performed by each counsel. The rules of evidence are relaxed. The arbitration panel, sometimes with input from all counsel, sets the time parameters for each side. In certain contractually based arbitrations, certain rules (i.e., American Arbitration Association, National Association of Security Dealers) may apply. Again, the arbitration award is non-binding unless the parties stipulate in writing in advance or have contractually agreed to be so bound.

The theory behind arbitration is that the parties, once apprised of an impartial panel's view, will have a basis for more productive negotiations. Of course, the parties may elect to ignore the panel's award.

2. **Moderated settlement conference.** The moderated settlement conference is a decision-rendering procedure very similar to arbitration, but less structured and with more interaction between the panelists, counsel, and the parties. Typically, a moderated settlement conference panel consists of three attorneys who hear an abbreviated presentation from each side, ask questions, and then render a non-binding decision on liability, damages, or both.

Again, as with arbitration, the premise is that the panel's decision will assist the parties in more constructive negotiations.

3. **Mini-trial.** In this decision-rendering ADR procedure, either a retired or sitting judge hears an abbreviated presentation of the evidence and renders a non-binding judgment on liability, damages, or both.

The premise behind the mini-trial is similar to that of arbitration and the moderated settlement conference. The only difference is that the parties may (or may not) give greater credence to the judgment of a respected judge.

4. **Summary jury trial.** In a summary jury trial, each side puts on an abbreviated summary of its case to six jurors selected from the jury roster. The jurors do not know and are not told that their verdict on liability and damages is purely *advisory*. Interestingly, most summary jury panels, despite the fact that evidence and testimony is presented narratively and summarily, do *not* know, until they are told, that a "normal" trial has not occurred (an amazing comment about the public's understanding of our legal system).

The premise behind this decision-rendering ADR form is that the parties get a better read as to what six representative jurors might do in their case.

Of course, parties who opt for such a procedure (even though the jury's decision is non-binding) must live and die with the verdict for purposes of the negotiations that will ensue after the summary jury panel renders its verdict.

5. **Med-arb.** The sixth, "unofficial" (although probably official to some) form of ADR is a hybrid called med-arb. This process, not surprisingly, blends together mediation and arbitration. The theory is that if the neutral can attain a consensual resolution through mediation, the matter is closed. But if the mediation process fails to produce an agreement, the neutral puts on his arbitration hat and renders a non-binding award that is designed to trigger more productive negotiations.

Admittedly, the concept is both seductive and creative, but in my admittedly very opinionated (albeit respectful) view, such a process seems flawed.

The concept of mediation is to empower the parties, facilitate a discussion, and create an environment conducive to consensual and self-determined resolution. The

Chapter 20
Using Multiple ADR Procedures

mediator is the catalyst. But ultimately, the parties uniquely possess responsibility to settle or not. The mediator is not present to let the parties off the responsibility hook.

The arbitration process is not as dynamic and interactive. Parties delegate responsibility to the panel to answer ultimate questions. In arbitration, the parties do not participate as actively as they do in mediation and do not determine their own fate.

I suppose it is a cynical, personal view to suggest that most human beings would prefer to delegate responsibility to a third party than to determine their fates. In essence, our legal system accomplishes just that. On the other hand, mediation participants bravely accept responsibility based on their determined views that a self-determined, consensual resolution is preferable.

Having stated that, the objection to the med-arb concept is based on human nature. Knowing the mediator may turn into an arbitrator, aren't most people likely to hold out or restrict their negotiations until such time as the mediator, now acting as arbitrator, rules? Or, to be objective and fair, does it work the other way? Are participants, fearful of the award, more likely to work harder to negotiate their own settlement and avoid such an award?

Well, the mediator in me feels better. Both premises have been stated. Maybe one's assessment of human nature affects one's view of the med-arb process. Typically, I am far more optimistic. But in more than 1,200 mediations, I have always felt (based on expressed words and implications) that the parties would love for me to render the opinion. Of course, their desire for such a ruling might change dramatically depending upon the opinion.

§20.2 Combining Forms

Now, armed with and aware of all ADR forms (and despite your absolute bias in favor of mediation), in what instances would you use other ADR forms and when and how might you combine ADR forms?

Chapter 20
Using Multiple ADR Procedures

Subject to the objection of the more scholarly, most (not all, of course) civil law-suits may be broken down into the following global categories:

1. Cases in which liability *and* damages are disputed.

2. Cases in which liability is virtually admitted, but damages are in dispute.

3. Cases in which liability is disputed, but if liability is found damages are not subject to serious dispute.

4. Cases that uniquely turn on an issue or issues of law.

5. Cases in which an absolute defensive bar (limitations, immunity, etc.), if successful, will totally eviscerate the plaintiff's claims.

Assume, for the sake of argument, that mediation will work successfully for all five categories. But in analyzing the respective categories, you will note that category four (cases that uniquely turn on an issue or issues of law) and category five (cases in which an absolute defensive bar is asserted) almost beg for an ADR mechanism that renders a non-binding decision or award. In these two categories, arbitration, moderated settlement conference, and mini-trial are logical preliminary ADR steps. The parties may need an "answer" to the legal question or to the validity of a defensive bar before they are able to negotiate.

And if independent negotiations in the wake of such a decision or award are unsuccessful, the parties are perfectly free to have the matter mediated. In such instances, the chances of a successful mediated resolution are enhanced because of the prior non-binding decision. Certainly, such decision may be re-visited during mediation; nonetheless, the parties start the mediation process with a "leg up" because a ruling by a neutral body has already been made.

The issue is: "Do the parties need a ruling before they will be able to negotiate?" If so, certain ADR procedures may meet that need.

Chapter 20
Using Multiple ADR Procedures

In conclusion, ADR itself provides a multiplicity of conflict resolution tools, which, of course, supplement trial and independent negotiation tools. From the lawyer's perspective, the only limitation is the lack of creativity.

From the other end, counsel may both decide that a case needs to be tried. The court or the jury renders a decision. One or both sides elect to appeal. No rule bars mediation after the jury renders a verdict or the court enters a judgment. Both sides are at risk pending appeal. But with the benefit of a verdict or a judgment, both sides may be in a better position to use mediation in an effort to resolve the dispute. Of course, by the time the trial is over, substantial costs have been incurred. But, the attendant risk and possibility of re-trial may make mediation a very appealing (pardon the pun) option.

Chapter 21

Building an ADR Practice

"If you build it, they will come."
— Field of Dreams

"To litigate is human. To mediate is divine."
— Lanier High School
Peer Mediation Class, Austin

"Just do it."
— Nike

§21.1 Background

Eleven years ago, when I first became involved in the ADR movement, the idea of writing a chapter on building an ADR practice would have been patently absurd. In truth, those of us who were pioneers in the ADR movement were motivated by the belief that ADR would provide necessary relief to an overburdened civil justice system and to consumers, both corporate and individual, who were frustrated by the tremendous costs and delays associated with the litigation process. While we perceived that economic realities would fuel the ADR revolution, we did not consider that the success of the ADR movement would result in the creation of one of the most dynamic practice areas of the past fifty years.

I now receive 10-15 telephone calls per week from lawyers across the country who are interested in developing an ADR practice.

I will confess, despite having served as a mediator in more than 1,200 cases and having created many institutional ADR training programs, that I am a bit uneasy writing what might be considered a guide to the development of a commercial ADR practice.

Chapter 21
Building an ADR Practice

Before we begin, you should consider why you want to create and build an ADR practice. If the primary reason for developing such a practice is economic, I would submit that the motivation is questionable and that your success as an ADR practitioner will be limited as a result.

Regrettably, abuses are already beginning to infiltrate the ADR practice. Some mediators are demanding and receiving excessive fees. As you are aware, ADR was in part predicated upon the notion that the process would provide a cost-effective alternative to litigation. I have heard of several mediators who are charging more than $500 per hour per party. While the mediator's total fee in such an in-stance may well be a mere fraction of the potential litigation costs, I find such a practice to be wholly inconsistent with the ADR concept.

Other mediators are adjusting up their rates based upon the amount in controversy. The fact that a claimant is making a $7 million demand may mean many things. The case may be worth $7 million. The case may be worth nothing. The case may be worth something in between. But the initial demand, simply because it is made, should not justify double, triple, or quadruple fees.

Finally, some courts, in jurisdictions in which statutes permit, are ordering parties into mediation on the court's motion *and* directing the parties to a particular mediator. Assuming non-consensual mediation is to occur, the parties should have the absolute right to select the mediator (based on quality, reputation, experience, and cost).

In my view, the economic woes confronting this country have had a substantial negative impact on the practice of law. ADR should not become monetary substitute for those practice areas that have been eviscerated as a result of the economic decline.

In short, this chapter is for the reader whose interest in ADR is a philosophical professional belief in the process. I am not suggesting that ADR is like a religion that requires an expression of belief, but I am suggesting that ADR was and is a

Chapter 21
Building an ADR Practice

result of a philosophical and professional commitment to the process, its value to our civil justice system, and its value to the consumers of legal services.

The remainder of this chapter, as is my custom, will be a practical, step-by-step guide to the development of a successful ADR practice.

§21.2 Education and Training

Regardless of whether the ADR statute in your jurisdiction (assuming you have such a statute) provides minimum educational and training requirements, the first step in developing an ADR practice is to receive necessary training and education.

With no disrespect to my arbitration colleagues, I think it is fair to say that mediation is and will remain the dominant and preferred ADR form. In Texas, for example, the Alternative Dispute Resolution Procedures Act provides for mediation, arbitration, moderated settlement conference, mini-trial, and summary jury trial. In the three years the Act has been in effect, I would estimate that 80% of the ADR practiced in Texas is mediation, 15% is arbitration, and the remaining 5% is divided evenly between the other three forms. Therefore, a lawyer who wants to build an ADR practice will very likely do so by being trained as a mediator.

In terms of training and education, I would recommend the following steps:

   1.   Through the ABA, your state bar, or your local bar, you should take a general ADR course and become familiar with all ADR forms, even if you intend only to mediate, because it is undeniably true that other ADR forms may be better suited to particular kinds of cases. For instance, you may find that a matter that is presented to you as a mediator might be handled better through a moderated settlement conference process. If you are educated in all ADR forms, you will be in a position to make such evaluations.

   2.   Again, through the ABA, your state bar, your local bar, or private training groups, you should receive *at least* 40 hours of mediation training. Because of the mediation boom, training programs are appearing everywhere. You must be careful in your selection of the training program. You should determine the qualifi-

Chapter 21
Building an ADR Practice

cations of the trainers, whether the program is accredited and by whom, the type of training offered, and the references of local lawyers in your area who have received the training. Call lawyers who have received the training and obtain their candid impressions of the program.

3.   As a corollary, I would recommend taking an extensive seminar on negotiation strategies and techniques. Such courses are offered by state, local, and national bars, but many superior seminars are offered by law schools across the country. In a way, mediation is a supervised negotiation. While negotiation courses are now offered in law schools, they were virtually non-existent for those of us who went to law school in the early 1970's or before. Most lawyers have a very limited understanding of the negotiation process. If you will in essence preside over negotiations, you will be well served by upgrading your understanding of the negotiation process.

4.   Education and training does not end with the attainment of minimum education and training requirements. You should make a commitment to take annual advanced ADR/mediation training or techniques courses. You will find, as with any area of practice, that the training process never ends.

5.   Self-study is also useful. Many excellent new publications on ADR exist and are worth reading.

§21.3 Participation in Bar ADR Sections

Most ADR practitioners are very involved in local bar, state bar, or national bar sections. These sections offer educational enhancement, consider ethical and practical ADR issues, and provide a collegial forum for ADR practitioners to get together and learn from each other. Further, such sections provide such necessary public functions as ensuring that ADR practices are not abusive or unethical, and implementing pro bono ADR programs. ADR practitioners, like those in any other area of practice, should be willing to make a pro bono commitment such as providing mediation services for indigents, participation in local settlement weeks, or setting up peer mediation programs in junior high and high schools.

Chapter 21
Building an ADR Practice

Of course, participation in an ADR section gets the word out in your legal community of your interest and expertise in the ADR area.

§21.4 Settlement Week Participation

Many local bar associations across the country, in conjunction with the courts, sponsor a settlement week once or twice a year.

Settlement week, as you are probably aware, is a week in which the local bar trains and provides volunteer mediators and pending civil cases are mediated. During settlement week, the courthouse in essence shuts down and no cases are tried.

Settlement week affords an opportunity for aspiring mediators to gain experience actually mediating disputes and to provide a good public service. Settlement week is a public-oriented way to demonstrate your commitment and interest in an ADR practice.

§21.5 Apprenticeships

Many mediation training programs require that one observe three mediations with experienced mediators to attain certification. Regardless of any such requirement, a brief apprenticeship is an excellent idea.

Obviously, an aspiring mediator will learn a great deal from observing an experienced mediator in action. Second, you will make contacts with the existing mediation community that will prove valuable in the future.

§21.6 Creating a Local ADR Society

As ADR practices begin to develop in your area, forming a local ADR/Mediation Society that consists of trained and committed neutrals makes good sense.

In Austin, for example, the Austin Mediators Society's goals are to engage in continuing education and training for ADR practitioners, to develop public-oriented ADR projects, to work with the state and federal courts on ADR projects, and to provide a collegial forum in which ADR practitioners may assemble and share experiences. At each monthly meeting, a society member offers a paper and presents a speech on an ADR topic.

The Austin Mediators Society includes lawyers, judges, law professors, psychologists, and other trained neutrals. Such societies enhance qualitative excellence in a local ADR community and can help in avoiding the regrettable political infighting that may occur in a developing ADR community. Further, such societies provide the opportunity for cross-referrals when conflicts occur or a matter falls outside of a member's expertise, and they help to legitimize ADR in a given community.

§21.7 Publications and Presentations

As you begin to develop expertise as an ADR practitioner, you may consider becoming a regular speaker on ADR topics for your local and state bar. Beyond providing helpful information to members of your bar, this will help you be identified as someone committed to an ADR practice.

You must remember that your "market," for the most part, is your fellow bar members. You must further remain aware that many members of your local or state bar have a minimal understanding of ADR and its benefits. Initially, you will find that your papers and presentations are directed primarily towards what ADR is and the benefits of using ADR procedures. Ultimately, you will find that your papers and presentations focus on ADR techniques and such things as mediation advocacy. Many lawyers do not know how to translate their litigation expertise into ADR forums. You may be able to help them understand how to do so.

§21.8 Public Projects

Lawyers who develop ADR practices should be as committed to public-oriented projects as they were to performing pro bono work. Among the possible public-oriented projects are:

    1. Developing peer mediation programs in the local junior high and high schools.

2. Developing pro bono mediation projects for the courts, especially in the areas of domestic relations and discovery related issues.

3. Working with state agencies and administrative bodies to develop institutionalized ADR programs.

Such ADR public projects help legitimize ADR within your community. More important, such projects demonstrate that ADR practitioners are committed to public service. The ADR movement will succeed, in my opinion, only if it makes public service a priority.

§21.9 Letters to Colleagues

You need to let the lawyers whom you have dealt with know that you have made a commitment to developing an ADR practice. I am not advocating a mass mail-out to members of your local bar. Rather, I am suggesting that you prepare a letter outlining your experience, training, and commitment, and mail that letter to lawyers you know or should know.

In such a letter, I would suggest you include:

1. Your prior experience in other legal areas.

2. Your training in ADR areas.

3. Your experience in ADR practice.

4. The reasons you have decided to engage in an ADR practice.

5. Your fee structures.

Such letters are usually very well received by your colleagues and will generate some initial mediation referrals. And if you mediate these cases completely and professionally, your colleagues will spread the word about your mediation skill and expertise.

Chapter 21
Building an ADR Practice

§21.10 Institutional Seminars

Many institutional groups, both private and public, are very interested in learning more about ADR and its benefits. You might consider putting on a seminar for any of the following groups:

1. Your local bar.

2. Your local chamber of commerce.

3. Your local small business association.

4. Private corporations in your area.

5. Civic groups.

I would further suggest that at such seminars you provide something written describing ADR procedures and their benefits. Also, such seminars are most effective when you adopt an interactive teaching model. You should consider, for example, creating a hypothetical dispute and having attendees role play as disputants and the mediator.

Initially, you will offer such seminars on a no-pay basis. You will discover that there is a tremendous interest in the public/business sector for information regarding ADR and mediation and you should have little difficulty attracting an audience. I would suggest that in the first two years of your ADR practice you attempt to offer such mini-seminars on a quarterly basis.

§21.11 ADR Newsletters

Once you have begun to mediate on a regular basis, you have begun to develop, perhaps without knowing it, a "client list." Your client list includes those attorneys who have appeared before you at mediations.

You may elect to prepare a focused ADR newsletter and mail it on a quarterly basis to those lawyers on your client list. Alternatively, you might consider sending copies of articles you publish to those lawyers on your client list.

Chapter 21
Building an ADR Practice

Such mailings, beyond any marketing purpose, are of real educational value to those lawyers who are only beginning to learn how to represent clients effectively in a mediation environment. Among the topics that may be of special value to lawyers who represent parties in a mediation are:

1. A mediation checklist that covers the process from beginning to end. I have attached a copy of the checklist I use as Appendix A, pages 183-194.

2. How to break impasses.

3. Negotiation strategies and techniques.

4. Preparing a party for a mediation.

5. Special factors that exist in certain types of mediations; i.e., medical mal-practice, family law, etc.

6. Identifying non-monetary interests present in a dispute.

§21.12 Creating an ADR Section in a Law Firm and Law Firm ADR Politics

Some of you will be attempting to develop an ADR practice in a law firm, often in the midst of a group of litigators. Is it possible to develop an ADR practice in a mid-size or large firm with a heavy litigation practice? The answer, happily, is "yes." The rub, of course, is how to make your colleagues comfortable with the notion. You might consider the following steps:

1. Involve your firm in your effort from the outset. You will need to educate your firm on *both* the ADR process and the economic benefits of such a practice.

2. Everyone is aware of the economic trends in the practice of law — insti-tutional efforts to cut litigation costs, for instance. The law firms that will succeed in the next century will be as qualitatively excellent in ADR as they are in litigation. Clients will demand such expertise. Circulate published articles supporting the use of ADR to your colleagues.

3. A law firm ADR commitment is an effective marketing tool for the firm. You distinguish your firm from others that have not made such a commitment. Your firm brochure should emphasize your ADR commitment. Also, your firm may wish to send a letter to its clients outlining the firm's ADR policy, expertise, and commitment.

4. Create articles or seminar topics that may be of benefit to your colleagues' clients.

5. If your firm is not ready to take the step of creating a formal ADR section, create an informal section. Involve lawyers from all areas of your firm in the effort. Your colleagues will better understand the global benefits of such a practice if they are involved in it. Further, some of your colleagues may decide to get training and develop their own ADR practices.

6. Develop a specific plan and a realistic timetable for developing your ADR practice. Your first year will be devoted to training and public service work. You will see a development in your practice by the second year. In the third year, your practice should be self-sustaining.

7. Do not abandon your current practice until you know that you are committed to an ADR practice. Most of us who have developed an ADR practice feel we have the best possible practice, but you may find that ADR does not suit your personality or that there is no market for an ADR practice in your area.

8. Assuming your efforts are successful, consider creating and establishing a law firm ADR policy that will be communicated to clients.

9. Keep your colleagues informed as to your progress.

I created my ADR practice in a large law firm with a heavy insurance defense practice. I found my colleagues to be very supportive and willing to help in any way possible.

Chapter 21
Building an ADR Practice

§21.13 Marketing in Communities Without Qualified Neutrals

ADR practices, not surprisingly, develop first in large metropolitan areas. As a result, many mid-size and small cities do not have qualified neutrals to mediate or arbitrate disputes. On the other hand, these same cities may have overcrowded litigation dockets. Also, many of these smaller cities have insulated legal communities in which all the lawyers know each other. As a result, such lawyers may be un-willing to "share their secrets" with one of their own even if a local lawyer receives the necessary training and is subject to absolute confidentiality.

In terms of expanding your practice to such venues, you might consider:

    1. Putting on an ADR seminar for the local bar.

    2. Drafting letters to your lawyer acquaintances in the area outlining your ADR experience and your commitment to ADR practice.

You will find after one successful mediation in a city that word travels very fast. The chances are excellent that with this success, you can develop a productive client base in the area.

§21.14 ADR Legislative Efforts

Many states do not have a comprehensive ADR statute. In Texas we have an excellent, comprehensive ADR statute, Civil Practice & Remedies Code §154, *et seq.*, the Alternative Dispute Resolution Procedures Act. See Appendix D, page 235.

In my view, the development of an ADR practice is improved by having a comprehensive ADR statute in place. Your efforts in working on such legislation will underscore your commitment to ADR and be a valuable public service. Also, your work in suggesting constructive amendments to an existing ADR statute, if one is in place, may be helpful.

Some of you may practice in jurisdictions with existing comprehensive ADR statutes. As you are aware, we are only beginning to understand fully the scope and dimensions of ADR issues. Important issues regarding confidentiality, qualifications, certification, and the like may not be fully covered by an existing ADR statute. As such, your continued involvement in the proper development of the ADR law will be of great public benefit.

§21.15 Advertising

Of course, advertising in your local or state bar journal is an option in developing an ADR practice. In my opinion, though, an ADR practice, perhaps more than any other, is developed by word of mouth. A mediator's reputation is built upon experience, maintenance of absolute impartiality and confidentiality, and a strong feeling of trust. Further, the selection of the mediator is probably, from the consumer's perspective, the most important step in the mediation process.

As a result, I think formal advertising is not an especially good idea in the early development of your ADR practice. Once you have your ADR practice in gear, you may evaluate the benefits and costs of such an advertising effort. In the event you elect to advertise, you must draft your ad carefully to avoid making any representations that are false, misleading, or deceptive.

§21.16 Plaintiff/Defense Issues

I was fortunate to have spent seven years litigating cases on the plaintiff's side of the docket and seven years trying cases on the defense side. As a result, I was virtually immune from any question regarding my impartiality or my ability to see and understand both sides of a case. But some of you who are aspiring to develop ADR practices may have spent your entire practice life on one particular side of the docket and may be subject to being considered "too plaintiff oriented" or "too defense oriented."

In your letters to your colleagues in your bar describing your ADR practice, I think you should squarely address this issue and explain how critical the maintenance of your impartiality is to your role. As a mediator, you are not the judge or jury. You are a facilitator. You are required to remain impartial.

Further, as you begin to engage in an ADR practice on a consistent basis, you will find that lawyers on both sides of the docket, if you have in fact been impartial, will be willing to serve as references if this concern comes up in the future.

Chapter 21
Building an ADR Practice

§21.17 Fees

As I stated at the outset of this chapter, ADR was predicated in part on providing cost-effective alternatives to litigation. I think it is critical that you always remain cognizant of this principle throughout your ADR practice.

While I have opinions regarding what I consider to be excessive billing practices, I have no desire to suggest standardized billing practices. I do think, however, that there is a logical and fair way to begin charging for your ADR services. As you gain experience and expertise, you will be the best judge of what may be a fair billing schedule.

Initially, I think an hourly rate structure plus expenses makes sense. Most lawyers are used to hourly rate billing practices. Over a two-year period, my hourly rate went from $150 per hour (*divided* by the parties) to $180 per hour to $220 per hour. Over the next two years, I expect that rate to rest ultimately at $300 per hour. In my opinion, especially given the cost of litigation, $150 per hour per party appears to be fair and reasonable based on the extent of my experience.

Some mediators set fees based on the number of parties or the amount in controversy. I am not certain, beyond the fact that more parties sometimes makes a mediation more complex, that the mere fact that more parties are involved should justify a higher fee. I am equally uncomfortable with the notion that the amount in controversy should create a higher charge. The amount in controversy may be reasonable or unreasonable. No one knows what the ultimate resolution will be prior to the process itself.

Finally, you should invite input regarding your fees from the lawyers who submit cases to you. You should remain open-minded regarding fees and be willing to discuss such matters freely.

§21.18 Office Environment and Facilities

Should you make the commitment to create an ADR practice, you must plan ahead to be certain that you have the office facilities to accommodate it. You will need, at a minimum:

Chapter 21
Building an ADR Practice

---

1. A large conference room for the initial collective session. In certain cases, you may have 30 people at the opening session. Typically, you will find eight to ten people involved in the majority of mediations you do.

2. At least two break-out rooms for your "separate caucuses" with each party. In multi-party cases, you may need three or four rooms. Each room must be acoustically designed to prevent anyone in any one room from hearing anyone in another room. In my office, the caucus rooms are non-contiguous.

3. A writing board or a drawing pad in each room.

4. In most instances, you will have lunches brought in during the mediation. You should arrange in advance with a restaurant or caterer how to handle this efficiently.

5. Coffee, water and soft drinks need to be available in each room.

When the parties and their counsel arrive at your office, they should perceive that you are prepared, organized, and have considered all logistical matters in advance.

§21.19 Develop a Mediation Coordinator

Most legal secretaries or paralegals know little about ADR or how to handle an ADR practice. Therefore, you will need to educate your staff person fully about the ADR process, confidentiality, scheduling, and how you want things to proceed (who goes where) when the parties arrive. You also want your staff person to be knowledgeable when counsel call to schedule mediations.

In my office, my wonderful mediation coordinator does the following:

1. Schedules all my mediations.

2. Sends out standard letters regarding what information I require from the parties in advance of the session.

3. Greets the parties when they arrive.

4. Explains to the parties when they arrive how the office is set up.

5. Provides information regarding telephone procedures.

6. Obtains lunch orders.

7. Prepares final bills, subject to my modifications and monitors collections.

I cannot emphasize enough how important it is having a qualified and knowledgeable coordinator. In many instances, you will be in a mediation or out of town mediating. You will need someone who understands your practice and who will mind the shop.

§21.20 Emerging ADR Practice Areas

An ADR practice, at least as we currently know it, involves primarily serving as a mediator or an arbitrator. But, as with any new practice area, we are only beginning to understand the scope and dimensions of such a practice. By the year 2100, I believe that ADR practice may include any of the following:

1. Consultant work with institutional clients to create ADR programs.

2. Consultant work with state agencies to create ADR programs.

3. Consultant work to train a body of in-house neutrals for a large corporation or agency.

4. Co-mediation teams who will tackle policy issues and mega-litigation matters.

5. ADR training programs directed to specific professional groups such as physicians, engineers, etc.

Simply stated, an ADR practice is by no means static or self-limiting. Further, given the ADR explosion, the ADR practice suffers from a future shock syndrome in the sense that the practice, as we know it, enlarges on an almost weekly basis.

Chapter 21
Building an ADR Practice

§21.21 Conclusions

Despite the ideas I have suggested in this chapter, I believe that a few tried and true things are required in any kind of successful ADR practice. First, you must be committed to doing whatever it takes to become qualified as an ADR practitioner. Second, you must consistently upgrade your education in this practice area and acquire more skills. Third, you must prepare fully for each mediation and treat every mediation as if it were the most important one. Fourth, you should always remain open to constructive criticism and new ideas.

Should you make the commitment to a qualitatively excellent and highly professional ADR practice, you will no doubt succeed — and you will also find the practice to be professionally rewarding and personally enriching. As you succeed, you will have a significant impact upon the administration of justice by assisting in facilitating early, sensible, and cost-effective resolutions of disputes.

Chapter 22

Looking Forward — the Future of ADR

Over the past three years, mediation in Texas has become a standard part of a practitioner's professional life. Eleven years ago, when ADR was first being discussed seriously in Texas, none of us who were part of that pioneering group would have thought the movement would have exploded as rapidly as it has. But today, if you take a commuter airplane from Austin to Houston and listen, you will find as many lawyers are going to attend a mediation as are going to a deposition or a court appearance. Times have changed.

The mediation profession, and it is a profession, must remain ever vigilant that this mediation explosion does not result in neutrals straying away from the guiding principles of ADR or failing to monitor their new profession to ensure that qualitatively excellent services are provided. Serious and difficult issues are ahead for the mediation profession and for our judicial system in terms of its use of ADR.

§22.1 Mandatory Use of ADR

Under the Texas ADR statute, a court on its own motion can compel the parties to engage in an ADR procedure. In Houston and Dallas, some courts are routinely exercising such power and referring many cases into mediation. Of course, the issue is whether the use of ADR should be a voluntary and consensual act by the parties or whether parties should be forced, sometimes kicking and screaming, into an ADR procedure.

Courts have a legitimate interest in moving their dockets, but shotgun and indiscriminate use of mandatory referrals as a docket-clearing mechanism will create an anti-mediation backlash, inspire negative attitudes, and decrease the chances of successful resolutions in those cases that are mandatorily ordered into mediation.

Chapter 22
Looking Forward — the Future of ADR

Despite my passionate belief in the efficacy of ADR, I think that ADR should remain largely voluntary and consensual, with only selective and cautious use of mandatory referrals.

But if mandatory referrals are not made selectively, both lawyers and parties will develop a negative feeling for ADR, and their participation may become half-hearted. A party may wish to have his day in court and might have absolutely no interest in settlement. This party may well resent a mandatory referral designed to explore settlement and consider it coercive. ADR was never intended to be a coercive process; in fact, a primary theme of ADR is its consensual nature. It seems paradoxical not to have the right to consent to the use of a process that, once entered, requires the parties' consent.

Cost is another concern with the issue of mandatory ADR referrals. ADR neutrals charge for their services — and properly so. Almost always, the cost of an ADR process pales in comparison to the litigation costs already expended or to be expended. Nonetheless, a party may want to expend its limited resources on the litigation and not an ADR procedure.

In many instances, courts are not only making mandatory referrals to mediation, but also ordering the parties to use a particular mediator. First, if the parties are forced into mediation, they should have the absolute right to select their own mediator. Second, the parties should not be forced to use a mediator who charges fees that may be significantly greater than other mediators. Third, mandatory referrals to a particular mediator may create the appearance of judicial impropriety.

I think there is a happy middle ground (very mediator-like, don't you think?) that achieves the courts' desired goals of reducing case loads and yet permits ADR to remain a largely voluntary process. I would suggest the following procedure:

1.   After all parties have answered the lawsuit, the court sends out an ADR questionnaire to all counsel, along with an information sheet explaining ADR procedure.

2. The questionnaire is designed to get all counsel's input as to whether ADR is desired, what ADR procedure is desired, when such a procedure would be appropriate, and specific reasons if an ADR procedure is opposed.

3. The questionnaire must be signed by all counsel *and* all parties. No hearing or trial date may be set until all questionnaires are returned to the court.

4. Based on the responses, the court may elect to make no ADR referral or specify a time by which the ADR procedure must be attempted.

5. Counsel have the right to agree upon and select a neutral. Should counsel not be able to agree, the court will appoint a neutral.

6. Counsel are required, one week after the ADR procedure, to send a notice of compliance to the court.

7. Should any party object to the referral, it may file a motion and get a hearing on the objection.

The benefits of such an approach are:

• Clients are directly advised of ADR options. Many clients will voluntarily opt for an ADR procedure.

• An ADR procedure will not be implemented too early, before all counsel have the ability to evaluate the case.

• ADR referrals will not be perceived as coercive.

• Parties will have the unfettered right to select a neutral.

• Inappropriate cases will not be involuntarily placed into ADR.

Certainly, the mechanics of such a program need to be fine-tuned and workable with a particular court's administrative approach to cases, but given public support for ADR, one may reasonably expect that parties, if so notified and educated, will try an ADR procedure in at least half of all cases. If so, the case backlog will be reduced without citizens and their counsel feeling forced to enter a procedure in which they have no interest in participating.

§22.2 ADR Litigation

ADR should not be and should never become a new forum for litigation. ADR was designed and intended to create resolutions, not to spawn a new area of litigation. Our district and appellate courts should zealously resist any attempts to permit litigation over ADR proceedings.

Two areas of controversy present themselves in this regard, both of which, in my view, are very easy issues.

1. **Negotiating in good faith.** Does a party to an ADR proceeding have a duty to negotiate "in good faith?" If ordered by the court, pursuant to either a voluntary or involuntary referral, the parties have an absolute obligation to attend, to have the ability to settle the dispute, and to "participate in the process"; i.e., listen, speak, meet with the mediator, etc. *No party is obliged to settle. No court may order the parties to settle.* The words "negotiate in good faith" are junk words and, in my view, dangerous to both sides of the docket.

Assume, going into a mediation, a plaintiff has a demand of $1 million and the defendant has an offer of zero. Conceptually, may the case settle for $1 million? The answer is yes. The plaintiff may, at mediation, persuade the defendant that $1 million is more than fair. Conceptually, may the case settle for zero? The answer is also yes. The plaintiff, as a result of mediation, may realize his case is worthless. Of course, the probabilities of a settlement at either extreme end are not great. The case could settle for $20,000, $150,000, $400,000, $925,000 — you can pick any number you wish. But is the plaintiff's failure to move off of the $1 million bad faith if he participates fully? The answer is no. Is the failure of defendant, if he participates fully, to move off the zero mark bad faith? The answer again is no. Few things in life, as mediators will attest, are black or white. This issue is. No non-binding ADR form may ever force any party to settle. No "law" needs to be made on this topic.

Chapter 22
Looking Forward — the Future of ADR

---

2. Failure to attend or to attend properly. The more difficult issue is whether sanctions should ever be imposed for lack of attendance at an ordered proceeding or lack of proper attendance. The first part of the issue is easy. The second part of the issue is more difficult.

Let's tackle the easy issue first. If the court orders an ADR proceeding and a party wholly fails to appear, an appropriate sanction would be as follows, failing a showing of good cause:

(1) The non-appearing party pays all costs (mediator, attorneys, travel costs, etc.) for the session that was not able to proceed.

(2) The non-appearing party must schedule and appear at a newly designated time and pay the entirety of the mediator's fee.

(3) Failing either of the above, more harsh and traditional sanctions may be ordered.

Even without specific legislation defining the remedy, and there is none, a court's ADR order is like any other order — subject to enforcement by the court. "Good cause" should be defined as such things as reasonably provable illness, family crisis, absence of notice, or unforeseen condition (i.e., car breaks down, flight cancelled due to weather, etc.). As stated, this part of the issue is a "no-brainer."

"Lack of proper attendance" is more difficult. It's the old "authority to settle" bugaboo in a different form.

This issue may be avoided in its entirety if the court's order specifically requires the parties to confer on this issue in advance of the session and reach an accord as to who will attend. The order should further specify that failing an agreement, the parties must confer with the mediator, and, still failing an agreement, resolve who will be required to attend with the court prior to the session. Such "hearings" may be held by telephone conference call. The courts must accept the responsibility, as opposed to dealing with motions regarding lack of "proper attendance."

Again, the guiding principle is: "No ADR litigation or motion practice, except in matters involving no appearance without good cause."

§22.3 Regulation and Certification of Mediators and Neutrals

At the risk of irritating many of my well-intentioned colleagues, my response to the issue of regulating mediators is: (a) avoid creating a new and unnecessary bureaucracy; (b) legislatively set out minimum standards and educational requirements; (c) promulgate a code of ethics; (d) set up an appropriate grievance process; and (e) avoid too much sub-specialization. Family law mediation, however, may well be an exception. Additionally, annual MCLE requirements in ADR should be imposed. Beyond the grievance process, mediators who violate their duties or who are negligent should be subject to lawsuits for such breaches.

§22.4 Mediator Fees

I have already discussed, in Chapter 3, pages 16-19, fee practices that I find abusive. Fee practices by neutrals may not be specifically regulated, just as they may not be with lawyers.

However, fee disputes should be the subject of a grievance mechanism. Courts should allow unfettered selection of mediators because fee structures vary and different types of cases require different kinds of fee structures, but there should be some institutionalized method of dealing with fee disputes outside of the court system. And no matter what fee structure is involved, mediator "contingency" fees should be expressly barred and prohibited.

Mediators perform valuable services and should be fairly compensated; however, the mediation community should not forget that cost-effective resolutions of disputes require fair and reasonable mediator fees.

§22.5 Law School Involvement

Our law schools must become increasingly involved in educating our future lawyers about alternative dispute resolution and, in particular, mediation. Law students will one day be lawyers representing parties to a mediation, mediators themselves,

Chapter 22
Looking Forward — the Future of ADR

or judges who may refer matters into alternative dispute resolution. Further, law students need to be aware of the full range of conflict resolution mechanisms if they are to be able to provide their clients with the full range of options.

Law schools must continue to provide ADR/mediation courses and to integrate such courses fully into the standard law school curriculum.

§22.6 Pro Bono/Public Service Mediation

Just as voluntary pro bono service is an important facet of a lawyer's professional life, a voluntary commitment to pro bono service should also be a part of a mediator's professional identity.

Many citizens, particularly in the family law area, cannot afford the cost of a mediator's services. Certainly dispute resolution centers, which usually charge fees on a sliding scale based on the parties' incomes, meet some of the need for reduced cost mediation services. But dispute resolution centers may not meet the entire need. Private mediators should consider making an ongoing commitment to providing pro bono mediation services.

Further, private mediators, as a form of pro bono service, may consider a variety of forms of public service.

For example, in many states, private mediators are offering mediation training to elementary, junior high, and high school students in order to create peer mediation programs. In such programs, students mediate (successfully) student/student disputes and provide great assistance to their schools. Mediation projects designed to reduce gang violence and mediation projects to assist the elderly or AIDS victims may also be valid public service projects.

§22.7 A Collaborative Mediation Community

Oddly enough, neutrals, who are trained to resolve conflicts, sometimes engage in bitter conflicts with other neutrals. Developing mediation communities may be ripped apart because of differences regarding mediation styles, fees, certification and qualification, or competing professional associations.

Chapter 22
Looking Forward — the Future of ADR

Such conflicts are unfortunate indeed. Mediation communities, by their very definition, should be collaborative and flexible in nature and absolutely dedicated to providing a continuum of mediation services and styles to their local communities. Mediators, from all facets of a mediation community, should find a way to come together. In Austin, we created the Austin Mediators Society for that purpose and to provide our members with continuing mediation education. The society's membership includes private lawyer mediators, non-lawyer mediators, law school professors, dispute resolution center members, and representatives from the judiciary.

For mediation to continue to gain acceptance and to improve qualitatively, neutrals in a mediation community must work together and apply to themselves the principles they communicate to others.

Every mediation is different. We never stop learning. And we should always strive to learn more, develop new techniques, and keep our minds open and flexible to accommodate good change.

In closing, I remain proud and privileged to be a lawyer. I am equally proud and privileged to be a mediator. My hope is that the legal profession and the mediation profession will engage in a continuous dialogue in order to work together efficiently and cooperatively to provide citizens with an array of conflict resolution mechanisms and to assist the administration of justice.

Mediation Checklist

I. Keys to a Successful Mediation

1. _____ Select a qualified mediator

2. _____ Prepare for the mediation

3. _____ Resolve authority to settle issues prior to the mediation

4. _____ Use mediation as soon as is practical

II. Selecting the Mediator

1. _____ At least six years litigation experience or at least six years practical experience in an area in which there is some exposure to litigation matters

2. _____ At least 40 hours of mediation training

3. _____ Actual mediation experience

4. _____ Uses case evaluation/separate caucus method

5. _____ Willing to discuss fee structure

6. _____ Able to provide neutral site for mediation

7. _____ Requires pre-mediation submissions

8. _____ Encourages lawyer participation

9. _____ Willing to reserve adequate time to mediate matter

10._____ Absence of any conflict

III. Pre-Mediation Submission Outline

1. _____ Provide a concise statement of issues and positions

2. _____ Identify strengths and possible weaknesses

3. _____   Provide a chronology

4. _____   Outline negotiations and proposals to date

5. _____   Specify who will be present at the mediation

6. _____   Provide copies of current pleadings

7. _____   Provide copies of pertinent appellate decisions

8. _____   Provide copies of key articles, critical excerpts from depositions, copies of key medical or expert witness reports

9. _____   Tab and index submission

10._____   Place submission in a three-ring binder

11._____   Mark submission as confidential

IV. Client Preparation for Mediation

1. _____   Explain the mediation process

2. _____   Explain the mediator's role

3. _____   Provide a copy of pre-mediation submission

4. _____   Explain your role at mediation and how it will be different from your role in court

5. _____   Explain that the client will actively participate

6. _____   Explain that the mediator may ask client questions

7. _____   Explain the separate caucus

8. _____   Explain benefits of mediation

9. _____   Anticipate initial unrealistic negotiating positions

10._____   Anticipate sensitive issues and formulate strategies to deal with such issues

Appendix A
Mediation Checklist

11._____ Provide the client with the mediator's background

12._____ Objectively evaluate strengths and weaknesses of case with client

13._____ Encourage patience, flexibility, open-mindedness, listening

14._____ Encourage polite, constructive approach

15._____ Anticipate impasses and need to work through impasses

16._____ Discuss authority issues

V. ADR Order

1. _____ Obtain prior to session

2. _____ Include confidentiality reference

3. _____ Include pursuant to ADR statute

4. _____ Include identity of mediator

5. _____ Include date, place, and time for mediation

6. _____ Include allocation of mediation costs

7. _____ Include non-binding

VI. Who Should Attend/Authority to Settle

1. _____ Counsel should attend

2. _____ Party should attend except in *rare* instances and *only* if agreed to in advance by all parties

3. _____ Insurance representative with authority to settle

4. _____ Preferable to have insurance representative with full authority to settle present

5. _____ Should logistical or economic factors make it impractical to have insurance representative with full authority able to attend:

Appendix A
Mediation Checklist

A. _____   Discuss matter with opposing counsel

B. _____   Have local representative with limited authority attend

C. _____   Agree that representative with full authority shall be available by telephone during the session

D. _____   Reduce such agreement to writing

6. _____   In exceptional cases, a critical expert witness may attend

7. _____   In cases in which a structured settlement is anticipated, the structure specialists should attend

VII. Objecting to a Motion to Refer or Overcoming Objections to a Motion to Refer

1. _____   Written objections must be filed within 10 days after receiving a notice of referral

2. _____   Court must find a *reasonable basis* for an objection to a referral

3. _____   "Reasonable basis" is not defined

4. _____   Standard is discretionary

5. _____   "I don't like ADR" is probably not a reasonable basis

6. _____   "Mediation will not work" is probably not a reasonable basis

7. _____   Significant economic hardship might be a reasonable basis

8. _____   Proof that referral is for delay purposes only might be a reasonable basis

9. _____   Proof that the referral is designed for abusive discovery purposes might be a reasonable basis

---

2. _____ Never refer to the other party by first name unless you have asked for permission to do so

3. _____ Never insult or criticize the mediator — especially in the other side's presence

4. _____ Anticipate volatile issues and *never* make comments to the other party that will trigger strong emotional responses

5. _____ Never undermine the other party's or other lawyer's dignity

6. _____ Never engage in theatrics; i.e., getting up to leave, etc.

XI. Collective Session Considerations (After Opening Statements by Lawyers)

1. _____ Have your client prepared to respond to the mediator's questions

2. _____ Have your client prepared to discuss his feelings

3. _____ Have your client prepared to speak in constructive, respectful terms

4. _____ Have your client prepared to express hope that the session will produce an agreement

5. _____ Have your client prepared to express his willingness to listen and work through problems

6. _____ Come prepared to exchange material that is otherwise discoverable

XII. Separate Caucus Phase

1. _____ Parties and counsel are placed in separate rooms and caucus privately with the mediator

2. _____ All communications are confidential save and except what the mediator is authorized to disclose to the party in the other room

3. _____ Initial caucus round typically lasts 30 minutes

Appendix A
Mediation Checklist

4. _____   Subsequent caucus rounds last 10-20 minutes

5. _____   Negotiating process typically begins after second round

6. _____   In the initial caucus, the mediator is attempting the following:

      A. _____   Getting to know the parties better (bonding)

      B. _____   Assessing who is the decision-maker (or makers)

      C. _____   Assessing the personality/negotiating styles of the parties

      D. _____   Mining for economic and non-economic issues

      E. _____   Permitting the expression of strong feelings

      F. _____   Identifying sensitive issues

7. _____   In the second caucus, the mediator is attempting the following:

      A. _____   Leading the parties in an objective evaluation of their case

      B. _____   Having the parties identify the strengths of their case on their own

      C. _____   Having the parties identify the weaknesses of their case on their own

      D. _____   Playing devil's advocate with the parties and assisting the parties in understanding or acknowledging possible weaknesses that the parties may not have listed on their own

8. _____   In caucus round three and thereafter, the mediator is attempting the following:

      A. _____   To get the parties "to dance"; i.e., begin the negotiations

Appendix A
Mediation Checklist

B. _____ To motivate the parties to negotiate reasonably and constructively

C. _____ To work through impasses

D. _____ To persistently force the parties to look at their case objectively

E. _____ To communicate proposals and messages; i.e., the mediator as shuttle diplomat

F. _____ To elect to re-convene the parties if appropriate to work through particular problems

G. _____ To hold a lawyer's caucus if special legal issues arise out of separate caucus

H. _____ To minimize negative reactions to proposals, to identify interests, and to keep the parties working through impasses

XIII. Memorandum of Agreement

1. _____ While not the final settlement documents, the agreement should clearly and specifically outline all terms of the agreement

2. _____ Agreement should be jointly drafted by all counsel so that it is not "one side's" agreement and so that the written agreement clearly reflects the agreement reached

3. _____ Should be signed by all counsel and parties

4. _____ All counsel and parties should receive copies of the fully exe-cuted agreement

XIV. Economic and Non-Economic Interests in Litigation

1. _____ Avoidance of risk

2. _____   Avoidance of delay

3. _____   Avoidance of cost

4. _____   Party's ability to decide own destiny

5. _____   Need to be listened to

6. _____   Need to be understood

7. _____   Integrity

8. _____   Reputation

9. _____   Possible future relationships

10. _____   Acknowledgement of responsibility

11. _____   Apology

12. _____   Sympathy

13. _____   Closure

XV. Impasses

1. _____   Present, often many times, in every mediation

2. _____   Often reflects limited or different negotiating styles of parties

3. _____   Ask "why questions" to overcome impasses; i.e., explain the basis of the proposal and the *needs* that are reflected in a proposal

4. _____   Encourage the other party to categorize needs

5. _____   If at an impasse, forge a new and agreed negotiating pattern

6. _____   Re-visit the other side's weaknesses with the mediator

Appendix A
Mediation Checklist

7. _____ Determine if meeting non-economic interests will help resolve the impasse

8. _____ Be patient. Some negotiators dance fast. Some negotiators dance more slowly

9. _____ Candidly express your frustration and concern regarding impasse to the mediator

Appendix A
Mediation Checklist

XVI. Outline of the Mediation Process

Select the Mediator

§

Enter Mediation Order

§

Pre-Mediation Submission

§

Mediator Introduction

§

Lawyers' Opening Statement

§

Collective Session/Brainstorming

§

Separate Caucus

§

Possible Second Joint Session

§

Possible Lawyers' Caucus

§

Drafting the Agreement

Mediation Notebook

Client: _____

Attorney: _____

Mediation Date: _____

Trial Date: _____

Case No.: _____

Case Name: _____

Mediator: _____

I. Parties:

Plaintiff(s)   Attorney(s)

_____   _____

_____   _____

_____   _____

_____   _____

Defendant(s)   Attorney(s)

_____   _____

_____   _____

_____   _____

_____   _____

Appendix B
Mediation Notebook

_____

Other Parties   Attorney(s)

_____   _____

_____   _____

_____   _____

_____   _____

II. Negotiation History:

First Demand   _____   Date

First Response   _____   Date

Second Demand   _____   Date

Second Response _____   Date

Third Demand   _____   Date

Third Response   _____   Date

III. Discovery Status

_____   No discovery

_____   Discovery partially completed

_____   Discovery substantially completed

_____   Discovery completed

IV. Costs and Expenses

Litigation costs to date_____

Estimated future litigation costs _____

Appendix B
Mediation Notebook

_____

Expenses incurred to date _____

Estimated future expenses _____

V. Posture of The Case

_____ Negligence in dispute

_____ Causation in dispute

_____ Damages in dispute

VI. Evaluation of the Case

Percentage chances of a negligence finding _____

Percentage chances of a causation finding _____

Estimated verdict range _____

Does venue play a role in verdict range?_____

VII. Mediator's Introduction (Significant Facts)

_____

_____

_____

_____

_____

_____

Appendix B
Mediation Notebook

_____

_____

_____

_____

VIII. Significant Points to Cover in Our Opening Statement

_____

_____

_____

_____

_____

_____

_____

_____

IX. Significant Points Covered By Opposing Counsel's Opening Statement

_____

_____

_____

_____

Appendix B
Mediation Notebook

_____

_____

_____

_____

_____

_____

_____

X. Significant Points Raised by Our Client's Opening Statement

_____

_____

_____

_____

_____

_____

_____

_____

_____

_____

XI. Significant Points Raised By Other Party's Opening Statement

_____

Appendix B
Mediation Notebook

_____

_____

_____

_____

_____

_____

_____

_____

XII. New Information Gained at Joint Session

_____

_____

_____

_____

_____

_____

XIII. First Caucus

A. Strengths Identified

_____

_____

_____

_____

_____

_____

_____

_____

_____

B. Weaknesses Identified

_____

_____

_____

_____

_____

_____

_____

_____

_____

_____

C. Significant Comments Made By Mediator

_____

_____

_____

_____

_____

_____

_____

_____

_____

D. Any Authorized Disclosures

_____

_____

_____

_____

_____

_____

_____

_____

_____

_____

_____

E. New Proposal Made

_____

_____

_____

_____

_____

_____

_____

_____

_____

F. New Proposal Received

_____

_____

_____

_____

_____

_____

_____

_____

_____

XIV. Second Caucus

_____

_____

_____

_____

_____

_____

_____

Appendix B
Mediation Notebook

XV. Third Caucus

XVI. Fourth Caucus

_____

XVII. Fifth Caucus

XVIII. Subsequent Joint Session Data

Appendix B
Mediation Notebook

_____

_____

_____

_____

_____

_____

_____

_____

XIX. Lawyer Caucus Data

_____

_____

_____

_____

_____

_____

_____

_____

_____

_____

XX. Mediation Results

    A. Was a settlement reached? _____

    B. If a settlement was reached, what was the settlement? _____

_____

_____

    C. If a settlement was not reached, why did impasse occur? _____

_____

_____

    D. If settlement was not reached, were issues narrowed? _____

    E. The mediator's skill and effort was:

    _____ Poor

    _____ Fair

    _____ Average

    _____ Good

    _____ Excellent

    F. If the case did not resolve, should mediation be tried again after additional discovery? _____

    G. The clients' reaction to the mediation was:

    _____ Very unfavorable

    _____ Unfavorable

_____ Neutral

_____ Favorable

_____ Very favorable

ATTACH COPY OF ANY SIGNED MEMORANDA OF AGREEMENT

Appendix B
Mediation Notebook

NEGOTIATIONS AT MEDIATION

First Offer   _____   Time _____

First Response   _____   Time _____

Second Offer   _____   Time _____

Second Response   _____   Time _____

Third Offer   _____   Time _____

Third Response   _____   Time _____

Fourth Offer   _____   Time _____

Fourth Response   _____   Time _____

Fifth Offer   _____   Time _____

Fifth Response   _____   Time _____

Sixth Offer   _____   Time _____

Sixth Response   _____   Time _____

Seventh Offer   _____   Time _____

Seventh Response   _____   Time _____

Eighth Offer   _____   Time _____

Eighth Response   _____   Time _____

Memorandum Of Agreement

On _____, the parties (and their counsel) assembled at
_____ for purposes of non-binding mediation. Upon completion of the mediation process, the parties, as evidenced by their signatures (and their counsel's signatures) below have reached a full and final settlement of their dispute.

The terms and conditions of this settlement are as follows:

1.

2.

3.

4.

5.

6.

7.

8.

9.

10.

The parties have read and fully understand this agreement and further understand that this agreement will finally and forever resolve this dispute. The parties further agree to be bound by this agreement.

_____,   _____(date)

_____,   _____(date)

_____,   _____(date)

Appendix C
Memorandum of Agreement

_____

_____, _____(date)

_____, _____(date)

_____, _____(date)

_____, _____(date)

_____, _____(date)

APPROVED BY COUNSEL:

_____, _____(date)

_____, _____(date)

_____, _____(date)

_____, _____(date)

_____, _____(date)

_____, _____(date)

_____, _____(date)

_____, _____(date)

BY:_____, Mediator

_____, (date)

Appendix D

State Statutes

Prepared by Professor Kimberlee K. Kovach

Each state has introduced mediation to the court system in a number of different ways. Some states have a completely integrated system, while others have just begun to discuss the concept. In late 1993, a survey to determine the status of mediation use in state courts was completed.[1]

An overview of the responses provides quite a variety of information and indicates that stages of progress differ. While the Alabama Supreme Court adopted rules for mediating civil cases, the implementation is very minimal.[2] Delaware is taking a year to experiment with court-annexed mediation, after which the Superior Court will consider full implementation.[3] Hawaii has been a leader in community, pre-litigation and voluntary mediation and mediation education in universities. However, the courts of Hawaii have not enacted a court-annexed mediation program.[4] Ohio does have court-annexed mediation, but it is primarily in small claims cases.[5] Oregon has been a leader in the use of ADR and mediation; however this has been primarily in the family law area, particularly custody and visitation cases. However, a new program for mediation in all civil cases has been initiated.[6] Tennessee has not experienced a lot of ADR activity, but currently has a committee charged with making recommendations to the legislature.[7] Wisconsin uses media-

---

1. Peter S. Chantilis, MEDIATION U.S.A. (1993).
2. Id. at 1.
3. Id. at 4.
4. Id. at 5.
5. Id. at 11.
6. Id. at 12.
7. Id. at 13.

Appendix D
State Statutes

---

tion only during settlement week, while Puerto Rico is very active, having referred cases since 1983.[8]

As is apparent, the variation is great. As more lawyers become educated and use mediation successfully and satisfactorily, no doubt its use will increase.

Sampling of State Statutes

Every state legislature has enacted some type of law advocating the use of mediation. These range from advocating its use in barber disputes[9] to a requirement that hospitals establish a mediation system for resolving disputes regarding the issuance of orders not to resuscitate.[10] Clearly, the applicability of mediation continues to increase.

The focus of this work is on the lawyer advocate and hence the use of mediation primarily within the legal system. This appendix consists of a sampling of statutes that implement the mediation process within the courts.[11]

---

8. Id. at 15.

9. Kan. Stat. Ann. §65-1824 (1993).

10. N.Y. McKinney's Pub. Health Law §2972 (1993).

11. For a complete review of all state statutes dealing with mediation see Nancy H. Rogers & Craig A. McEwen, MEDIATION: LAW, POLICY, PRACTICE Appendix C (1989 & Supp. 1993).

Appendix D
State Statutes

COLORADO
Colorado Revised Statutes, Title 13

§13-22-311. Court referral to mediation — duties of mediator

(1) Any court of record may, in its discretion, refer any case for mediation services or dispute resolution programs, subject to the availability of mediation services or dispute resolution programs; except that the court shall not refer the case to mediation services or dispute resolution programs where one of the parties claims that it has been the victim of physical or psychological abuse by the other party and states that it is thereby unwilling to enter into mediation services or dispute resolution programs. In addition, the court may exempt from referral any case in which a party files with the court, within five days of a referral order, a motion objecting to mediation and demonstrating compelling reasons why mediation should not be ordered. Compelling reasons may include, but are not limited to, that the costs of mediation would be higher than the requested relief and previous attempts to resolve the issues were not successful. Parties referred to mediation services or dispute resolution programs may select said services or programs from mediators or mediation organizations or from the office of dispute resolution. This section shall not apply in any civil action where injunctive or similar equitable relief is the only remedy sought.

(2) Upon completion of mediation services or dispute resolution programs, the mediator shall supply to the court, unless counsel for a party is required to do so by local rule or order of the court, a written statement certifying that the parties have met with the mediator.

(3) In the event the mediator and the parties agree and inform the court that the parties are engaging in good faith mediation, any pending hearing in the action filed by the parties shall be continued to a date certain.

(4) In no event shall a party be denied the right to proceed in court in the action filed because of failure to pay the mediator.

FLORIDA
Florida Statutes, Section 44.102. Court-ordered mediation

(1) Court-ordered mediation shall be conducted according to rules of practice and procedure adopted by the Supreme Court.

(2) A court pursuant to rules adopted by the Supreme Court:

(a) May refer to mediation all or any part of a filed civil action; and

(b) In circuits in which a family mediation program has been established and upon a court finding of a dispute, shall refer to mediation all or part of custody, visitation, or other parental responsibility issues as defined in s. 61.13. A court shall not refer any case to mediation if it finds there has been a significant history of domestic abuse which would compromise the mediation process.

(3) Each party involved in a court-ordered mediation proceeding has a privilege to refuse to disclose, and to prevent any person present at the proceeding from disclosing, communications made during such proceeding. Notwithstanding the provisions of s. 119.14, all oral or written communications in a mediation proceeding, other than an executed settlement agreement, shall be exempt from the requirements of chapter 119 and shall be confidential and inadmissible as evidence in any subsequent legal proceeding, unless all parties agree otherwise. This exemption is subject to the Open Government Sunset Review Act in accordance with s. 119.14.

(4) There shall be no privilege and no restriction on any disclosure of communications made confidential in subsection (3) in relation to disciplinary proceedings filed against mediators pursuant to s. 44.106 and court rules, to the extent the communication is used for the purposes of such proceedings. In such cases, the disclosure of an otherwise privileged communication shall be used only for the internal use of the body conducting the investigation. Prior to the release of any disciplinary files to the public, all references to otherwise privileged communications shall be deleted from the record. When an otherwise confidential communication is used in a mediator disciplinary proceeding, such communication shall be inadmissible as evidence in any subsequent legal proceeding. "Subsequent legal proceeding" means

any legal proceeding between the parties to the mediation which follows the court-ordered mediation.

(5) The chief judge of each judicial circuit shall maintain a list of mediators who have been certified by the Supreme Court and who have registered for appointment in that circuit.

(a) Whenever possible, qualified individuals who have volunteered their time to serve as mediators shall be appointed. If a mediation program is funded pursuant to s. 44.108, volunteer mediators shall be entitled to reimbursement pursuant to s. 112.061 for all actual expenses necessitated by service as a mediator.

(b) Nonvolunteer mediators shall be compensated according to rules adopted by the Supreme Court. If a mediation program is funded pursuant to s. 44.108, a mediator may be compensated by the county or by the parties. When a party has been declared indigent or insolvent, that party's pro rata share of a mediator's compensation shall be paid by the county at the rate set by administrative order of the chief judge of the circuit.

(6)(a) When an action is referred to mediation by court order, the time periods for responding to an offer of settlement pursuant to s. 45.061, or to an offer or demand for judgment pursuant to s. 768.79, respectively, shall be tolled until:

1. An impasse has been declared by the mediator; or

2. The mediator has reported to the court that no agreement was reached.

(b) Sections 45.061 and 768.79 notwithstanding, an offer of settlement or an offer or demand for judgment may be made at any time after an impasse has been declared by the mediator, or the mediator has reported that no agreement was reached. An offer is deemed rejected as of commencement of trial.

LOUISIANA
Louisiana Statutes 9:332-333

§332. Custody or visitation proceeding; mediation

A. The court may order the parties to mediate their differences in a custody or visitation proceeding. The mediator may be agreed upon by the parties or, upon their failure to agree, selected by the court. The court may stay any further determination of custody or visitation for a period not to exceed thirty days from the date of issuance of such an order. The court may order the costs of mediation to be paid in advance by either party or both parties jointly. The court may apportion the costs of the mediation between the parties if agreement is reached on custody or visitation. If mediation concludes without agreement between the parties, the costs of mediation shall be taxed as costs of court. The costs of mediation shall be subject to approval by the court.

B. If an agreement is reached by the parties, the mediator shall prepare a written, signed, and dated agreement. A consent judgment incorporating the agreement shall be submitted to the court for its approval.

C. Evidence of conduct or statements made in mediation is not admissible in any proceeding. This rule does not require the exclusion of any evidence otherwise discoverable merely because it is presented in the course of mediation. Facts disclosed, other than conduct or statements made in mediation, are not inadmissible by virtue of first having been disclosed in mediation.

§333. Duties of mediator

A. The mediator shall assist the parties in formulating a written, signed, and dated agreement to mediate which shall identify the controversies between the parties, affirm the parties' intent to resolve these controversies through mediation, and specify the circumstances under which the mediation may terminate.

B. The mediator shall advise each of the parties participating in the mediation to obtain review by an attorney of any agreement reached as a result of the mediation prior to signing such an agreement.

C. The mediator shall be impartial and has no power to impose a solution on the parties.

Appendix D
State Statutes

MAINE
Maine Revised Statutes, Title 19

§214 (4) Mediation. Except as provided in subsection 4-A, prior to a contested hearing under this section when there are minor children of the parties, the court shall refer the parties to mediation; except that, for good cause shown, the court, prior to referring the parties to mediation, may hear motions for temporary relief, pending final judgment on any issue or combination of issues for which good cause for temporary relief has been shown. Upon motion supported by affidavit, the court may, for extraordinary cause shown, waive the mediation requirement under this subsection. Any agreement reached by the parties through mediation on any issues must be reduced to writing, signed by the parties and presented to the court for approval as a court order. When agreement through mediation is not reached on any issue, the court must determine that the parties made a good faith effort to mediate the issue before proceeding with a hearing. If the court finds that either party failed to make a good faith effort to mediate, the court may order the parties to submit to mediation, may dismiss the action or any part of the action, may render a decision or judgment by default, may assess attorney's fees and costs or may impose any other sanction that is appropriate in the circumstances. The court may also impose an appropriate sanction upon a party's failure without good cause to appear for mediation after receiving notice of the scheduled time for mediation.

§214(4-A) Waiver of mediation; questions of law. The court may hear motions to waive mediation in cases in which there are no facts at issue and all unresolved issues are questions of law.

§665 Court authority to order mediation

The court may, in any case under this subchapter, at any time refer the parties to mediation on any issues. Any agreement reached by the parties through mediation on any issues shall be reduced to writing, signed by the parties and presented to the court for approval as a court order. When agreement through mediation is not reached on any issue, the court must determine that the parties made a good faith effort to mediate the issue before proceeding with a hearing. If the court finds that

---

either party failed to make a good faith effort to mediate, the court may order the parties to submit to mediation, may dismiss the action or any part of the action, may render a decision or judgment by default, may assess attorney's fees and costs or may impose any other sanction that is appropriate in the circumstances. The court may also impose an appropriate sanction upon a party's failure without good cause to appear for mediation after receiving notice of the scheduled time for mediation.

Appendix D
State Statutes

MASSACHUSETTS
Massachusetts General Laws, chapter 211B

§19. Mandatory alternative dispute resolution program

The chief administrative justice may establish and promulgate rules for a mandatory alternative dispute resolution program for civil actions within the trial court subject to the approval of the supreme judicial court; provided, however, that the parties to a dispute resolution shall not be bound by the results thereof. The office of the chief administrative justice shall supervise and establish standards for the implementation of such program.

MINNESOTA
Minnesota Statutes

§484.74 Alternative dispute resolution

Subdivision 1. Authorization. In litigation involving an amount in excess of $7,500 in controversy, the presiding judge may, by order, direct the parties to enter nonbinding alternative dispute resolution. Alternatives may include private trials, neutral expert fact-finding, mediation, minitrials, and other forms of alternative dispute resolution. The guidelines for the various alternatives must be established by the presiding judge and must emphasize early and inexpensive exchange of information and case evaluation in order to facilitate settlement.

Subd. 4. Application. This section applies only to the second and fourth judicial districts, which will serve as pilot projects to evaluate the effectiveness of alternative forms of resolving commercial and personal injury disputes. The state court administrator shall evaluate the pilot projects and report the findings to the chairs of the house and senate judiciary committees by January 15, 1991, in the case of the fourth judicial district and by January 15, 1992, in the case of the second judicial district.

§484.76. Alternative dispute resolution program

Subdivision 1. General. The supreme court shall establish a statewide alternative dispute resolution program for the resolution of civil cases filed with the courts. The supreme court shall adopt rules governing practice, procedure, and jurisdiction for alternative dispute resolution programs established under this section. Except for matters involving family law the rules shall require the use of nonbinding alternative dispute resolution processes in all civil cases, except for good cause shown by the presiding judge, and must provide an equitable means for the payment of fees and expenses for the use of alternative dispute process.

Subd. 2. Scope. Alternative dispute resolution methods provided for under the rules must include arbitration, private trials, neutral expert fact-finding, mediation, minitrials, consensual special magistrates including retired judges and qualified attorneys to serve as special magistrates for binding proceedings with a right of

Appendix D
State Statutes

---

appeal, and any other methods developed by the supreme court. The methods provided must be nonbinding unless otherwise agreed to in a valid agreement between the parties. Alternative dispute resolution may not be required in guardianship, conservatorship, or civil commitment matters; proceedings in the juvenile court under chapter 260; or in matters arising under section 144.651, 144.652, 518B.01, or 626.557.

Appendix D
State Statutes

NEW MEXICO
New Mexico Statutes, chapter 40

40-4-8. Contested custody; appointment of guardian ad litem.

A. In any proceeding for the disposition of children when custody of minor children is contested by any party, the court may appoint an attorney at law as guardian ad litem on the court's motion or upon application of any party to appear for and represent the minor children. Expenses, costs and attorneys' fees for the guardian ad litem may be allocated among the parties as determined by the court.

B. When custody is contested, the court:

(1) shall refer that issue to mediation if feasible unless a party asserts or it appears to the court that domestic violence or child abuse has occurred, in which even the court shall halt or suspend mediation unless the court specifically finds that:

(a) the following three conditions are satisfied: 1) the mediator has substantial training concerning the effects of domestic violence or child abuse on victims; 2) a party who is or alleges to be the victim of domestic violence is capable of negotiating with the other party in mediation, either alone or with assistance, without suffering from an imbalance of power as a result of the alleged domestic violence; and 3) the mediation process contains appropriate provisions and conditions to protect against an imbalance of power between the parties resulting from the alleged domestic violence or child abuse; or

(b) in the case of domestic violence involving parents, the parent who is or alleges to be the victim requests mediation and the mediator is informed of the alleged domestic violence.

NORTH CAROLINA
General Statutes of North Carolina, chapter 7A

§7A-38. Court ordered, mediated settlement conferences in superior court civil actions.

(a) Purpose. This section is enacted in order to provide for a pilot program in judicial districts selected by the Director of the Administrative Office of the Courts in which parties to superior court civil litigation may be required to attend a pretrial settlement conference conducted by a mediator. The purpose of the pilot program is to determine whether a system of mediated settlement conferences may make the operation of the superior courts more efficient, less costly, and more satisfying to the litigants.

(b) Definitions as used in this section:

(1) "Mediated settlement conference" means a court ordered conference between or among the parties to a civil action and their representatives conducted by a mediator prior to trial.

(2) "Mediation" means an informal process conducted by a mediator with the objective of helping parties voluntarily reach a mutually acceptable settlement of their dispute.

(3) "Mediator" means a neutral person who acts to encourage and facilitate a resolution of a pending civil action. A mediator does not render a judgment as to the merit of the action.

(c) Selection of districts. This procedure may be implemented in a judicial district or any party of a judicial district if the Director of the Administrative Office of the Courts and the senior resident superior court judge of that district determine that use of this program may assist in achieving objectives stated in subsection (a) of this section. The Director of the Administrative Office of the Courts may terminate any pilot program after consultation with the senior resident superior court judge.

(d) Rules of mediated settlement conferences. The Supreme Court may adopt rules to implement this section.

(e) Judge to select cases for mediated settlement conferences. The senior resident superior court judge of any district participating, in whole or in part, in any pilot program may order a mediated settlement conference for all or any part of a superior court civil action pending in the pilot area, except as limited by the rules of the Supreme Court adopted under the authority of this section.

(f) Attendance of parties. The parties to a civil action in which a mediated settlement conference is ordered, their attorneys, and other persons having authority to settle the parties' claims shall attend the conference unless excused by rules of the Supreme Court or by order of the senior resident superior court judge.

(g) Selection of mediator. The parties shall have the right to stipulate to a mediator subject to the standards and rules established by the Supreme Court. Upon failure of the parties to agree within the time established by the rules, a mediator shall be appointed by the senior resident superior court judge.

(h) Sanctions. Upon failure of a party or attorney to attend a court ordered mediated settlement conference to the extent required by this section and rules promulgated by the Supreme Court, a resident or presiding judge may impose any lawful sanction, including but not limited to the payment of attorneys' fees, mediator fees, and expenses incurred in attending the conference, contempt, or any other sanction authorized by G.S. 1A-1, Rule 37(b).

(i) Standards for mediators. The Supreme Court is authorized to establish standards for the qualification and conduct of mediators and mediator training programs. An administrative fee may be set by the Administrative Office of the Courts to be charged to applicants for approval as mediators and mediator training programs.

(j) Immunity. A mediator acting pursuant to this section shall have judicial immunity in the same manner and to the same extent as a judge of the General Court of Justice.

(k) Costs of mediated settlement conference. Costs of the mediated settlement conference shall be paid: one share by the plaintiffs, one share by the defendants, and one share by any third-party defendant, unless otherwise ordered by the court or agreed to by the parties. The rules established by the Supreme Court under subsection (d) of this section shall set out a method whereby the parties found by the court to be unable to pay the costs of the mediated settlement conference are afforded an opportunity to participate without cost.

(*l*) Inadmissibility of negations. All conduct or communications made during a mediated settlement conference are presumed to be made in compromise negotiations and shall be governed by Rule 408 of the North Carolina Rules of Evidence.

(m) Evaluation. The pilot program authorized by this section shall be evaluated for a reasonable period of time under the direction of the Administrative Office of the Courts. The Director of the Administrative Office of the Courts shall report the results of the evaluation to the General Assembly.

(n) Funding of the pilot program. The Administrative Office of the Courts may solicit funds from private sources to establish, conduct, and evaluate this pilot program. No State funds shall be used to establish, conduct, or evaluate this program.

(o) Report on pilot program. The Administrative Office of the Courts shall file a written report with the General Assembly on the evaluation of the pilot program on or before May, 1, 1995. The pilot program shall terminate on June 30, 1995.

(p) Right to jury trial. Nothing in this section or the rules promulgated by the Supreme Court implementing this section shall restrict the right to jury trial.

General Statutes of North Carolina, chapter 50

§50-13.1 Action or proceeding for custody of minor child.

(a) Any parent, relative, or other person, agency, organization or institution claiming the right to custody of a minor child may institute an action or proceeding for the custody of such child, as hereinafter provided. Unless a contrary intent is clear, the word "custody" shall be deemed to include custody or visitation or both.

(b) Whenever it appears to the court, form the pleadings or otherwise, that an action involves a contested issue as to the custody or visitation of a minor child, the matter, where there is a program established pursuant to G.S. 7A-494, shall be set for mediation of the unresolved issues as to custody and visitation before or concur-

Appendix D
State Statutes

rent with the setting of the matter for hearing unless the court waives mediation pursuant to subsection (c). Issues that arise in motions for contempt or for modifications as well as in other pleadings shall be set for mediation unless mediation is waived by the court. Alimony, child support, and other economic issues may not be referred for mediation pursuant to this section. The purposes of mediation under this section include the pursuit of the following goals:

(1) To reduce any acrimony that exists between the parties to a dispute involving custody or visitation of a minor child;

(2) The development of custody and visitation agreements that are in the child's best interest;

(3) To provide the parties with informed choices and, where possible, to give the parties the responsibility for making decisions about child custody and visitation;

(4) To provide a structured, confidential, nonadversarial setting that will facilitate the cooperative resolution of custody and visitation disputes and minimize the stress and anxiety to which the parties, and especially the child, are subjected; and

(5) To reduce the relitigation of custody and visitation disputes.

(c) For good cause, on the motion or either party or on the court's own motion, the court may waive the mandatory setting under Article 39A of Chapter 7A of the General Statutes of a contested custody or visitation matter for mediation. Good cause may include, but is not limited to, the following: a showing of undue hardship to a party; an agreement between the parties for voluntary mediation, subject to court approval; allegations of abuse or neglect of the minor child; allegations of alcoholism, drug abuse, or spouse abuse; or allegations of sever psychological, psychiatric, or emotional problems. A showing by either party that the party resides more that fifty miles from the court shall be considered good cause.

(d) Either party may voice to have the mediation proceedings dismissed and the action heard in court due to the mediator's bias, undue familiarity with a party, or other prejudicial ground.

(e) Mediation proceeding shall be held in private and shall be confidential. Except as provided in this Article, all verbal or written communications from either or both parties to the mediation or between the parties in the presence of the mediator made in a proceeding pursuant to this section are absolutely privileged and inadmissible in court. The mediator may assess the needs and interests of the child, and may interview the child or others who are not parties to the proceedings when he or she thinks appropriate.

(f) Neither the mediator nor any party or other person involved in mediation sessions under this section shall be competent to testify to communications made during or in furtherance of such mediation sessions; provided, there is no privilege as to communications made in furtherance of a crime or fraud. Nothing in this subsection shall be construed as permitting an individual to obtain immunity from prosecution for criminal conduct or as excusing an individual from the reporting requirements of G.S. 7A-543 or G.S. 108A-102.

(g) Any agreement reached by the parties as a result of the mediation shall be reduced to writing, signed by each party, and submitted to the court as soon as practicable. Unless the court finds good reason not to, it shall incorporate the agreement in a court order and it shall become enforceable as a court order. If some or all of the issues as to custody or visitation are not resolved by mediation, the mediator shall report that fact to the court.

(h) If an agreement that results from mediation and is incorporated into a court order is referred to as a "parenting agreement" or called by some similar name, it shall nevertheless be deemed to be a custody order or child custody determination for purposes of Chapter 50A of the General Statutes, G.S. 14-320.1, G.S. 110-139.1, or other places where those terms appear.

Appendix D
State Statutes

OREGON
Oregon Revised Statutes Annotated 36.185-36.205

36.185. Referral of civil dispute to mediation; objection; information to parties

After 30 days have passed following the appearance by all parties in any civil action, except proceedings under ORS 107.700 to 107.730, a judge of any district or circuit court may refer a civil dispute to mediation under the terms and conditions set forth in ORS 36.180 to 36.210. When a party to a case files a written objection to mediation with the court, the action shall be removed from mediation and proceed in a normal fashion. All civil disputants shall be provided with written information describing the mediation process, as provided by the Dispute Resolution Commission, along with information on established court mediation opportunities. Filing parties shall be provided with this information at the time of filing a civil action. Responding parties shall be provided with this information by the filing party along with the initial service of filing documents upon the responding party.

36.190. Stipulation to mediation; selection of mediator; stay of proceedings

(1) On written stipulation of all parties at any time prior to trial, the parties may elect to mediate their civil dispute under the terms and conditions of ORS 36.180 to 36.210.

(2) Upon referral or election to mediate, the parties shall select a mediator by written stipulation or shall follow procedures for assignment or a mediator from the court's panel of mediators.

(3) During the period of any referred or elected mediation under ORS 36.180 to 36.210, all trial and discovery time lines and requirements shall be tolled and stayed as to the participants. Such tolling shall commence on the date of the referral or election to mediate and shall end on the date the court is notified in writing of the termination of the mediation by the mediator or one party requests the case be put back on the docket. All time limits and schedules shall be tolled, except that a judge shall have discretion to adhere to preexisting pretrial order dates, trial dates or dates relating to temporary relief.

Appendix D
State Statutes

36.195. Presence of attorney; authority and duties of mediator; notice to court at completion of mediation

(1) Unless otherwise agreed to in writing by the parties, the parties' legal counsel shall not be present at any scheduled mediation sessions conducted under the provisions of ORS 36.100 to 36.175.

(2) Attorneys and other persons who are not parties to a mediation may be included in mediation discussions at the mediator's discretion, with the consent of the parties, for mediation held under the provisions of ORS 36.180 to 36.120.

(3) The mediator, with the consent of the parties, may adopt appropriate rules to facilitate the resolution of the dispute and shall have discretion, with the consent of the parties, to suspend or continue mediation. The mediator may propose settlement terms either orally or in writing.

(4) All court mediators shall encourage disputing parties to obtain individual legal advice and individual legal review of any mediated agreement prior to signing the agreement.

(5) Within 10 judicial days of the completion of the mediation, the mediator shall notify the court whether an agreement has been reached by the parties. If the parties do not reach agreement, the mediator shall report that fact only to the court, but shall not make a recommendation as to resolution of the dispute without written consent of all parties or their legal counsel. The action shall then proceed in the normal fashion on either an expedited or regular pretrial list.

(6) The court shall retain jurisdiction over a case selected for mediation and shall issue orders as it deems appropriate.

36.200. Mediation panels; qualification; procedure for selecting mediator

(1) A district or circuit court providing mediation referral under ORS 36.180 to 36.210 shall establish mediation panels. The mediators on such panels shall have such qualifications as set by the Dispute Resolution Commission. Formal education in any particular field shall not be a prerequisite to serving as a mediator.

---

(2) Unless instructed otherwise by the court, upon referral by the court to mediation, the clerk of the court shall select at least three individuals from the court's panel of mediators and shall send their names to legal counsel for the parties, or to a party directly if not represented, with a request that each party state preferences within five judicial days. If timely objection is made to all of the individuals named, the court shall select some other individual from the mediator panel. Otherwise, the clerk, under the direction of the court, shall select as mediator one of the three individuals about whom no timely objection was made.

(3) Upon the court's or the parties' own selection of a mediator, the clerk shall:

(a) Notify the designated person of the assignment as mediator.

(b) Provide the mediator with the names and addresses of the parties and their representatives and, with copies of the order of assignment, the pleadings and any scheduling or pretrial order that has been entered.

(4) The parties to a dispute that is referred by the court to mediation may choose, at their option and expense, mediation services other than those suggested by the court, and entering into such private mediation services shall be subject to the same provisions of ORS 36.180 to 36.210.

(5) Disputing parties in mediation shall be free, at their own expense, to retain jointly or individually, experts, attorneys, factfinders, arbitrators and other persons to assist the mediation, and all such dispute resolution efforts shall be subject to the protection of ORS 36.180 to 36.210.

36.205. Confidentiality; disclosure of materials and communications

(1) If there is a written agreement between any parties to a dispute that mediation communications will be confidential, then all memoranda, work products and other materials contained in the case files of a mediator or mediation program are confidential. Any communication made in or in connection with such mediation which relates to the controversy being mediated, whether made to the mediator or a party, or to any other person if made at a mediation session, is confidential. However, a

mediated agreement shall not be confidential unless the parties otherwise agree in writing.

(2) Confidential materials and communications are not subject to disclosure in any judicial or administrative proceeding except:

(a) When all parties to the mediation agree, in writing, to waive the confidentiality;

(b) In a subsequent action between the mediator and a party to the mediation for damages arising out of the mediation; or

(c) Statements, memoranda, materials and other tangible evidence, otherwise subject to discovery, that were not prepared specifically for use in and actually used in the mediation.

(3) When there is a written agreement as described in this section, the mediator may not be compelled to testify in any proceeding, unless all parties to the mediation and the mediator agree in writing.

TEXAS
Texas Civil Practice & Remedies Code
Chapter 154. Alternative Dispute Resolution Procedures

Acts 1987, 70th Leg., ch. 1121, §1, eff. June 20, 1987.

Subchapter A. General Provisions

Section

154.001   Definitions.
154.002   Policy.
154.003   Responsibility of Courts and Court Administrators.
[Sections 154.004 to 154.020 reserved for expansion]

Subchapter B. Alternative Dispute Resolution Procedures

Section

154.021   Referral of Pending Disputes for
           Alternative Dispute Resolution Procedure.
154.022   Notification and Objection.
154.023   Mediation.
154.024   Mini-Trial.
154.025   Moderated Settlement Conference.
154.026   Summary Jury Trial.
154.027   Arbitration.
[Sections 154.028 to 154.050 reserved for expansion]

Subchapter C. Impartial Third Parties

154.051   Appointment of Impartial Third Parties.
154.052   Qualifications of Impartial Third Party.
154.053   Standards and Duties of Impartial Third Parties.
154.054   Compensation of Impartial Third Parties.
154.055   Qualified Immunity of Impartial Third Parties.
[Sections 154.055 to 154.070 reserved for expansion]
154.071   Effect of Written Settlement Agreement.
154.072   Statistical Information on Disputes Referred.
154.073   Confidentiality of Communications in Dispute Resolution Procedures.

Appendix D
State Statutes

Subchapter A. General Provisions

§154.001 Definitions

In this chapter:

(1) "Court" includes an appellate court, district court, constitutional county court, statutory county court, family law court, probate court, municipal court, or justice of the peace court.

(2) "Dispute resolution organization" means a private profit or nonprofit corporation, political subdivision, or public corporation, or a combination of these, that offers alternative dispute resolution services to the public.

§154.002 Policy

It is the policy of this state to encourage the peaceable resolution of disputes, with special consideration given to disputes involving the parent-child relationship, including the mediation of issues involving conservatorship, possession, and support of children, and the early settlement of pending litigation through voluntary settlement procedures.

§154.003 Responsibility of Courts and Court Administrators

It is the responsibility of all trial and appellate courts and their court administrators to carry out the policy under Section 154.002.

[Sections 154.004 to 154.020 reserved for expansion]

Subchapter B. Alternative Dispute Resolution Procedures

§154.021 Referral of Pending Disputes for Alternative Dispute Resolution Procedure

(a) A court may, on its own motion or the motion of a party, refer a pending dispute for resolution by an alternative dispute resolution procedure including:

(1) an alternative dispute resolution system established under Chapter 26, Acts of the 68th Legislature, Regular Session, 1983 (Article 2372aa, Vernon's Texas Civil Statutes);

(2) a dispute resolution organization; or

(3) a nonjudicial and informally conducted forum for the voluntary settlement of citizens' disputes through the intervention of an impartial third party, including those alternative dispute resolution procedures described under this subchapter.

(b) The court shall confer with the parties in the determination of the most appropriate alternative dispute resolution procedure.

§154.022 Notification and Objection

(a) If a court determines that a pending dispute is appropriate for referral under Section 154.021, the court shall notify the parties of its determination.

(b) Any party may, within 10 days after receiving the notice under Subsection (a), file a written objection to the referral.

(c) If the court finds that there is a reasonable basis for an objection filed under Subsection (b), the court may not refer the dispute under Section 154.021.

§154.023 Mediation

(a) Mediation is a forum in which an impartial person, the mediator, facilitates communication between parties to promote reconciliation, settlement, or understanding among them.

(b) A mediator may not impose his own judgment on the issues for that of the parties.

§154.024 Mini-Trial

(a) A mini-trial is conducted under an agreement of the parties.

(b) Each party and counsel for the party present the position of the party, either before selected representatives for each party or before an impartial third party, to define the issues and develop a basis for realistic settlement negotiations.

(c) The impartial third party may issue an advisory opinion regarding the merits of the case.

(d) The advisory opinion is not binding on the parties unless the parties agree that it is binding and enter into a written settlement agreement.

§154.025 Moderated Settlement Conference

(a) A moderated settlement conference is a forum for case evaluation and realistic settlement negotiations.

(b) Each party and counsel for the party present the position of the party before a panel of impartial third parties.

(c) The panel may issue an advisory opinion regarding the liability or damages of the parties or both.

(d) The advisory opinion is not binding on the parties.

§154.026 Summary Jury Trial

(a) A summary jury trial is a forum for early case evaluation and development of realistic settlement negotiations.

(b) Each party and counsel for the party present the position of the party before a panel of jurors.

(c) The number of jurors on the panel is six unless the parties agree otherwise.

(d) The panel may issue an advisory opinion regarding the liability or damages of the parties or both.

(e) The advisory opinion is not binding on the parties.

§154.027 Arbitration

(a) Nonbinding arbitration is a forum in which each party and counsel for the party present the position of the party before an impartial third party, who renders a specific award.

(b) If the parties stipulate in advance, the award is binding and is enforceable in the same manner as any contract obligation. If the parties do not stipulate in advance that the award is binding, the award is not binding and serves only as a basis for the parties' further settlement negotiations.

Appendix D
State Statutes

Subchapter C. Impartial Third Parties

[Sections 154.028 to 154.050 reserved for expansion]

§154.051 Appointment of Impartial Third Parties

(a) If a court refers a pending dispute for resolution by an alternative dispute resolution procedure under Section 154.021, the court may appoint an impartial third party to facilitate the procedure.

(b) The court may appoint a third party who is agreed on by the parties if the person qualifies for appointment under this subchapter.

(c) The court may appoint more than one third party under this section.

§154.052 Qualifications of Impartial Third Party

(a) Except as provided by Subsections (b) and (c), to qualify for an appointment as an impartial third party under this subchapter a person must have completed a minimum of 40 classroom hours of training in dispute resolution techniques in a course conducted by an alternative dispute resolution system or other dispute resolution organization approved by the court making the appointment.

(b) To qualify for an appointment as an impartial third party under this subchapter in a dispute relating to the parent-child relationship, a person must complete the training required by Subsection (a) and an additional 24 hours of training in the fields of family dynamics, child development, and family law.

(c) In appropriate circumstances, a court may in its discretion appoint a person as an impartial third party who does not qualify under Subsection (a) or (b) if the court bases its appointment on legal or other professional training or experience in particular dispute resolution processes.

§154.053 Standards and Duties of Impartial Third Parties

(a) A person appointed to facilitate an alternative dispute resolution procedure under this subchapter shall encourage and assist the parties in reaching a settlement of their dispute but may not compel or coerce the parties to enter into a settlement agreement.

(b) Unless expressly authorized by the disclosing party, the impartial third party may not disclose to either party information given in confidence by the other and shall at all times maintain confidentiality with respect to communications relating to the subject matter of the dispute.

(c) Unless the parties agree otherwise, all matters, including the conduct and demeanor of the parties and their counsel during the settlement process, are confidential and may never be disclosed to anyone, including the appointing court.

§154.054 Compensation of Impartial Third Parties

(a) The court may set a reasonable fee for the services of an impartial third party appointed under this subchapter.

(b) Unless the parties agree to a method of payment, the court shall tax the fee for the services of an impartial third party as other costs of suit.

§154.055 Qualified Immunity of Impartial Third Parties

(a) A person appointed to facilitate an alternative dispute resolution procedure under this subchapter or under Chapter 152 relating to an alternative dispute resolution system established by counties, or appointed by the parties whether before or after the institution of formal judicial proceeding, who is a volunteer and who does not act with wanton and willful disregard of the rights, safety, or property of another, is immune from civil liability for any act or omission within the course and scope of his or her duties or functions as an impartial third party. For purposes of this section, a volunteer impartial third party is a person who does not receive compensation in excess of reimbursement for expenses incurred or a stipend intended as reimbursement for expenses incurred.

(b) This section neither applies to nor is it intended to enlarge or diminish any rights or immunities enjoyed by an arbitrator participating in a binding arbitration pursuant to any applicable statute or treaty.

Appendix D
State Statutes

[Sections 154.056 to 154.070 reserved for expansion]

§154.071   Effect of Written Settlement Agreement

(a) If the parties reach a settlement and execute a written agreement disposing of the dispute, the agreement is enforceable in the same manner as any other written contract.

(b) The court in its discretion may incorporate the terms of the agreement in the court's final decree disposing of the case.

(c) A settlement agreement does not affect an outstanding court order unless the terms of the agreement are incorporated into a subsequent decree.

§154.072   Statistical Information on Disputes Referred

The Texas Supreme Court shall determine the need and method for statistical reporting of disputes referred by the courts to alternate dispute resolution procedures.

§154.073 Confidentiality of Communications in Dispute Resolution Procedures

(a) Except as provided by Subsections (c) and (d), a communication relating to the subject matter of any civil or criminal dispute made by a participant in an alternative dispute resolution procedure, whether before or after the institution of formal judicial proceedings, is confidential, is not subject to disclosure, and may not be used as evidence against the participant in any judicial or administrative proceeding.

(b) Any record made at an alternative dispute resolution procedure is confidential, and the participants or the third party facilitating the procedure may not be required to testify in any proceedings relating to or arising out of the matter in dispute or be subject to process requiring disclosure of confidential information or data relating to or arising out of the matter in dispute.

(c) An oral communication or written material used in or made a part of an alternative dispute resolution procedure is admissible or discoverable if it is admissible or discoverable independent of the procedure.

Appendix D
State Statutes

(d) If this section conflicts with other legal requirements for disclosure of communications or materials, the issue of confidentiality may be presented to the court having jurisdiction of the proceedings to determine, in camera, whether the facts, circumstances, and context of the communications or materials sought to be disclosed warrant a protective order of the court or whether the communications or materials are subject to disclosure.

UTAH
Utah Code chapter 31b: Alternative Dispute Resolution

78-31b. Definitions

(1) "ADR" means alternative dispute resolution.

(2) "Arbitration" means the procedures in Title 78, Chapter 31a, Utah Arbitration Act.

(3) "Certified dispute resolution provider" means a person or a private or non-profit corporation, political subdivision, or public corporation, or a combination of these, who has voluntarily qualified for certification and offers alternative dispute resolution services to the public according to the rules and standards of the board.

(4) "Court" means any trial court of record or not of record in the state.

(5) "Mediation" means a forum in which one or more impartial persons, acting as mediators, facilitate communication between parties to a controversy to promote a mutually acceptable resolution or settlement among them.

(6) "Mini-trial" is a meeting of parties to a legal action held under the procedures of this chapter, where the parties present their positions to define the issues and develop a basis for realistic settlement negotiations.

(7) "Moderated settlement conference" is a meeting of parties to a legal action, held under the procedures of this chapter, where the parties present their positions to one or more ADR providers.

(8) "Summary jury trial" means the parties to a legal action present their positions to a panel of jurors under the procedures of this chapter.

78-31b-2. Court authority and parties' participation

(1) Any court of competent jurisdiction may, on its own motion or the motion of a party, refer any pending civil dispute for ADR by an ADR provider certified under Title 58, Chapter 39a.

(2)(a) If a court determines a pending dispute is appropriate for referral to an ADR procedure, the court shall notify the parties in writing.

(b) The court shall confer with the parties in determining the most appropriate alternative dispute resolution procedure.

(3)(a) Any party to the dispute may file a written objection within ten days of receiving the notice of referral to ADR.

(b) If the court finds there is a reasonable basis for the objection, the court may not refer the dispute to ADR.

78-31b-3. Procedure for court referral

(1) If the court refers a pending dispute for resolution by an ADR procedure under this chapter, the court may appoint one or more certified ADR providers to facilitate the procedure.

(2) The court may appoint one or more certified ADR providers who are agreed upon by the parties to the dispute.

(3)(a) If a prosecutor has filed a criminal complaint for an offense other than an infraction against one of the parties to the civil dispute, the advice of counsel for the defendant party shall be obtained before the case may be referred to an ADR procedure.

(b) This subsection does not preclude the defendant from knowingly and voluntarily waiving the right to counsel. The court shall encourage a defendant who desires to waive the right to counsel to consult with the public defender or private counsel, as appropriate, before waiving the right.

78-31b-4. Reporting of court ADR referrals

(1) The Office of the Court Administrator shall provide annually to the Legislature on or before October 1 a report of the following information for the prior year of July 1 through June 30;

(a) the number of referrals made, including a subtotal of the number of referrals the parties objected to;

(b) the categories of cases referred and the number of referrals in each category;

(c) the number and types of cases resolved by referral to ADR;

(d) the number of persons participating in the ADR process through court referral more than once in the reporting year; and

(e) the duration and estimated cost of the ADR procedures handled by court referral.

(2) The report shall maintain the confidentiality and anonymity of the persons participating in ADR through court referral.

78-31b-5. ADR agreement enforcement

(1) An agreement reached through ADR procedures is enforceable as a contract among the parties if the agreement:

(a) includes an acknowledgment that the agreement is enforceable as a contract; and

(b) is executed in writing.

(2) This section applies to ADR conducted either through court referral or independent of the court.

(3) The ADR provider shall encourage the parties to the dispute to obtain individual legal advice and legal review of the agreement before signing it.

(4) This section does not apply to arbitration procedures conducted under Title 78, Chapter 31a, Utah Arbitration Act.

78-31b-6. Tolling of time requirements

(1)(a) During the period of court-referred ADR all trial and discovery time requirements are tolled regarding the participants in the ADR, except under Subsection (2).

(b) The tolling begins on the date the dispute is referred for ADR and ends on the date the court receives notice in writing from the provider that the ADR procedure has been terminated.

Appendix D
State Statutes

---

(2) Under this section the court may in its discretion adhere to preexisting pretrial order dates, trial dates, or dates relating to temporary relief.

78-31b-7. Confidentiality

(1)(a) Except as provided in Subsection (3) and (4), all communications relating to the subject matter of any civil or criminal dispute made by a participant in an ADR procedure, whether before or after the institution of formal judicial proceedings, are confidential.

(b) These communications are not subject to disclosure, and may not be used as evidence against the participant in any judicial or administrative proceeding.

(2) Any record made at an ADR procedure is confidential. The participants or the third party facilitating the procedure may not be required to testify in any proceedings relating to or arising out of the matter in dispute.

(3) Confidential communications and materials are subject to disclosure when:

(a) all parties to the ADR procedure agree in writing to waive the confidentiality regarding specific communications or materials;

(b) there is a subsequent action between the ADR provider and a party to the ADR procedure for damages arising out of the mediation; or

(c) the statements, memoranda, materials, and other tangible evidence, otherwise subject to discovery, were not prepared specifically for use in and actually used in the ADR procedure.

(4)(a) A person providing ADR as defined in this chapter is subject to the child abuse reporting requirements of Section 62A-4-503 and the criminal penalty for failure to report under Section 62A-4-511. The confidentiality provisions of Section 62A-4-513 apply to records made under this subsection.

(b) If the ADR provider determines a participant in the procedure has made an immediate threat of physical violence against a readily identifiable victim or against the provider, communications involving the threat are not confidential.

Appendix D
State Statutes

WASHINGTON
Revised Code of Washington chapter 5.60

5.60.070. Mediation — Disclosure — Testimony

(1) If there is a court order to mediate, a written agreement between the parties to mediate, or if mediation is mandated under RCW 7.70.100, then any communication made or materials submitted in, or in connection with, the mediation proceeding, whether made or submitted to or by the mediator, a mediation organization, a party, or any person present, are privileged and confidential and are not subject to disclosure in any judicial or administrative proceeding except:

(a) When all parties to the mediation agree, in writing, to disclosure;

(b) When the written materials or tangible evidence are otherwise subject to discovery, and were not prepared specifically for use in and actually used in the mediation proceeding;

(c) When a written agreement to mediate permits disclosure;

(d) When disclosure is mandated by statute;

(e) When the written materials consist of a written settlement agreement or other agreement signed by the parties resulting from a mediation proceeding;

(f) When those communications or written materials pertain solely to administrative matters incidental to the mediation proceeding, including the agreement to mediate; or

(g) In a subsequent action between the mediator and a party to the mediation arising out of the mediation.

(2) When there is a court order, a written agreement to mediate, or when mediation is mandated under RCW 7.70.100, as described in subsection (1) of this section, the mediator or a representative of a mediation organization shall not testify in any judicial or administrative proceeding unless:

(a) All parties to the mediation and the mediator agree in writing; or

(b) In an action described in subsection (1)(g) of this section.

Appendix D
State Statutes

7.70.100. Mandatory mediation of health care claims — Procedures

(1) All causes of action, whether based in tort, contract, or otherwise, for damages arising from injury occurring as a result of health care provided after July 1, 1993, shall be subject to mandatory mediation prior to trial.

(2) The supreme court shall by rule adopt procedures to implement mandatory mediation of actions under this chapter. The rules shall address, at a minimum:

(a) Procedures for the appointment of, and qualifications of, mediators. A mediator shall have experience or expertise related to actions arising from injury occurring as a result of health care, and be a member of the state bar association who has been admitted to the bar for a minimum of five years or who is a retired judge. The parties may stipulate to a nonlawyer mediator. The court may prescribe additional qualifications of mediators;

(b) Appropriate limits on the amount or manner of compensation of mediators;

(c) The number of days following the filing of a claim under this chapter within which a mediator must be selected;

(d) The method by which a mediator is selected. The rule shall provide for designation of a mediator by the superior court if the parties are unable to agree upon a mediator;

(e) The number of days following the selection of a mediator within which a mediation conference must be held;

(f) A means by which mediation of an action under this chapter may be waived by a mediator who has determined that the claim is not appropriate for mediation; and

(g) Any other matters deemed necessary by the court.

(3) Mediators shall not impose discovery schedules upon the parties.

**7.70.110.   Mandatory mediation of health care claims —
Tolling statute of limitations**

The making of a written, good faith request for mediation of a dispute related to damages for injury occurring as a result of health care prior to filing a cause of action under this chapter shall toll the statute of limitations provided in RCW 4.16.350 for one year.

**7.70.120.   Mandatory mediation of health care claims —
Right to trial not abridged**

RCW 7.70.100 may not be construed to abridge the right to trial by jury following an unsuccessful attempt at mediation.

**7.70.130.   Mandatory mediation of health care claims —
Exempt from arbitration mandate**

A cause of action that has been mediated as provided in RCW 7.70.100 shall be exempt from any superior court civil rules mandating arbitration of civil actions or participation in settlement conferences prior to trial.

Appendix D
State Statutes

WYOMING
Code of Civil Procedure; Wyoming Statutes chapter 43: Mediation

§1-43-101. Definitions

(a) As used in this act:

(i) "Communication" means any item of information disclosed during the mediation process through files, reports, interviews, discussions, memoranda, case summaries, notes, work products of the mediator, or any other item of information disclosed during the mediation, whether oral or written;

(ii) "Mediation" means a process in which an impartial third person facilitates communication between two (2) or more parties in conflict to promote reconciliation, settlement, compromise or understanding;

(iii) "Mediator" means an impartial third person not involved in the conflict, dispute or situation who engages in mediation;

(iv) "Party to the mediation" means a person who is involved in the conflict, dispute or situation and is rendered mediation services by a mediator or consults a mediator with a view to obtaining mediation services;

(v) "Representative of the mediator" means a person employed by the mediator to assist in the rendition of mediation services;

(vi) "Representative of the party" means a person having authority to obtain mediation services on behalf of the party to the mediation or to act on advice rendered by the mediator;

(vii) "This act" means W.S. 1-43-101 through 1-43-104.

§1-43-102. General rule of confidentiality

Any communication is confidential if not intended to be disclosed to third persons other than those to whom disclosure is in furtherance of the mediation process or those reasonably necessary for the transmission of the communication.

Appendix D
State Statutes

---

§1-43-103. General rule of privilege; claiming privilege; exception

(a) A party to the mediation has a privilege to refuse to disclose and to prevent all mediation participants from disclosing confidential communications.

(b) The privilege under this section may be claimed by a representative of the party or by a party, his guardian or conservator, the personal representative of a deceased party, or the successor, trustee or similar representative of a corporation, association, or other organization, whether or not in existence. The person who was the mediator may claim the privilege but only on behalf of the party. The mediator's authority to do so is presumed in the absence of evidence to the contrary.

(c) There is no privilege under this section if any one (1) of the following conditions is met:

(i) All the parties involved provide written consent to disclose;

(ii) The communication involves the contemplation of a future crime or harmful act;

(iii) The communication indicates that a minor child has been or is the suspected victim of child abuse as defined by local statute;

(iv) The communication was otherwise discoverable prior to the mediation;

(v) One of the parties seeks judicial enforcement of the mediated agreement.

§1-43-104. Immunity

Mediators are immune from civil liability for any good faith act or omission within the scope of the performance of their power and duties.

Federal Court Overview

Prepared by Professor Kimberlee K. Kovach

Summaries of Federal Court/Mediation Programs

While all of the Federal District Courts have submitted plans in accordance with the directives of the Civil Justice and Reform Act (28 U.S.C.A. §§ 471-482), not all plans include specific mediation or ADR programs. Some are silent with regard to ADR; others merely recommend its use, and a few have created specific programs. The court programs highlighted here are generally those that have advocated implementation of a recommended or mandatory mediation program. As the following are only brief summaries, and modifications take place during the implementation process, it is necessary to check with the court for the particulars of the program.

ALABAMA — Middle District

Informal program encouraging settlement.

CALIFORNIA — Northern District

Has had a long history of Early Neutral Evaluation. Mediation program has been added as a pilot program. Lawyers encouraged generally to discuss ADR with clients. In accordance with General Orders 36 and 37, cases assigned to pilot must select an ADR process, including mediation.

CALIFORNIA — Southern District

Mediators are volunteers without compensation. After an Early Neutral Evaluation (ENE) Conference, which occurs within forty-five (45) days of filing answer, if no settlement is reached, the court may refer the case to mediation. The mediation is to occur within forty-five (45) days in even-numbered simple contract and simple tort cases (excluding FTCA cases) where potential judgment does not exceed $100,000, and in every even-numbered trademark and copyright case. Mediation procedure governed by Rule 600-7, General Order No. 387.

Appendix E
Federal Court Overview

DELAWARE

Parties must certify to the court that they have discussed the possibility of using mediation or arbitration to effectuate settlement.

FLORIDA— Middle District

Governed by chapter 9 of the local rules. Court-ordered mediation requires use of mediators from the court's roster. Mediator's fees are uniform in accordance with a standing order. Parties can also stipulate to mediation and not be governed by court rules for the process.

FLORIDA — Southern District

Governed by Rule 16.2: All civil cases referred to mediation. A number of exceptions: habeas corpus; motion to vacate sentence under 28 U.S.C. §2255, social security cases, foreclosures, civil forfeitures, IRS summons enforcement actions; bankruptcy proceedings including appeals and adversary proceeding, land condemnation, default proceeding, student loan cases, VA loan overpayment cases, naturalization proceedings filed as civil actions, review of administrative agency actions; statutory interpleader actions, Truth-In-Lending Act cases not brought as class actions, Interstate Commerce Act cases, labor management relations or ERISA actions seeking recovery for unpaid employee welfare benefit and pension funds; civil penalty cases and any other case expressly exempted by Court order.

The mediation must take place not later than sixty (60) days before scheduled trial date, with mediator chosen by party agreement from an available list with 15 days of referral order. Barring agreement of parties, a mediator is designated by the Clerk of Court on a blind, random basis. All parties to attend and representatives to have full settlement authority; failure to do so may result in sanctions. All mediation proceedings privileged in all respects.

IDAHO

Mediation may occur during periodic voluntary settlement weeks.

Appendix E
Federal Court Overview

INDIANA — Northern District

Judicially hosted (other than the judge before whom the case is to be tried) settlement conferences/mediation. One division, Ft. Wayne, has been most active in referring cases to mediation.

INDIANA — Southern District

Court to encourage settlement actively, including early neutral evaluation by magistrates in non-consent cases. Clerk of Court to include in Practitioner's Handbook descriptions of the ADR mechanisms, including mediation. Brochure for litigants and attorneys describing processes to be distributed. Litigants can voluntarily access outside mediators.

KANSAS

By Rule 214 the court encourages settlement by various proceedings including mediation, but cannot require such. Cases may be referred to a settlement conference before mediator, an attorney-mediator chosen from panel of local attorneys, a magistrate judge or any consenting trial judge. Attendance by party representative with settlement authority is mandatory, and the proceeding is confidential. Costs of mediator, attorney-mediator, or panel of attorney-mediators assessed to parties in proportions determined by trial judge.

KENTUCKY — Eastern District

Adoption and implementation of a voluntary mediation program, and unanimously opposed any mandatory ADR. Mediation upon request of a party, with the option to back out at any time without repercussion. Any party may object to the use of mediation.

KENTUCKY — Western District

Court initiating small scale pilot mediation project.

LOUISIANA — Eastern District

Court generally makes known to lawyers and litigants the availability of judicial officers for settlement conference at any time upon request. Plan authorizes court to employ ADR techniques. At court's discretion, upon determination that case will benefit from ADR, case is referred to private mediation.

MASSACHUSETTS

Rule 4.03 authorizes a judicial officer to refer appropriate cases to an ADR program, including mediation. The mediator will be compensated as agreed by parties, subject to approval of court. Communications will be confidential; and no admission, representation, statement, etc. is discoverable or admissible as evidence. Courts encouraged to use the Boston Bar Association's federal mediation program.

MICHIGAN — Eastern District

Governed by Local Rule 53.1. Court may submit any civil case where monetary relief is sought to mediation. Exclusion: cases where United States a party. Panel of mediators assume evaluative role, and issue award.

MICHIGAN — Western District

Governed by Local Rule 42. Court may submit any civil case to mediation. Mediation by a panel of three lawyers who evaluate the case and issue a decision within ten days after the hearing.

MINNESOTA

At pretrial conferences, the Judge will determine if a case is appropriate for ADR after consultation with the parties. The Judge may appoint an ADR provider who is considered skilled enough to reach settlement. Fees are to be paid by the parties. At the conference, attorneys must have authority to bind parties on reports of settlement prospects, negotiations, whether to go to formal mediation either before or at completion of discovery, and the advisability of court ordered mediation or early neutral evaluation.

MISSOURI — Eastern District

No formal program but parties can request court to refer case to mediation.

Appendix E
Federal Court Overview

MISSOURI — Western District

Experimental program through which every third case filed, (excepting excluded types of cases) is randomly assigned to an Early Assessment Program for choice of ADR, including mediation. Control group of cases can volunteer to participate. Administration meets with litigants to choose process, and in absence of choice Administration selects.

MONTANA

In process of establishing program for mediation.

NEW JERSEY

Local Rule 47C.2 expanded to permit parties to participate in any available form of ADR, including mediation. Seminars to be conducted for both the court and the bar. Court to divert selected civil cases to mediation or summary jury trial to assess strengths and weaknesses of each process.

NEW MEXICO

Courts to offer parties option of ADR, including mediation. Clerk of court to establish panel of mediators and designate method of selection and training of mediators.

NEW YORK — Eastern District

Court to establish program of court-annexed mediation for civil cases filed on or after June 30, 1992. Voluntary participants to chose: a) using a mediator from the court's panel of volunteers; b) selecting a mediator on their own; or c) seeking assistance of reputable neutral ADR organization in selection of mediator. Court to publish and distribute pamphlet describing various ADR mechanisms. Administrator to supervise all ADR programs and educate bar.

NEW YORK — Southern District

Mandatory court-annexed mediation for all expedited cases and other cases where monetary damages only are sought, excluding social security cases, tax matters, prisoners' civil rights cases, and pro se cases. Civil case manager designates cases for mediation and supervises the procedure. Mediators qualify by being a member of the bar of any state for at least five years, are admitted to practice in Southern District of NY, are certified by Chief Judge as competent to perform duties of mediator and mediate without compensation. Mediation to be held no later than 150 days after filing last responsive pleading. Failure or refusal to attend mediation may result in sanctions. Attorneys and clients attend and mediator may require party representatives with settlement authority to attend. Proceedings are confidential.

OHIO — Northern District

Local rules incorporate a broad menu of non-binding, court-annexed ADR processes. Judicial officers refer cases to ADR, including a number of cases to mediation.

OHIO — Southern District

Referral to private mediation primarily during settlement weeks.

OKLAHOMA — Western District

Local Court Rule 46 provides for a court-annexed mediation program to augment previously existing ADR procedures, and is intended as a mechanism for especially early resolution of civil cases. Mediators must be admitted to practice of law for at least 5 years and a member of the bar or a professional mediator who would otherwise qualify as a special master, and whom the court determines competent to perform the duties of mediator. Completion of appropriate training as the court may from time to time determine and direct. Mediator's fees are borne equally by the parties. If settlement is not accomplished and case is later concluded by trial or otherwise, the prevailing party, upon motion, may recover as costs in the instant action fees paid to the mediator. Mediation clerk shall maintain list of certified mediators, which is to be made available to counsel and the pubic. Court has discretion to refer any civil action of portion thereof to mediation. Parties to choose mediator, within 10 days of order of referral, from list available from court or barring agreement, the mediation clerk will make selection. Counsel and parties with full settlement authority to attend. Sanctions pursuant to Local Rule 17(E) may apply for failure to attend. Proceedings are confidential.

OREGON

Voluntary mediation program pursuant to Local Rule 240-2. Parties are encouraged to pursue mediation as first approach to settlement. List of volunteer mediators maintained by Clerk and selection made by agreement of parties or failing same, designation by court. Attorneys to attend, with clients available. Mediator decides if clients are present in conference room, and if and how they are to participate. Representatives (insurance companies) shall attend and must have binding settlement authority. Failure to attend may result in sanctions. Settlement agreements to be reduced to writing and are binding upon the parties.

PENNSYLVANIA — Eastern District

Local Civil Rule 15: Court-Annexed Mediation (Early Settlement Conference); experimental program; "odd" number docketed cases placed in program, except social security cases, cases in which prisoner is a party, cases eligible for arbitration pursuant to Local Civil Rule 8, asbestos cases, and any case which a judge determines, sua sponte, or on application by interested party (including the mediator) is not suitable for mediation.

Mediators must be member of the bar of the highest court of a state for at least 15 years, be admitted to practice in this district and receive no compensation or reimbursement of expenses. Mediation is considered a pro bono service. Mediators picked by random selection by Clerk of Court from list maintained by Clerk's Office. Mediation attended by counsel of record and any unrepresented party. Failure to attend may result in sanctions. Confidential proceedings; only written settlements signed by parties or their counsel are binding. No recording or transcript of proceedings.

TENNESSEE — Western District

Court authorized to determine, at initial Rule 16(b) conference, what particular ADR method, including mediation, should be used.

Appendix E
Federal Court Overview

TEXAS — Eastern District

ADR utilized at discretion of court. Includes mediation and is governed by Local Rules 1-18. Clerk's office maintains roster of mediators.

TEXAS — Northern District

Judge may refer to ADR, including mediation, on the motion of any party, agreement of the parties or on the Judge's own motion. A party opposing a referral or provider must file written objections within 10 days of the order of referral, giving reasons for opposition. All counsel, party representatives with authority to negotiate and all necessary persons for settlement, including insurance carriers, must attend. All communications are confidential, protected from disclosure and do not constitute waiver or any privileges or immunities.

TEXAS — Southern District

ADR is governed by Local Rule 22: the court is to explore ADR possibility at the initial pretrial conference and may refer case to ADR (including mediation) upon its own motion or motion or agreement of the parties. Parties may chose, but court retains discretion to suggest or require a particular ADR mechanism. Mediators must be licensed to practice for at least ten years, be admitted to practice in this district and must complete at least 40 hours training in dispute resolution techniques. Party representatives with authority to negotiate settlement and all other persons necessary to negotiate settlement (including insurance carriers) must be present at session. Fees are determined by provider and litigants, although court can review reasonableness.

TEXAS — Western District

Governed by Local Civil Rule 88. Counsel must certify to court consideration of ADR, including mediation, use. Court may order ADR. Clerk's office maintains list of mediators. ADR proceedings must occur within 45 days of entry of referral order.

UTAH

Voluntary, experimental plan. Parties considering mediation to also participate in court-sponsored mediation education program.

Appendix E
Federal Court Overview

WASHINGTON — Eastern District

List of mediators made available to parties on a voluntary basis.

WASHINGTON — Western District

Governed by Civil Rule 39.1. Court maintains register of attorneys who have volunteered to serve as mediators. Any civil case can be designated by court for mediation. All proceedings to be excluded from the court.

WEST VIRGINIA — Northern District

Expansion of use of mediation in Settlement Week Conferences to a minimum of three per year.

WEST VIRGINIA — Southern District

Mandatory mediation program with selection of cases made by court. Cases typically included in program: commercial and other contract cases, personal injury matters, civil rights employment, ERISA, tax matters, debt collection, asbestos cases, FELA, labor-management employment, and miscellaneous civil action. Cases typically not included: administrative agency appeals, habeas corpus and other prisoner petitions, forfeitures of seized property and bankruptcy appeals. However, even these matters could be included on a case-by-case basis, but special problems suggest typically not included. Cases must be at least six months old and discovery either complete or close to completion if being actively and aggressively pursued by parties. May still be considered for mediation if case has languished. Attorneys anonymously "suggest" cases for referral to mediation.

Mediators drawn from experienced litigators in district who donate their time. Mediator selected from panel of three named by district judge with each party having right to strike one, with remaining one automatically select for the case. Absolute confidentiality of proceedings.

WISCONSIN — Eastern District

Judicial officer at Rule 16 conference to determine if case appropriate for mediation or other ADR process.

Appendix E
Federal Court Overview

WISCONSIN — Western District

General mediation along with mediation by a magistrate judge to be encouraged. Clerk's office to distribute information on ADR.

WYOMING

Local Rule 220 makes services of a magistrate judge available upon request for settlement conferences held in accordance with the Rule. A standing committee on local rules shall amend current local rules for consideration by court to utilize other ADR techniques on an ad hoc basis when they are deemed appropriate.

VIRGIN ISLANDS

Court-annexed mediation plan. Court may order referral to mediation upon agreement of parties. Actions excluded from mediation referral: criminal actions, appeals from rulings of administrative agencies, forfeitures of seized property, habeas corpus and extraordinary writ, declaratory relief, any case assigned by court to multidistrict tribunal, litigation expedited by statute or rule, except issues of parental responsibility, or other matters as may be specified by order of presiding judge in district. Mediators are chosen by agreement within ten days of order of referral or appointed by court barring agreement of parties.

Counsel to parties *do not participate* in, interfere with, or attend any portion of mediation conference. Attorneys' role limited to general consultation. Mediation has duty to define and describe the process including circumstances under which mediator may meet alone with either party or with any other person and the confidentiality provision as provided for by Title 5, Section 854 of the Virgin Islands Code. Agreements reached must be by mutual consent. Each party has privilege to refuse to disclose or prevent any person present at proceeding from disclosing communications made during proceeding. Other than executed settlement agreement (signed by parties and counsel), all processes of proceeding are inadmissible. Failure to appear at mediation may result in sanctions, including an award of mediator and attorney's fees and other costs. Representatives appearing at mediation must have full settlement authority without further consultation. Discovery may continue

---

throughout mediation but may be delayed or deferred upon agreement of parties or by order of the court.

While not every court has embraced the use of mediation in their civil cost justice expense and delay reduction plan, it is likely that as more courts implement their respective plans and the use of mediation produces favorable results, the process will be considered by additional courts. The model plan designed by the Judicial Conference of the United States includes four alternate methods by which a court can implement mediation. No doubt within the next few years, ADR, and in particular, mediation, will be an integral part of federal pretrial procedure.

In addition to mediation at the trial level, some federal courts have recognized the benefit of mediation for cases at the appellate level. Two such circuits are the 9th Circuit in California and the 10th Circuit in Colorado.

Appendix E
Federal Court Overview

Index

Index

Index